Horse Racing Logic

A Guide for the Serious Horseplayer

Glendon Jones

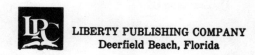

Second Edition: December, 1994

LIBERTY PUBLISHING COMPANY
Deerfield Beach, Florida

Published by:
Liberty Publishing Company, Inc.
440 South Federal Highway
Deerfield Beach, Florida 33441

ISBN 0-89709-203-1

Publisher's Note

Manufactured USA

For Doreen and Jeff

Contents

Flexibility

Flexibility

Ask ten average horseplayers if the races can be beaten and probably nine of them will respond negatively (the other one will, too, after a little more experience). This response, of course, is due mainly to the notable lack of success experienced by most racegoers. While there are many horseplayers who consider racetrack betting merely as an exciting but unprofitable diversion, there are numerous others who hold, or at some time held, aspirations of earning regular profits from race betting. Nearly all fail.

They fail for several reasons, including inadequate funding, poor money management, inability to cope with the emotional and financial pressures, and insufficient handicapping knowledge. But primarily they fail because of ignorance—ignorance about the realities of the restricted money-making opportunities at the track, ignorance of the handicapping techniques required to locate the truly profitable betting opportunities, and ignorance about the essential personal qualities that must be developed to become a successful horseplayer. The primary objective of this book is to enlighten the serious horseplayer in these areas. Toward this goal, this book will

- deal candidly and logically about the existence of the relatively few but highly profitable betting situations that arise most days at the track;
- demonstrate sophisticated and flexible handicapping techniques to help identify horses that are overbet and underbet (the real secret of profitable horseplaying);
- and present an insightful discussion of the psychological or inner battle that all successful players must win in order to profit consistently at the track.

The Shortcomings of Most Handicapping Methods

There are dozens of horse race betting methods available that deal with the mechanics of handicapping and that describe systematic methods to select contenders and ultimately the best horse in a race. While many of these are useful in providing tools for distinguishing ability and form among horses, as a class they fail in two important respects.

First, they do not fully recognize and promote handicapping as being a complex craft or art that can only be learned through years of intelligent practice and flexible application of a broad set of fundamentals. Rather, they focus on a few handicapping techniques and build an approach or method around them. In particular, most methods are based on the measurement of a horse's race times (speed handicapping), or the determination of its inherent class (class handicapping), or some combination of the two factors. The use of speed is considered the cornerstone of so many handicapping methods because of the obvious positive correlation between a horse's speed ratings and ability. Class is considered important because of a similar relationship between the calibre of the company a horse usually keeps and its talent. There is no doubt that both speed and class techniques are important handicapping tools. There are, however, serious drawbacks to limiting the selection of horses for betting to speed and class methods.

Methods based on speed are not reliable for comparing young, maturing horses, especially in the first part of the racing season, because these horses demonstrate unpredictable improvement. Similarly, class methods fail for two- and three-year-old horses because of their rapidly changing maturation rates. Lengthy periods of wet and cold weather, as occur in the spring and fall, can also invalidate the premise on which speed and class methods are built, because many horses perform above or below par on different race surfaces and in different seasons. The tendency of trainers to try their runners at turf racing is another variable that seriously affects that predictability of methods utilizing speed and class measurement. Many horses will not extend themselves on grass; others highly favor the surface.

Even methods based on more subtle handicapping factors have their effective and ineffective periods. For instance, an approach based on a track or post bias can work well when the bias holds up, but breaks down when it changes. And methods based on winning consistency are ineffective at the start of the racing season because a horse's consistency must be reestablished; they are also ineffective at the end of the season because there are so many races filled with horses that have won frequently during the year.

For these reasons, many professional horseplayers achieve their results by mastering specialized areas of the game, confining their betting to well-understood, but relatively restricted situations. For example, one operator may look for bets only in dry track sprint races open to older horses; another in high-class distance races in which a single quality horse is present; a third in grass races in which a wake-up prospect on breeding may be entered; and another may wait for biases to appear on the running surface and bet with the bias. Enormous patience is required to wait for these infrequent betting opportunities.

Unfortunately, techniques associated with many handicapping methods have a tendency to force a player to look for such special situations. This occurs because the serious player eventually comes to realize that the methods only work under certain conditions and cannot be applied at all times. Another goal of this book is to show how a thorough background in all important fundamentals can help provide the flexibility necessary to properly assess almost any handicapping situation, and thereby increase the overall chance of profit.

The second, and more serious failing of most handicapping methods, is their inadequate or nonexistent treatment of the critical art of judging comparative probabilities of winning among the top race contenders. The business of making accumulating profits at the races over the long term is dependent entirely on the regular betting of horses having a substantially higher chance of winning than their odds suggest. This is the only possible way to consistently make profits, a fact little understood by many racing fans, including a good number of players who try seriously to beat the game. These players feel that all they must do, in order to make a profit, is to pick a higher percentage of winners. This, most emphatically, is not the high road to profits at the track.

The real secret of beating the races is to be selective, by passing races (and missing winners) when the logical choice is overbet and by restricting bets to selections that are underbet. A player who is able to achieve an average of 25 to 30 percent winners cannot possibly reap consistent and substantial profits over long periods if betting each race, but will show handsome returns restricting bets to horses that are solidly underbet in relation to their true chance of winning. This concept is developed in detail later, along with techniques to determine if a selection is properly or poorly bet by the public.

Apprenticeship of a Horseplayer

My first experience at a racetrack (Woodbine, 1966) was a winning one. I wanted a two-dollar bet on number four but bungled the request and was given a four-dollar bet on number two. At that point I was so excited about having a ticket that I kept it and paid the four bucks. Naturally the two horse won, returning something like $20. Beginners luck, of course!

I enjoyed the excitement of the races but never gave it a serious thought until 1967 when a local newspaper racing writer wrote a story about a man who had sold his business because of union conflicts and decided to try earning a living by betting on thoroughbreds. He related that it took him a couple of years to learn the ropes, and that for five years he had earned about $35,000 a year by betting the horses, playing the local circuit in summer and the Florida circuit in winter.

This success story intrigued me, and I began to study the game seriously, reading most of the available books and articles on the subject. At the time I was completing a postgraduate degree in applied statistics and felt that my background in this field would give me a big edge on other horseplayers, because the process of picking winners appeared to be one involving the assessment of numbers—how fast can a horse run, how much money has it won, how long since its last race, and so on.

I went as far as to computerize my equine studies, hoping that this would somehow produce a sophisticated formula for picking winners and thereby give me a big advantage over the average player. I coded dozens of factors for a few thousand races, entered the data into computer storage, and began testing the factors for significance using a complex analysis technique called multiple regression. This is a statistical method that permits examination of multiple factors simultaneously to determine if they have a significant predictive relationship with a particular event—in this case, a horse's chance of winning.

The study picked out a number of important factors, including: speed in the first half mile of previous recent races, last race recency and finish, weight allotted, jockey, and consistency. These factors were assigned weights by the statistical calculations and summarized in an equation. I then used this equation to rank contenders in subsequent races.[1]

The formula was able to pick about 25 percent winners, but produced no long-term profit. Most of the selections were confirmed by the public as favorites or second choices, with only a smattering of long shots. Similar work carried out by others has shown this tendency, and to my knowledge no such derived method shows a worthwhile profit. Profitability may be possible with a formula derived from much more data and an approach that permits the calculation of probabilities of winning.

Horse Sense

My results were disappointing, but did convince me that the computer was not likely going to be the useful tool for horse racing that it was for science

1. *This technique is the basis of the horseracing pocket calculators and computer programs in vogue today. The selection equation is stored in the memory of the calculator or computer. When specific handicapping factors for each horse are keyed into the calculator or computer they are automatically plugged into the equation and rankings quickly generated. The horse with the highest ranking is the computer's choice to win the race.*

and business. Shortly after, I read a book called *Horse Sense* by Burton Fabricand, which gradually changed my approach in a positive way. This well-researched book describes a complex mechanical system for finding favorites (and some second and third betting choices) that are bet less than they should be.

The underlying principle is that when horses in a race have recent form that looks similar to the favorite's form, then these "similar" horses will be too heavily bet because the public gets confused (Principle of Maximum Confusion). The public overbets the similar-looking nonfavorites because their form appears almost the same as the favorite's.

The overbetting of these horses leaves the favorite underbet and therefore a profitable bet when considered over a long series of such races. When the system indicates that a favorite is overbet, then the second betting choice is tested in a similar manner to determine if it is underbet. The third choice can also be considered if the second choice is also deemed overbet.

The author claims the system produces a winning percentage of 40 percent or so on an average of two or three plays per day, and yields a long-term return of 30 to 40 percent on monies wagered. I tested the system on paper several years ago and found that it worked when favorites were consistently winning 33 percent or more of the races (equivalent to the national average), but failed badly when the winning percentage of favorites fell below this level for periods of several weeks. The losses for the system were substantial then. Over the full three-month test period, during which the favorite won 32 percent of the races, the system produced a marginal profit of twelve percent.

Superiority of a Flexible Approach

The results of my test were disappointing in two respects. First, the system forced me to bet favorites even during periods when they were not winning their normal share; and second, the total return was, for my sample, inadequate. I feel that the financial and emotional pressures that are likely to build up while applying the mechanical system with real money during these lengthy dry periods could be devastating. In spite of these drawbacks, the system opened my eyes to the concept that long-term consistent profits can only be attained by restricting bets to horses that are significantly underbet in relation to their true chances of winning.

I hold the view that an expert horseplayer, combining good handicapping techniques with a nose for value, should do well even when favorites and other heavily bet choices are not winning their usual high proportion of races. My experience suggests that during these periods it is not difficult to find good bets on other formful horses. In the extreme, unformful long shots will occasionally win with surprising regularity for brief periods. When this happens, my approach is to exercise caution by reducing the usual number of bets until things get back to normal. These are periods when flexibility, impossible with a mechanical system, carries the day.

There is no doubt in my mind that greater overall profits and less variability of results are available to those who wish to approach the game as an art, rather than a science, which subjects it to categorization. The player who views horseplaying as an art brings to it dimensions that separate humans from computers, namely, observation, flexibility, and adpatability.

The remainder of this book is divided into the following themes:

- the principle of the underlay and overlay and a discussion of why bets must be based on their occurrence;
- a set of advanced handicapping tools to assist in finding profitable betting opportunities;
- identifying and profiting by underlays and overlays when they occur at the track;
- a conservative betting approach for the serious bettor;
- a discussion of some of the mental and emotional factors that a successful player must develop and cope with—the inner struggle.

Betting Principles

Betting Principles

It can safely be said that many casual racing fans have a limited or mistaken understanding of the fundamentals of racetrack betting. It is common at the track to overhear punters pontificate about racing matters, and over the years I have rarely heard anyone reveal significant insights. On the contrary, most of the time these garrulous horseplayers have demonstrated serious misconceptions.

Two of the more serious misunderstandings include the views that the betting public is incompetent in selecting the best horse in a race and inaccurate in setting odds. This perception is unfortunate. Nearly all horseplayers fail to recognize and take advantage of the valuable information generated by the collective thoughts and betting of the public. This chapter is meant to clear up these misconceptions and direct the horseplayer to make better use of the public's betting savvy and tendencies.

The Winning Percentage of Favorites

Public favorites win 32 to 34 percent of thoroughbred races year after year. This is a well-known statistic. It holds true for nearly all classes of races and for most tracks over any lengthy period. Although a few tracks do show a long-term winning percentage a point or two above the 33 percent mark, it is usually due to smaller than average race field sizes. The fewer the horses, the higher the percentage of winning favorites, and conversely. This fact also accounts for the higher percentage of winning favorites in stakes and handicap races, because these races tend to attract smaller fields than average.

The Experts' Betting Record

There are many public handicappers to be found in and around every city where racetracks operate. Their numbers include the racing paper handicappers, newspaper selectors, official program handicappers, and tout sheet operators. These people are paid to make race selections for their clients, and many work very hard at their craft. How well do they do?

The best public selectors usually achieve a 25 to 30 percent winning percentage. This range may seem low, but it compares favorably with an expected random-chance percentage that varies between approximately 8 and 15 percent depending on race field size. The expert's record is demonstrated in table 1 below, which presents the 1981 results for several highly regarded professional race selectors, including the Daily Racing Form expert consensus, in New York and Toronto.

The top handicappers in each city (Harris in New York, Bannon in Toronto) compiled almost identical winning percentages of 29 percent for the full year. Losses associated with these percentages averaged around 15 percent of monies wagered. This negative return is virtually the same as the expected loss of about 14 percent to 18 percent, the track take, indicating that the expert's selections are fully discounted at the betting window.

Interestingly, this expected loss can be achieved simply by random selection—expert handicapping is not required! The winning percentage obtainable by random selection (8 to 15 percent) is much lower than that achievable using a good handicapping method; however, the higher average price paid on winners obtained through random selection compensates for their lower winning percentage, with the result that losses on money wagered average the track take.

The Superiority of the Betting Public

Who, then, can do better than the experts? Answer: the betting public. The public's top choice, the post time favorite, wins about 33 percent of the time, a figure which is usually several percentage points higher than the winning percentage of the top-rated experts. Moreover, the loss incurred from betting favorites is lower than the expected loss (the track take). It averages around ten to twelve cents on each dollar wagered. Not exciting, but better than the fifteen cents or so loss expected by chance alone.

Another demonstration of the public's ability to cope with complex information and sort it out with accuracy can be seen in the way odds are assigned to horses. Tote board odds reflect the distribution of money wagered by the public on their choices to win a race. The more bet on one horse in relation to the others, the lower its odds. This in turn means higher odds on the others, because odds are determined by the relative amounts bet on individual horses. The public, by observing the odds distribution on the tote board during the betting period and by making decisions about monetary imbalances, has an uncanny ability to establish odds by post time that accurately reflect, on average, the true probability of winning.

Table 1.

Results for the Top Three Public
Handicappers in New York and Toronto

New York

Top Pick—Win %

Harris (Daily News) 29.4%
Consensus (DRF) 29.2%
Sweep (DRF) 27.2%

Money Won/Lost

Trackman (DRF) .... (−11.7%)
Handicap (DRF) .... (−14.4%)
Harris (Daily News) .... (−16.5%)
Average .... (−14.2%)

Toronto

Top Pick—Win %

Bannon (OJC) 29.3%
Program (OJC) 27.0%
Consensus (DRF) 26.6%

Money Won/Lost

Slater (Star) .... (−13.6%)
Bannon (OJC) .... (−15.3%)
Trackman (DRF) .... (−16.5%)
Average .... (−15.1%)

This is demonstrated in a remarkable table based on the 10,000-race sample of the *Horse Sense* study. Table 2 presents the results. It shows the winning probabilities associated with 22 odds ranges. These figures are calculated by converting the midpoint value of each odds range to a probability, after the removal of track takeout percentage. The formula used was:

probability = (1 − .15)/(weighted midpoint of odds range + 1)

where the number .15 represents the average track take proportion (15 percent). The resulting value was converted to a percentage by multiplying by 100.

The resulting value represents the percentage of horses that theoretically should win in an odds range if the public odds at post time (adjusted for track take) matched those horses' true chances. To the right is a column showing the actual percentages of horses that won in each odds grouping. Comparing the two columns, the case for the public's collective ability is clear. The odds they set are, on average, accurate estimates of probabilities of winning. The public demonstrates noticeable bias only at odds range extremes; they consistently underbet strong favorites and overbet longshots.

The table also proves conclusively that random favorites are better bets than random long shots; that is, the loss when betting favorites is less than the loss when betting long shots. Those favorites that went to post at odds of 8:5 and less produced losses considerably smaller than the track take of 15 percent, and for one small subgrouping at the lowest odds range actually produced a profit. Contrasted with this were the high losses associated with the random betting of long shots. Horses going to post at odds at 20:1 and higher produced a staggering 54 percent loss on monies wagered.

The overbetting of long shots and underbetting of favorites, as shown in table 2, demonstrates the symmetry of the public's odds line. The overbetting of long shots assures that another group of horses (in this case heavy favorites) is underbet. While this principle is apparent in a tabulation that shows the frequency of odds for 10,000 races, it applies directly to individual races as well. The effect is similar to that when walking on a water bed: stepping down with one foot pushes the other foot up. At the track, the overbetting of one or more horses results in higher odds on other horses.

It should be clear from table 2 that the public deserves much credit for sorting out the many variables in a complex game and estimating accurately the probabilities involved. My experience has been that even serious handicappers look down on the public and their post time favorites. I have even heard supposed experts suggest that the betting crowd is a mindless mob that simply follows the lead of the public handicappers. This quite obviously is not the case.

Table 2.

Comparison of True Winning Probabilities with the Winning Probabilities Determined by the Public.

Odds Range	Public's Prob- ability	"True" Prob- ability	No. of horses and winners		% loss of amount bet
0.40– 0.55	56.9%	71.3%	129–	92	(Profit)
0.60– 0.75	50.2	55.3	295–	163	7.1%
0.80– 0.95	44.9	51.3	470–	241	3.8
1.00– 1.15	40.6	47.0	615–	289	2.4
1.20– 1.35	37.1	40.3	789–	318	8.1
1.40– 1.55	34.1	37.9	874–	331	6.1
1.60– 1.75	31.5	35.5	954–	339	4.8
1.80– 1.95	29.3	30.9	1051–	325	10.5
2.00– 2.45	26.3	28.9	3223–	933	6.5
2.50– 2.95	22.8	23.0	3623–	835	13.5
3.00– 3.45	20.1	20.9	3807–	797	11.0
3.50– 3.95	18.0	18.6	3652–	679	11.6
4.00– 4.45	16.2	16.1	3296–	532	15.3
4.50– 4.95	14.8	15.5	3129–	486	10.6
5.00– 5.95	13.2	12.3	5586–	686	20.1
6.00– 6.95	11.4	11.0	5154–	565	18.0
7.00– 7.95	10.0	9.9	4665–	460	16.4
8.00– 8.95	9.0	8.2	3990–	328	21.8
9.00– 9.95	8.1	8.2	3617–	295	14.7
10.00–14.95	6.5	6.0	12007–	717	20.7
15.00–19.95	4.7	4.0	7041–	284	26.4
20.00–99.95	2.5	1.4	25044–	340	54.0

93011–10035

My intentions in demonstrating the betting public's general expertise and biases are threefold. First, it presents a strong counterargument to those who think that to beat the races they must simply pick more winners. It is exceedingly difficult to beat the winning percentage of the post time favorites. It is also very difficult to overcome the track take by attempting to bet more winners. The experts are not able to do it, so good luck to those who think they can.

Second, the public's bias toward overbetting horses going to post at odds of 5:1 and higher presents compelling evidence of the difficulty inherent in trying to beat the races by playing long shots in an impulsive or arbitrary way. Even systematic ways to play long shots must be given little chance to consistently succeed because the unfavorable bias is so large.

Finally, the public's record strongly suggests that any betting decision should stem from a careful scrutiny of betting odds, as well as from an analysis directed toward picking a horse with a strong chance of winning. This study of betting odds should lead to feelings that a horse is properly bet, overbet, or underbet by the public. Only when this is determined should a decision to bet or not bet be made.

The remainder of this chapter explores this area in more detail.

Underlays and Overlays

An "underlay" is track parlance for a horse having too much money bet on it to a degree that is out of proportion to its chance of winning. Long shots are usually underlays, a fact clearly demonstrated in table 2. Their chances of winning tend to be overestimated by the public, due in part to the number of racegoers who bet them simply so as to not miss big payoffs. I have known players who catch many long shots only because they bet three or four of them each race. This type of multiple wagering is particularly common for bets involving daily doubles, exactas, trifectas, and the like. When they win, these players boast loudly; but unfortunately they lose more money than other bettors, and substantially more than players of favorites or "chalk eaters."

While I am not in any way advocating that a steady diet of favorites is the way to beat the game, it is important to keep in mind that the frequent betting of long shots and other large payoff wagers is the worst possible approach. Some will argue that since big triactor payoffs can go as high as fifty thousand dollars or more, it is worthwhile to bet them. Newspapers often report on these big payoffs by showing a picture of a happy winner who bet the combination using a system based on his wife's age, number of kids, and license plate number. These exotic bets are miniature lotteries, with expected losses of upwards of 50 percent when betting in such an arbitrary manner. They are exciting perhaps, and undeniably popular, but very difficult to integrate into any handicapping method designed to earn regular and substantial profits at the track.

At the other end of the wagering scale is the "overlay." An overlay is a horse that has too little money bet on it in relation to its real chances of winning. A horse going to post at betting odds of 5:1 (a one-in-six chance) when its true odds are 2:1 (a one-in-three chance), is an overlay. Table 2 demonstrates that low-priced favorites are, on average, overlays in that bets on them are not as unprofitable as expected on the basis of the track take. Taking a moment to summarize the past few pages, it has been demonstrated from a frequency table of odds ranges that the betting public

- produces winning probabilities for most odds ranges, which, on average, are quite accurate, but
- tends to heavily overbet long shots, and
- significantly underbet very low-priced favorites.

By inference, then, it can be said that the public also significantly underbets or overbets some horses that are neither low-priced choices nor long shots.[2] If we accept that the public does well on average but slips up from time to time for all odds ranges, we can proceed to . . . *the secret.*

The Secret of Beating the Races

Simply stated, identifying and taking advantage of significant underlays and overlays is the secret of beating the races. (*Significant* here implies that the underlay or overlay is large enough to overcome the track take by a wide margin so that meaningful long-run betting profits are assured.) In terms of betting behavior, this means that when a pronounced underlay at low odds is found then it should be bet against; when a substantial overlay is found it should be bet. There is no other way to consistently win profits at the race track.

This "secret" should not come as a surprise to anyone having a sound understanding of betting principles. It requires no further justification or explanation; however, it raises a couple of natural questions: (1) If the

2. The proof of this is not demonstrated in table 2 because it shows only averages. In fact, it cannot be proven mathematically because it is impossible to ever determine a horse's true odds of winning. However, my own year-to-year wagering results empirically prove that the public sometimes errs in setting odds in all ranges. The Horse Sense *study results confirm this.*

public on average sets relatively accurate odds, then how often are horses significantly underbet and overbet? and (2) how can we identify the underbet and overbet horses?

I can only answer the first question from my own experience. With regard to favorites, I estimate the public significantly underbets their top choice about 20 percent of the time, and overbets it another 20 percent of the time. About 60 percent of all favorites, in my judgement, are more or less properly bet. Horses other than the favorite get misbet, too, but as odds increase, the likelihood is that the public errs in the direction of overbetting. At 5:1 odds, I would say that only one in ten horses is significantly underbet; at 10:1 odds perhaps one in twenty; and at 20:1 odds and higher, fewer than one in fifty are underbet enough to profit from.

These estimates may seem low to many horseplayers. It may be that they are, but not by much. It defies logic to suggest that there are many more horses underbet by an amount significantly greater than the track take. Favorites would win far less than 33 percent of the time if horses were so poorly bet.

Given that there are usually some underbet horses going to the post each day, the critical question is not how many significantly underbet horses there are, but how they can be identified. The next section provides the clues, and chapters four and five provide specifics.

Finding Underlays and Overlays—General Principles

When people ask me if I have a special system with which I "beat the races," my response is always the same: "No," I tell them. "I have no system. I treat the game as an art." At this point, the inquirer usually responds with a nod and an incredulous smile, then changes the subject. While the neophyte horseplayer may also respond this way, the really good horse-player knows better.

The "art" begins where Racing Form analysis ends and when public betting commences. It involves the mental assessment of odds on the top contenders to determine if, and by how much, horses are overbet or underbet. This is an art that requires a finely tuned feel for relative odds among contenders. There are no definitive odds cutpoints that can be used to distinguish between overbet, properly bet, and underbet horses. The difficulty of the task is magnified by the confusing fact that the majority of strongly bet horses tend to be slightly underbet or properly bet.

Again, this is not meant to imply that the public is ever 100 percent accurate in producing a betting line. As demonstrated in table 2 and discussed previously, the public sets odds quite accurately *on average*. Even so, probably all races at post time contain horses which, to at least a very small degree, are underlayed and at the same time other horses which are overlayed; however, the majority of races are reasonably properly bet, with overlayed and underlayed amounts being too small to profit by. For betting purposes, only large imbalances are of importance, those large enough to reverse the unfavorable track take percentage and large enough to yield healthy long-term profits.

This last point must be emphasized. It behooves the horseplayer to bet only those races in which large betting imbalances exist. Why? For one thing, large imbalances are far more readily identifiable; for another, they are more profitable. Betting those situations arising from small imbalances increases the frequency of unprofitable bets and contributes to the reduction or elimination of profits from optimal situations.

Returning to the discussion of finding underlays and overlays, one point needs to be clarified now. While it is true that profitable bets can only be made on overlays, there are actually two methods of finding them. The more common way (for me) involves the public overbetting one or more of their top choices, resulting in another horse (or horses) receiving too little support, i.e., overlaid. In this situation, the horse neglected most in the betting is the best overlay (although there may be other profitable overlays among the other horses). So this is one way to find an overlay.

The second method involves the detection by the handicapper of important but hidden or unobvious information about a specific horse. This happens relatively infrequently, because the public is generally expert at finding and properly weighting even less obvious features of a horse's form. When some relevant information does slip past the public, overlays do occur.

Turning our focus now to the relative difficulty of finding each type of overlay, a generalization can be made: detecting a horse in the Form with high potential to be overbet is an easier task than digging out a horse with potential to be underbet. Horses that attract heavy public support usually have obvious good form and are easy for all horseplayers to spot. On the other hand, contenders with positive but obscure form factors are usually only found by digging deeply into the past performance records for significant information. For this reason the information may not be assessed completely or accurately by the public.

An overlay arising from the heavy overbetting of another horse is relatively simple to find, then. Once a horse with potential for being overbet is located in the Form, only two things remain to be done to find a good contender from the remaining horses in the race and to observe if public betting action confirms the underlay. If the handicapper makes a thorough analysis of the race contenders to find a potential counterbet, then chances are the horse selected by this process will be the one likely to be most underbet. The greatest difficulty associated with finding overlays of this kind is in accepting that the obvious choice will probably be overbet and then redoing the analysis to find the best of the remaining contestants. It is natural to want to accept the obvious choice as the best bet for the race. One must be ever aware that the obvious choice is usually the worst horse to bet, in that it has no long-term profit potential. It may win the race at low odds and provide immediate cashing gratification to those who bet it, but long-run betting on these overbet types will eventually wipe out the bankroll.

Which betting situations have most potential for overlays of this kind? As a rule, races in which the favorite or second choice is overbet provide the most profitable opportunities for these types of overlays, because the top two public choices usually receive more than half of the betting support and thereby contribute maximally to betting imbalances if they exist. When one or both are highly overbet, then another horse or other horses will be significantly underbet. By exactly the same reasoning, when only one of the top two public choices is heavily overbet, the other is usually the horse that is underbet.

Thus, the majority of profitable bets (overlays) arise from the public underbetting favorites, second, or third choices and are discovered by first determining whether one or more of the other low-priced horses in the race are definitely overbet.

The other method of finding overlays is less productive in my experience. As described earlier, it occurs when obscure information is ferreted out from a horse's record, information that points out the runner as a very strong contender under today's conditions, and yet information that the general public almost certainly underweights. In these situations, the underbetting is not done because the favorite or second choice is grossly overbet. It occurs because the postive information about the overlayed horse is well concealed and results in several low-priced horses receiving somewhat stronger betting than they should. The horseplayer should not be as concerned, in this instance, with identifying a specific overbet horse, because several will be bet too heavily. The main concern should be to affirm the race-readiness and superiority of the supposed overlayed horse.

Just Picking Winners Is Not the Answer

Many horseplayers have at least some inkling about the betting principles discussed in this chapter. They rarely apply them, however, succumbing instead to the lure of having a bet on the winner in every race. They take the view that the more winners, the more chance of beating the game. They also think that they are, in many cases, betting overlays simply by avoiding low-priced horses. This is usually not the case unless it happens by accident, because a large majority of longer-priced horses are overbet.

This kind of vague feeling or hope about the underlay-overlay relationship existing among the competing horses is simply not adequate to produce profitable returns. Locating most of the truly profitable betting opportunities requires that a careful analysis of each of the top two, three, and sometimes four betting choices be made to determine the existence of meaningful underlay and overlay possibilities. If the analysis points out that the top public choices are more or less properly bet, then the chances of a sizeable overlay existing are very remote. Races of this kind should not be bet regardless of having a preference for one horse or another.

What is needed now is a set of practical tools to enable the horseplayer to thoroughly analyse the past performance data, so that decisions about betting imbalances can be made with relative accuracy and ease. The next chapter presents a wide range of techniques to enhance a horseplayer's ability to assess the potential of each race contender. Later, in chapter four, it is explained in detail how to identify horses that are likely to be overbet or underbet by the betting public, and specific advice is given on how to take advantage of significant betting imbalances.

Handicapping Tools

Handicapping Tools

This chapter presents a variety of handicapping precepts for use in analysing the Racing Form past performances. The purpose of their presentation is to describe some out-of-the-ordinary situations in which certain subtle handicapping factors are especially valuable. They should help any player take a more complete and flexible approach to assessing the relative merits of a racing field.

Some of the handicapping tools presented here have associated with them rough rules for usage. The rules are merely guidelines and not dogma. I often break these rules of thumb, usually by only small degrees, but sometimes by margins so great that the rules become meaningless. When selected horses lose under these circumstances, there can be a great temptation to feel that the losses could have been avoided by sticking rigidly to rules that may have at that time been bent or broken. But this is erroneous reasoning. No set of rigid handicapping rules can work as well as a flexible and thoughtful approach, in the long run.

The Importance of Flexibility

A few words here about flexibility are in order before discussing the handicapping tools. The single most important factor in regard to the mechanics of successful handicapping is flexibility. Good handicapping requires the ability to adapt an analysis to a specific race situation because of wide race-to-race variation in factors such as race surface, age and experience of horses, distance, track, sex, and so on. A specific race analysis approach may be useful in one circumstance but worthless in another. This is one reason why "systems" do not work. The limited rules of mechanical systems prevent adaptation to the large variety of circumstances encountered from race to race.

By way of contrast, the betting public demonstrates an ability to adapt efficiently, and to such a degree that the winning percentage of favorites remains constant within all kinds of race categorizations. The collective approach of the public is flexible enough to ensure that, on average, proper weights are assigned to handicapping factors in all circumstances. A handicapper who wishes to select the top contenders in every situation must be just as flexible.

The other important reason for flexibility is to facilitate the assessment of a horse's chances relative to the chances of the other contenders, so that the player can take advantage of overlays and underlays if they arise. This means that in order to benefit by the mistakes made by the public, the impact of race circumstances on the chance of winning for all the race candidates must be understood. An inflexible method would therefore miss the mark in two ways: by not focusing the selection procedure toward the best candidate to win in every circumstance, and in inadequately assessing the relative merits of all the contenders.

There is no easy way to develop a flexible approach. It is only achieved through wide experience, which contributes to the understanding of the significance of handicapping factors under varying circumstances, and by making a concerted effort to adapt a method to the requirements of each race. Old and rigid habits must be broken and replaced with a thinking approach, one able to adapt to the new problems faced in each race. An approach that worked well in the last race may not be (likely is not) suitable for the next race. The spectacular winners of the past cannot be obtained now or ever again in precisely the same way, because no two sets of racing circumstances are ever identical.

The Tools

The handicapping factors are presented here in general order of importance in my handicapping scheme. This means that I usually put more emphasis on earlier appearing factors in the race assessment. But this is not always the case. For some races a factor well down in the list takes on prime importance. Some of these situations are discussed.

Another word of caution: these and other handicapping factors cannot be used in isolation. They must all be integrated into the complete handicapping picture in a thorough, analytical way.

Many of the handicapping points are accompanied by examples. The examples used in this section and throughout the remainder of the book originate from the Daily Racing Form Past Performances and Results Charts.

Dates of Races and Workouts

When handicapping a race, the first variables I look at in the Form are the dates of the horses' races and workouts. I quickly check the dates of every race, not just the last one or two. A complete scan reveals a great deal about a horse: recent activity, usual frequency of running, and layoff history. This information is valuable in providing clues about the horse's physical condition (both in a fitness and health sense), the stage of its form cycle, its physical toughness, and the trainer patterns used in preparing the horse for a sharp effort.

There are several race frequency patterns, both positive and negative, which can be used in conjunction with form cycle considerations to classify a horse as a contender or likely loser. These are presented below.

Positive Date Patterns

Positive Date Patterns—Recent Layoff

Horses that have had a three-to-eight-week layoff in the midst of a racing campaign and are now running their second, third, or fourth race since returning, often run their best races. In many cases these horses will improve to a greater degree than indicated by their latest race finish position. It is helpful to consider a horse's best race as an ability and form benchmark in this circumstance, rather than its last race, because it is quite possible the horse will run back to its best performance.

The same reasoning applies to horses coming back to racing after a longer layoff (such as after a winter break) except that they sometimes require four or more races before running back to their best level of output. More on this later.

Mito's Touch — B. m. 6, by Gentle King—Hasty Mito, by Mito
Own.—Killeen W T — $35,000 — Br.—Walldov G G (Fla) — Tr.—Levine Bruce — 117
Lifetime 52 9 10 6 $123,736

2May87- 1Aqu	fst	6f	:22$\frac{2}{5}$	:45$\frac{4}{5}$	1:11		ⒻClm 35000	2	6	2^{hd}	1^{hd}	$2^{1\frac{1}{2}}$	$4^{4\frac{1}{4}}$	Samyn J L	b 117	12.70	82-19	KissingBooth$117^{2\frac{3}{4}}$Crlingfor
16Apr87- 1Aqu	fst	6f	:22$\frac{4}{5}$	:46$\frac{3}{5}$	1:11$\frac{2}{5}$		ⒻClm 45000	1	6	6^{6}	$7^{5\frac{3}{4}}$	$7^{6\frac{3}{4}}$	$7^{8\frac{1}{4}}$	Badamo J J^{5}	b 108	11.90	76-22	Peace Keeper 115^{nk} Peacefı
9Oct86- 7Crc	fst	6$\frac{1}{2}$f	:22$\frac{4}{5}$	:46$\frac{2}{5}$	1:19$\frac{3}{5}$	3↑	ⒻClm 40000	7	1	2^{hd}	$3^{1\frac{1}{2}}$	4^{4}	6^{6}	Paynter L A^{5}	111	4.10	81-23	Classy Chasse 112no Jay'sJe
25Sep86- 9Crc	fst	6f	:22$\frac{2}{5}$	:45$\frac{3}{5}$	1:11$\frac{4}{5}$	3↑	ⒻAlw 18800	3	3	2^{hd}	2^{1}	$3^{4\frac{1}{2}}$	$2^{5\frac{1}{2}}$	Paynter L A^{5}	110	8.60	86-16	ClndestineAffir$115^{5\frac{1}{2}}$Mito'sT
12Sep86- 5Crc	fst	6f	:22$\frac{3}{5}$	:46$\frac{1}{5}$	1:12$\frac{1}{5}$	3↑	ⒻClm 50000	1	2	2^{hd}	3^{2}	$3^{3\frac{1}{2}}$	5^{2}	Paynter L A^{5}	111	6.80	88-14	SupremeLuck109^{1}DonIsACa
27Aug86- 9Crc	fst	6f	:22	:45$\frac{3}{5}$	1:11$\frac{4}{5}$	3↑	ⒻRaintree H	1	3	$1^{\frac{1}{2}}$	2^{1}	5^{5}	$7^{9\frac{3}{4}}$	Velez J A Jr	112	43.80	82-22	Classy Tricks$116^{\frac{3}{4}}$KlondikeK
15Aug86- 7Crc	sly	7f	:22$\frac{3}{5}$	:46$\frac{2}{5}$	1:25	3↑	ⒻAlw 19900	6	3	$2^{2\frac{1}{2}}$	$2^{\frac{1}{2}}$	3^{3}	$6^{6\frac{1}{2}}$	Velez J A Jr	116	9.50	84-16	MademoiselleJolie120^{5}FirstI
1Aug86- 9Crc	fst	7f	:23$\frac{2}{5}$	:47$\frac{2}{5}$	1:25$\frac{4}{5}$	3↑	ⒻAlw 18300	3	3	$3^{1\frac{1}{2}}$	4^{3}	$4^{5\frac{1}{2}}$	$4^{9\frac{1}{2}}$	Velez J A Jr	121	*1.30	77-14	SlipOnToGlory117^{1}GentleSc
19Jly86- 7Crc	fst	6f	:22$\frac{2}{5}$	:46$\frac{3}{5}$	1:13$\frac{1}{5}$	3↑	ⒻAlw 17800	3	5	3^{2}	$3^{1\frac{1}{2}}$	2^{2}	2^{hd}	Velez J A Jr	116	*1.00	85-14	GretBirdie116^{hd}Mito'sTouch
9Jly86- 9Crc	fst	7f	:22$\frac{3}{5}$	:45$\frac{3}{5}$	1:25$\frac{3}{5}$	3↑	Ⓕ[R]Zippy DoH	10	3	2^{2}	4^{1}	2^{2}	2^{2}	Velez J A Jr	116	22.80	86-17	MdemoisellJoli118^{2}Mito'sTo

LATEST WORKOUTS May 25 Aqu 5f fst 1:03$\frac{2}{5}$ b ● Apr 10 Aqu 6f fst 1:15$\frac{2}{5}$ h

Strategic Heir

Dk. b. or br. g. 5, by Strategic Command—Victorian Heirloom, by Vict Era

DRIEDGER I	118	Br.—Sills & Stranks (Ont-C)
Own.—Mann D		Tr.—Campbell D J $25,000

1987 5 1 0 1 $
1986 15 2 1 3 $
Lifetime 47 7 5 8 $82,027

```
19Jun87-5WO  6½f :222 :454 1:18 ft   26 118  63½ 52½ 34 32½   Driedger I 2   25000 80-23 Koiro, Goose Green, Strategic H
6May87-8WO   1  :492 1:15 1:494ft  *8-5e116  1½ 11½ 13½ 13    Driedger I 5   24000 60-33 StrategicHeir,Let'sDnce.Cndin H
24Apr87-9Grd 7f :231 :471 1:263ft  3½e118  109 86½ 56 45      Clark D 8      20000 77-24 Royal Cape, Bubblestach, State
1Apr87-7Grd  6½f :233 :473 1:193ft   19 118  75½ 75½ 59 56½    Clark D 4      25000 82-17 NorthrnTribut,WGordi,CndinCh
4Apr87-8Grd  4½f :23 :473 :533sy     39 115  6 6² 69½ 59½      Clark D 4      30000 78-19 AgntfNmss,CmmndFlght,Rnwy
11Dec86-9Grd 1½ :474 2:351 3:024ft   3e115  2hd — — —         ClairBT 2 Valdictory H  — — RoylTresurr,SongofDom,KidSh
11Dec86—Pulled up
9Dec86-6Grd  7f :224 :463 1:253ft    2e116  43½ 22 48 57½      Clair B T 3    30000 79-17 Boukephlos,RedyToExplod,Roy
24Nov86-7Grd 1  :474 1:122 1:384gd   5½ 115  53½ 56 713 816½   Clark D 2      30000 69-23 OldGunPowder,HonordCounsl,D
17Nov86-7Grd 6½f :233 :47 1:212ft    6 116  56 35 33½ 3nk      Clark D 4      24000 79-32 Denin,RedyToExplode,Strtegicl
21Aug86-8WO  7f :23 :46 1:243ft     11e124  1hd 11 57½ 810½    King R Jr 5    Aw17500 75-22 CoinDuBanc,Boukephalos,Essa
```

Jun 14 WO 4f ft :491 b   May 24 WO 4f ft :503 b   May 17 WO 4f ft :504 b   May 2 WO 4f ft :494 b

Positive Date Patterns—Last Race within Seven Days

Many of the horses that race again within a week or so of their previous race are sharp and on a form cycle upswing. Rather than waste a sharp horse's fitness by waiting the usual 12 to 15 days between races, a trainer will often send it right back to the racetrack in order to win a purse. As a rule these runners should always be considered as preliminary contenders.

Positive Date Patterns—Frequent Races with Short Layoff

A layoff of about three weeks since a horse's last race is often useful if the horse has raced frequently in the past couple of months. It is important, in this instance, for the horse to have worked a few times during the layoff and to have run at least five or six times in the past 50 to 60 days. These fit and rested horses often come back to run a big race after the short break.

Play The King *(TODAY'S DATE JUNE 28)*

Dk. b. or br. g. 4, by King Of Spain—Whisper, by Laugh Aloud

SEYMOUR D	126	Br.—Kinghaven Farms Ltd (Ont-C)
Own.—Kinghaven Farms Limited		Tr.—Attfield Roger

1987 7 3 2 1 $192,233
1986 6 4 1 0 $54,352
Lifetime 13 7 3 1 $246,585

```
7Jun87-10Cby 6½f :222 :444 1:161ft  *9-5 121  1½ 1½ 2hd 43½    HrnndR 6 Chaucer C H  96-07 Don'sIrshMlody,Suproyl,ChfStwrd 14
25May87-9Aks 6f :213 :442 1:10 ft    3½ 122  74½ 54½ 34½ 23    SymorDJ 4 Aksarben H  84-24 CreoleDncer,PlyThKing,ChifStwrd 10
2May87-9WO   7f :223 :45 1:252ft   *2-5 125  1½ 11½ 12½ 11½    Platts R 3  Vigil H  82-25 PlyThKing,Introspctiv,StrsN'Strips 5
2May87—Grade III-C
19Apr87-9Grd 7f :223 :454 1:24 ft   *1-3 121  12½ 14½ 14 15    Platts R 2  [S]J Cartier  95-21 PlyThKng,OldGunPowdr,BshopBob 6
11Apr87-8Aqu 6f :213 :44 1:09 ft     13 121  33 22 2² 31½      HrnndzR 6 Bold Ruler  94-23 PineTreeLne,LovThtMc,PlyThKing 7
```

● Jun 24 WO tr.t 5f gd :59 b   Jun 20 WO tr.t 4f ft :404 b   ● Jun 3 Cby 5f ft :574 h   ● May 21 WO 5f ft :582 h

Positive Date Patterns—Regular Racing

Regular racing in the positive sense means racing every 10 to 16 days or thereabouts, optimally with workouts used by the trainer to keep the horse sharp between races. Horses that run regularly are usually sound and fit and should be considered carefully.

There are limits, however, to the amount of constant racing that horses can cope with, each horse having its own tolerance level. So while regular racing is by and large a positive factor, there is a fine line between the positive aspect of it and the negative—that of too much racing. This topic is discussed in a later section; however, as a general rule, it is prudent to consider for detailed analysis any horse with a regular racing pattern.

Positive Date Patterns—Layoff Specialists

Some horses run best when given regular periods of rest (three or more weeks) between races. If the chart of a rested horse shows at least a couple of instances of finishing first or second while running on or near the pace after a previous layoff, then it is a potential winner now. (Off-pace runners showing the layoff pattern tend to be less reliable, but can also be considered in this group provided they run consistently well.

***Jeff** — Ch. g. 8, by Sharp-Eyed Quillo—Jeanne d'Arc, by Jardiniere
Own.—Valentine Mrs M
Br.—Haras Geoffrey Bushell (Chile)
Tr.—Cocks W Burling
115 — Lifetime 22 9 4 3 $75.019

7Jun87-	8Del	fm	5f	Ⓣ:21⅖	:44⅘	:57	3↑Post Card	2	9	95¼	52¾	2hd	11	Fitzgerald J F	110	2.40	96-08	Jeff 1101 Bryantown 1111 Se
17May87-	9Del	fm	5f	Ⓣ:21⅖	:44⅗	:57	3↑Alw 9000	5	3	21	22	2hd	2½	Fitzgerald J F	116	*1.70	95-04	Revenged 116½ Jeff 116nk So
1Nov86-	2Fai	fm	*7f	Ⓣ		1:27⅗	3↑Alw 2500	4	10	84¼	32½	42	34¾	Hendriks R	150	*1.40	— —	Major Event 1592¾ Lee De G
12Oct86-	8Pha	fm	5f	Ⓣ:22⅖	:45⅖	:57⅗	3↑Handicap	4	6	52½	1½	11½	2no	Fitzgerald J F	114	14.80	97-08	Bryantown 116no Jeff 114½ W
8Nov85-	5Med	sf	5f	Ⓣ:22⅘	:47⅖	1:00⅕	3↑Alw 20000	5	4	2hd	2hd	22	55	Terry J	115	*1.00	77-27	Banker'sJet1172MissSharpe1
20Oct85-	7Bel	fm	7f	Ⓣ:24	:46⅗	1:22⅖	3↑Alw 36000	4	3	1½	2hd	56	711¾	Vasquez J	115	4.80	80-18	Dominating Dooley 115nk Ch.
13Oct85-	7Pen	fm	5f	Ⓣ		:57⅗	3↑Handicap	3	4	53¼	41¼	2hd	1hd	Colton R E	125	*.90	92-27	Jeff 125hd Doubly Clear 1281½
4Jly85-	6Pen	fm	5f	Ⓣ		:56⅘	3↑Handicap	5	6	42	42	42	11	Terry J	121	*.60	96-16	Jeff 1211LowellPremier119no
19May85-	8Del	yl	*5f	Ⓣ		:58⅗	3↑Alw 7200	2	2	1½	12	12½	13¼	Terry J	122	*.90	97-10	Jeff 1223¼ Cutting Thru 113nk
1Nov84-	9Med	yl	5f	Ⓣ:22⅗	:47	:59⅘	3↑Alw 20000	5	3	31½	1½	2½	32	McCarron G	117	3.10	82-29	Alev 1171 Shananie 1191 Jeff

LATEST WORKOUTS May 14 Del 4f fst :50⅕ b

Positive Date Patterns—Start of Season

Early in the year many horses return for another season of racing after layoffs of several months. Because of the lack of recent races, their prospects must be judged from their workouts, trainer, natural speed, and consistency. Digging through old racing forms to see how a horse has returned from a similar winter layoff can also be informative on occasion.

In any case, a horse should show some evidence of good and frequent activity in the morning, with the most recent workout occurring within three or four days of the horse's seasonal bow. The longer this first race is, the longer and more frequent the workouts should be. If a horse is running its initial start in a very short sprint (five furlongs or less), then it should show some evidence of sharp speed in the workouts.

As confirmation of the benefits of the workouts, the freshened horse should also look fit, lean, and sharp in the paddock.

Dear Effie — Ch. m. 5, by Full Pocket—Miss McGuire, by Mickey McGuire
$16,000 Br.—Alexander & Johnson (Ky) — Tr.—Hall Timothy — **116** — Lifetime 12 1 1 2 $18,225
Own.—Moss J S

30Oct86- 2Aqu	fst	6f	:22⅗	:46⅖	1:11⅘	3↑ ⒻClm 25000	5	8	42½	42	31½	53½	Davis R G	b 117	6.00	78-21	DawnBreak110nkPlatinumPos
6Oct86- 3Bel	fst	6f	:22⅗	:46	1:10⅘	3↑ ⒻClm 35000	4	7	77¾	611	610	613¼	Venezia M	b 117	5.20	75-24	Solohi 1141¼ Forever Special
15Sep86- 1Bel	fst	6f	:23	:46⅘	1:11⅗	3↑ ⒻClm 35000	1	2	31	2½	2hd	3nk	Venezia M	b 117	7.90	85-15	MerryWidowWaltz113hdSoloE
9Aug86- 2Sar	fst	6f	:22⅗	:46	1:11⅖	3↑ ⒻClm 30000	1	3	2hd	3½	31½	33¾	Venezia M	b 113	9.10	79-17	ProHarmony1173¼HighlndSin
24Jly86- 1Bel	fst	6f	:22⅗	:46	1:10⅘	3↑ ⒻClm 42500	5	6	53	33	46½	710	Venezia M	b 115	10.60	78-15	Teriyaki Stake 1174 Oaxaca 1
5Jly86- 3Bel	fst	7f	:23⅗	:46⅘	1:24	3↑ ⒻAlw 24000	2	6	11	22½	511	719¼	Guerra W A	b 117	*1.10	63-15	Pasampsi 1123¼ Unlimited Ac
15Jun86- 6Bel	fst	7f	:23⅖	:46⅗	1:25⅖	3↑ ⒻAlw 24000	5	1	11½	11½	1½	2¾	Venezia M	b 117	5.10	74-21	Give A Toast 114¾ Dear Effie
17Jan86- 9SA	fst	1	:45⅘	1:10⅗	1:36⅖	ⒻClm 62500	4	1	13	11½	54	89½	Valenzuela P A	b 115	7.10	76-15	Stemware 1161¼ Pet Bird 114
17Jan86-Placed seventh through disqualification																	
26Dec85- 6SA	fst	6f	:21⅘	:44⅕	1:09⅖	3↑ ⒻAlw 24000	6	3	41¼	36	49	511¾	Meza R Q	b 115	6.50	79-13	Doff 11710 Soul Light 117nk H
1Dec85- 5Hol	gd	7f	:21⅘	:44⅘	1:23⅗	ⒻⓇDsrt Lw	6	1	2hd	41¾	511	513¾	Meza R Q	b 115	3.30	72-16	Wild Kitty 115¾ Affirmed's D

LATEST WORKOUTS May 30 Mth 4f fst :49 b May 23 Mth 6f fst 1:13 hg ●May 15 Mth 5f fst 1:01⅖ h

Negative Date Patterns

Negative Date Patterns—Too Much Racing

Many horses (especially cheaper ones) cannot race at the top of their form cycle for more than a few weeks. Once the horse has passed the form peak and shows a race or two in which it failed in the stretch, it can be considered a likely loser today.

A study of the race dates and stretch drives provides the clues to determine if a horse is showing the signs of tired form. A horse that continues to race regularly (every 10 to 16 days or so) after the form cycle peak is passed will often fade in a stretch drive because of fatigue. It is in need of a rest.

Exceptions to the rule are usually found among consistent winning horses that have had an easy last race. Generally, an easy race means a race in which the horse was not forced to compete on or near the lead, and which resulted in an out of the money finish. The form of these animals must be studied carefully, with particular attention devoted to the easy appearing races. There should exist reasonable excuses for poor or mediocre performances. (One of the best excuses in this instance occurs when a consistent speed horse is unable to get control of a fast-paced race, finishing back in the pack. More on the topic of excuses later.)

Two poorish races in a row by a horse that normally finishes near the winner is an emphatic sign of fatigue or physical deterioration. Consistent horses that show clear signs of tiredness from too much hard racing tend to be heavily overbet.

Island Victory * B. m. 5, by Victory Stride—Malhoa, by Monterey
$5,000 Br.—Mittman & Murty Farm (Okla) 119 Lifetime 51 9 7 7 $55,290
Own.—Nash T D Tr.—Aristone Philip

17Jun87- 4Pha	fst	7f	:22⅗	:46⅖	1:26⅘	3↑ⒻClm 6500	2	5	2^{5}	2^{3}	4^{4}	$3^{5\frac{1}{2}}$	Aristone M	b	116	6.00	67-25	Bewitching Bee116$^{1\frac{1}{2}}$Broadw
10Jun87- 5GS	fst	170	:47⅗	1:14⅘	1:46⅗	3↑ⒻClm 6500	6	4	$4^{4\frac{1}{2}}$	2^{hd}	$3^{\frac{1}{2}}$	3^{7}	Aristone M	b	116	2.20	59-31	Inca Gold 109½ Binn N' Bea
1Jun87- 2GS	fst	$1\frac{1}{16}$	:48⅘	1:14⅗	1:48⅕	3↑ⒻClm c-5000	3	1	$1^{\frac{1}{2}}$	2^{hd}	$3^{2\frac{1}{2}}$	$3^{5\frac{1}{2}}$	Fitzgerald J F	b	122	2.30	61-27	All In Free 116^{3} Hidden Fan
18May87- 6Pen	sly	170	:47	1:13⅕	1:45⅖	ⒻClm 7500	5	3	3^{4}	$3^{\frac{1}{2}}$	2^{1}	2^{nk}	Aviles R B	b	114	4.90	73-29	Akkurate Dancer 110^{nk} Islar
6May87- 7Del	fst	$1\frac{1}{16}$	:48	1:14	1:50	3↑ⒻClm 5000	2	1	2^{hd}	2^{hd}	1^{hd}	1^{nk}	Fitzgerald J F	b	119	*2.10	58-33	IslndVictory119^{nk}Shesnoord
29Apr87- 6Pen	fst	$1\frac{1}{16}$	:47⅘	1:13⅗	1:48⅕	ⒻClm 5000	1	2	1^{hd}	$1^{\frac{1}{2}}$	1^{2}	$1^{1\frac{1}{4}}$	Aviles R B	b	116	*1.60	65-28	Island Victory 116$^{1\frac{1}{4}}$ IDon'tS
20Apr87- 4Pen	fst	170	:48	1.13⅘	1:45⅘	ⒻClm 5000	9	3	2^{2}	3^{nk}	3^{3}	3^{6}	Johnston D Jr	b	116	7.00	65-25	Knave's Lark 122^{hd} County
10Apr87- 8Pen	fst	$1\frac{1}{16}$	:49⅕	1:13⅘	1:48	ⒻClm 5000	5	4	$5^{2\frac{3}{4}}$	$4^{2\frac{1}{2}}$	$5^{6\frac{1}{2}}$	5^{6}	Sanchez F C	b	116	5.00	60-22	Trumpet Vine 116^{4} CountyJ
23Mar87- 8Pen	fst	$1\frac{1}{16}$	:48⅖	1:13⅗	1:48	ⒻClm 5000	3	2	2^{hd}	1^{hd}	1^{hd}	3^{nk}	Aviles R B	b	116	5.90	66-24	County Joy116^{hd}Appomatto
15Mar87- 4Pen	fst	170	:48⅕	1:13⅗	1:44⅘	ⒻClm 3200	1	1	$1^{1\frac{1}{2}}$	1^{3}	1^{6}	$1^{8\frac{1}{4}}$	Appleby D L Jr	b	116	8.10	76-20	Island Victory 116$^{8\frac{1}{4}}$ Held O

LATEST WORKOUTS May 30 CT 3f fst :38 b

Negative Date Patterns—Frequent Layoffs

A great many thoroughbred race horses cannot physically stand up to continuous racing. After a few races they go sore in one or more vulnerable body sites. When this happens the trainer will usually rest the horse until it feels better. These layoffs range from three weeks to many months. Some skilled trainers can bring these horses back to winning form immediately after layoffs. This is the exception, however.

As a rule, a horseplayer should downgrade the chances of frequently laid-off horses unless multiple workouts are evident in the form or the horse has shown a liking for infrequent racing. Normally the public properly bets horses that have run infrequently; however, laid-off horses are sometimes heavily overbet if their last race prior to the layoff was a good one. The public tends to expect a repeat of the horse's latest race in spite of its absence from racing.

Negative Date Patterns—No Workouts Between Races

Horses away from racing for 14 to 20 days or so should show at least one workout in the interim. I suspect the physical condition of horses not worked under these circumstances. Occasionally a trainer will schedule a workout for his horse but because of bad weather or track conditions be forced to cancel or postpone it. A long spell of poor track conditions might even prevent a trainer from rescheduling a trial. If this appears to be the case, check to see if workouts were given between previous races. The horse can usually be forgiven if it has a history of between-race workouts and the weather recently restricted on-track training. Otherwise it is risky to consider an unworked horse for a bet unless it is a layoff specialist or has had a high frequency of races in the past few months.

Negative Date Patterns—First Race of Season

Generally, horses that have not worked within four or five days of their seasonal bow should not be considered for a bet. An exception is the dominant speedball running a short sprint (five furlongs or less). This kind of horse normally has enough natural speed to run a short distance without a substantial base of workout conditioning. Its physical condition, though, should always be verified visually. Look for a tightness in the girth and chest area, with a bit of ribs showing. Fat horses that have not run in months should be considered as likely losers.

Sharp Form and Signs of Sharp Form

The next aspect of a horse's form that must be examined in conjunction with race and workout dates is sharpness. A horse must show signs of sharpness in the recent past (within two weeks or so for sprinters, within about 25 days for routers) if it is to be considered as a genuine contender. It is required that a horse show obvious sharp form, but at the least shows signs of improving fitness.

Indications of sharp form follow below.

Sharp Form Factors—Fast Final Times

This positive factor is ascertained through a comparison of a horse's previous race times with times of races run by the other horses in the race. Times from any race run in the past three weeks or so are acceptable, but last race figures are the more reliable indicators.

Final times meeting the sharp horse criteria for sprints are those within a couple of fifths of the top recent times of the fastest contender. A wider range (about a full second) should be used for routes. (Assessing the final times of turf races presents a more difficult problem because of their high variability. This topic is discussed in detail shortly.)

I recommend that dirt race times be adjusted by a daily variant in order to make day-to-day comparisons valid. The method I use to adjust time figures for daily variation of track condition is described below.

Adjusting Final Times for Track Condition

There are complex methods available for calculating a daily variant. The best are usually based on a comparison of the final time of a race against a well-established "standard" associated with class, age, distance, and other conditions of each race field.

The idea behind the use of a daily track variant is that track conditions vary from day to day, thereby contributing to variations in final times. This extraneous variation in final times can be removed by subtracting or adding a figure representing the difference between the final times and a standard or par time for each racing field. These par figures are computed, for each distance-age-class category of race run at the track, by averaging the times from many races run on normal fast-track days. The figures must be updated regularly because track speed can show secular changes. I have no quarrel with those wishing to do the considerable work to establish and maintain this kind of sophisticated system, providing care is exercised in application.

The variant I use, however, is much simpler, takes only a few minutes to compute each week, and works adequately well. The basis of it is a familiarity with the older horses running at the track. The variant is estimated by comparing race times of horses familiar to me with the time I expect them to run under normal fast-track conditions. For instance, if a group of familiar, older horses run a six furlong race in 1:12 on a given day when I know they can run it in 1:10⅗ under normal fast-track conditions, then I can compute a variant of plus seven fifths of a second for that day at six furlongs. Ideally there should be another race or two available on that day at or near the same distance for other known older horses to confirm the observation. The estimate of plus seven may change depending on the results of these other races. When two or more good observations are available, then a simple average of the variants can be computed.

A variant for route times can be estimated in a similar manner if longer races are run during the racing card.

A sprint variant should be used to adjust all sprint times for the day; a route variant used for the route times. If one of the two variants is considered unreliable or uncertain, it can be estimated from the other: for routes add half again as much to the sprint variant, for sprints divide the route variant by 1.5. This calculation should also be done when both a route and sprint variant are estimated independently, in order to validate the figures. The two methods should produce roughly similar figures, otherwise the estimates are suspect.

Comparing Adjusted Times

Care must be exercised when comparing adjusted final times for different distances. Racing Form speed ratings should not be used because infrequently run distances often have relatively slow track record times and produce higher speed ratings than races run by similar horses at more popular distances. There is a better way to compare times run at different distances. It may be a bit rough for the purists, but it works well for me.

The adjustment requires that several seconds be added to or subtracted from times to make them comparable. The idea is to adjust each time to a common distance to make quick comparisons possible. As a rule of thumb, final times from different sprint distances can be adjusted by about $6\frac{3}{5}$ seconds for each half-furlong difference between the two distances. This rough guide can be reduced by one or two fifths for short sprints ($4\frac{1}{2}$, 5, and $5\frac{1}{2}$ furlongs).

For routes, the corresponding rule of thumb adjustment is $6\frac{4}{5}$ or 7 seconds. Longer routes ($1\frac{1}{4}$ miles and up) require an extra fifth or so in the adjustment to make times from short routes and long routes comparable. Knowledge of the peculiarities of a track and common sense should be your guide to finding the best adjustment.

Comparing route times with sprint times can be tricky and should only be done on a general scale. It is nearly impossible to compare short sprint times (6 furlongs and less) with route times, because sprinters with good times often produce slow times in routes, and vice versa. Times from 7-furlong races are somewhat more extendible to route distances by extrapolation, since most routes are only a furlong and a half longer in distance. In any case, the sprinter moving to a route should show evidence of stamina, and the router moving to a sprint should possess some speed. These topics are discussed in more detail later.

A Word of Caution in Using a Variant

My variant is essentially a quick estimate, not a rigid calculation. Blind variant calculations using time standards can, in my experience, often produce a variant far out of line with reality because races for two and three year olds (especially early in the year) cannot be assigned proper class-time standards. A day during which races for young horses are frequent may yield a variant that is unrealistic due to spectacular improvement by a couple of youngsters. In addition, days on which the dirt track is sloppy or muddy may produce some overly fast times in easily won races, because of the penchant some runners have for an off-track. Winning times from these races would not truly reflect the reduced speed of the racing strip, and a variant based on the final times would therefore be too low. Care must be taken to adjust or reject such time figures, as well as the figures from races in which the pace was controlled by a single front-runner or pair of dueling speed merchants. Front-runners that are permitted to relax on the lead and speed duelers fighting every inch of the way sometimes produce times that are faster than those possible under more usual pace circumstances.

Adjustment to the variant must also be made when the condition of the racing surface changes during the day, as when rain falls in the morning and the track dries gradually during the afternoon, or when rain suddenly falls part way through the session. Under these conditions, the track speed is not likely to be consistent throughout the race card. Extremely variable weather and track conditions may even require that a variant be estimated for individual races. Here again, knowledge of the horses can help produce a graduated variant.

Turf Race Variant

Computing a variant for turf races presents a more difficult problem because of the wide variability in surface conditions as well as the periodic use of dogs or rails by the management to protect the inside part of the course. Rather than calculate a variant, I prefer to do a careful check of the competitiveness within each turf race.

There are some valuable clues about the speed of a race to be gleaned from the way a race is run. For example, a race in which many of the horses were separated at the finish by a relatively small margin suggests that the time truly reflected the abilities of a matched field, and lacking evidence to the contrary should be considered an average to slow time. It would be an oddity if the time for this race represented a truly fast clocking, because the chances are low that a majority of the horses in any one race would be especially sharp. A race in which a smaller group of runners (two or three) finished well ahead (by at least three or four lengths) of the majority of the field is another story, however. Times from these races are often quite fast, because the median ability of the field is more accurately reflected in the time clocked by the leader of the second (larger) flight of finishers. If the small group of first flight runners produced much faster times than this median, then the race was indeed probably run very rapidly. This conclusion is not warranted if the field was markedly weak, however. This can be ascertained by a quick review of the past performances for the race in question.

Another valuable clue to the significance of grass race times within a given day is provided when more than one race was run on the same turf course. If the difference between times (adjusted for distance) was proportional to the differences between the basic classes, then probably the times were not exceptional, since no single time stood out. On the other hand, a time that seemed overly fast relative to other times would be worth noting. Remember to consider how the field was spread out in that race at the finish. It may be that only a few horses ran to good time, not the whole field.

Due to these considerations, instead of computing a daily variant I record a qualitative assessment of the final time for each grass race. I use such terms as "very fast time," "slow time," "average time," et cetera. Comparison of turf race performances by horses that ran on different days must be made on the basis of these qualitative assessments and class levels.

These comparisons might lead to conclusions such as: an "average" time for a $10,000 race is worse than an "average" time for a $12,000 race, or a "very fast" time at the $15,000 level may be better than a "slow" time at $20,000, et cetera. This practice is sure to offend the speed purists, some of whom spend hours each week computing a numeric variant. But the method has worked well for me in contributing to a better feel for relative worth among contenders.

EIGHTH RACE
Hialeah Park
DECEMBER 8

1 ⅛ MILES.(Turf). (1.46²) ALLOWANCE. Purse $14,000 (plus $3,500 FOA). 3-year-olds and upward which have never won a race other than maiden, claiming or starter. Weights: 3-year-olds, 119 lbs.; Older, 122 lbs. Non-winners of a race other than claiming at a mile or over since September 15, allowed 3 lbs. Of such a race since August 1, 5 lbs.

Value of race $17,500; value to winner $11,900; second $2,520; third $1,400; fourth $560; balance of starters $140 each.

Mutuel pool $66,708. Perfecta PI $31,165 Quinella PI $20,029 Trifecta PI $66,143

Last Raced	Horse	M/Eqt.A.Wt	PP	St	¼	½	¾	Str	Fin	Jockey	Odds $1
19Nov91 7Hia²	Sitz High	L	3 114	10	10	8²	8hd	6¹	5hd	1no	Martin C W	3.40
27Nov91 4Hia¹	Firing Fuse-Fr	L	3 114	4	11	12	12	11⁶	6³½	2⁴½	Castillo H Jr	10.00
12Nov91 7Hia²	Nez Perce	Lb	5 117	6	5	2²	2²½	1²	2hd	3hd	Gaffalione S	7.20
12Nov91 7Hia³	Siempre	L	3 116	9	9	9³	9⁴	5²½	4¹	4no	Velez J A Jr	5.10
19Nov91 3Hia¹	Anywhere North	L	4 117	5	2	4½	7¹½	4½	3¹½	5²½	Ramos W	29.60
20Nov91 8Hia⁵	David Dunnit	Lb	3 114	2	3	7²	6²	3¹	1hd	6³	Guerra W A	93.70
16Nov91 3Grd¹	Dorsan		3 119	3	4	10¹½	11²½	9²	8²	7nk	Penna D	3.80
6Jly91 6Lrl⁵	Spectacular Mitch	L	3 114	8	7	5¹	5½	7¹½	7hd	8hd	Vasquez J	4.80
28Nov91 9Hia¹	Go Robert Go	Lb	3 114	12	12	11¹½	10hd	10²½	10⁵	9³	Rodriguez P A	17.10
26Nov91 8Hia¹⁰	Crafty Tonage	Lb	3 114	1	1	1¹½	11	2²	9hd	10³	Lester R N	11.20
27Nov91 5Hia¹	Silver Kris	L	3 114	11	8	6¹	4¹	8hd	11	11	Terry J	29.00
6Nov91 6Crc⁴	For Me	L	4 117	7	6	3½	3²½	12	—	—	St Leon G	30.60

SIXTH RACE
Hialeah Park
NOVEMBER 24

1 $\frac{1}{16}$ MILES.(Turf). (1.39^3) CLAIMING. Purse $12,000 (plus $3,000 FOA). 3-year-olds and upward. Weights: 3-year-olds, 119 lbs.; Older, 122 lbs. Non-winners of two races at a mile or over since October 15, allowed 3 lbs. Of such a race since then, 5 lbs. Claiming price $40,000; for each $2,500 to $35,000, 2 lbs. (Races when entered to be claimed for $30,000 or less not considered.)

Value of race $15,000; value to winner $10,200; second $2,160; third $1,320; fourth $600; balance of starters $120 each. Mutuel pool $65,364. Perfecta Pl $34,168 Quinella Pl $18,967 Trifecta Pl $67,085

Last Raced	Horse	M/Eqt.	A.	Wt	PP	St	¼	½	¾	Str	Fin	Jockey	Cl'g Pr	Odds $1
14Oct91 ^{9}Lrl^{5}	Cafe Creme	L	6	117	5	8	8^1	$7\frac{1}{2}$	3^{hd}	3^3	$1\frac{1}{2}$	Ramos A	40000	11.70
12Oct91 ^{7}Crc^{5}	Gun Deck	Lb	7	117	4	7	7^4	$6\frac{1}{2}$	$8^{1\frac{1}{2}}$	$7^{2\frac{1}{2}}$	$2\frac{1}{2}$	Castillo H Jr	40000	5.50
9Nov91 ^{2}Crc^{1}	Atom Action	L	4	113	9	3	$2^{1\frac{1}{2}}$	1^{hd}	1^{hd}	1^{hd}	3^{nk}	Duarte J C	35000	4.70
2Nov91 ^{13}Crc^{2}	Inishpour-Ir	L	9	113	7	6	$4^{2\frac{1}{2}}$	$3\frac{1}{2}$	2^2	2^{hd}	4^{hd}	Felix J E	35000	8.00
9Oct91 ^{7}Kee^{4}	Kings Casino	Lb	3	114	8	9	10	10	$6^{1\frac{1}{2}}$	6^{hd}	$5^{2\frac{1}{2}}$	Thibeau RJJr	40000	5.50
9Nov91 ^{11}Crc^{8}	Coach Digger	Lb	4	117	3	10	9^{hd}	9^1	$4^{1\frac{1}{2}}$	$4^{1\frac{1}{2}}$	$6^{2\frac{1}{2}}$	Sipus E J Jr	40000	1.30
12Nov91 ^{7}Hia^{7}	Dancer's Light	Lb	3	110	6	4	$6\frac{1}{2}$	8^1	$9^{3\frac{1}{2}}$	8^1	$7^{2\frac{1}{2}}$	Nunez E O	35000	68.80
17Nov91 ^{8}Hia^{2}	Wish Tonite	b	3	114	10	5	$5^{1\frac{1}{2}}$	$5^{1\frac{1}{2}}$	$5\frac{1}{2}$	5^{hd}	$8^{2\frac{1}{2}}$	St Leon G	40000	17.30
12Oct91 ^{6}Crc^{7}	Ocean Mistery	L	5	108	1	1	1^{hd}	2^1	7^{hd}	9^5	9^{10}	Martinez RR^7	35000	22.40
10Nov91 ^{8}Hia^{10}	Soft Halo	b	4	113	2	2	3^2	$4^{2\frac{1}{2}}$	10	10	10	Daigle E T	35000	86.20

OFF AT 2:54 Start good Won driving Time, 1:45^2 Course good.

$2 Mutuel Prices:			
5-CAFE CREME	25.40	9.60	5.60
4-GUN DECK		6.80	5.00
9-ATOM ACTION			3.60

$2 PERFECTA 5-4 PAID $174.80 $2 QUINELLA 4-5 PAID $73.20 $2 TRIFECTA 5-4-9 PAID $1,359.20

Sharp Form Factors—Early Speed in a Recent Race

By definition, early speed means that a horse led the field or was much closer than usual to the lead in the early part of a recent race, while fading to finish out of the money. An early speed performance can be due to several factors, including improving fitness, maturation (young horses), slow early pace, outside or inside post position, trainer intentions (hidden workout), poor jockey strategy, or a combination of factors. What are the signs of positive early speed?

The best pattern occurs when unexpected speed is flashed for no more than the first two calls, after which the horse drops well back out of the money. As a result, the horse's sharpness is not completely noticed by the public in its next race. This kind of speed is a sign of improving fitness, especially if the horse displaying it has returned recently from a layoff or, in the case of a young horse, has had limited racing experience. The angle has greater strength if the horse's final clocking was close to the top times of contenders today or if the horse ran in a higher class than today.

Fast early race fractions lend added strength to the indicator. This applies particularly in short sprints (races of 6 furlongs or less), in which the ability of a front-runner to break away from the pack is an important consideration. The comparison of first and second quarter fractional times among contenders can often point out the top candidate in these short sprints and is especially useful in assessing the ability of two-year-olds.

Early speed in a horse's next to last race can be a positive sign under certain circumstances. The race in which the speed was displayed should have been run within 25 days or so of today's race, preferably within 15 or 20 days. The last race should have looked dull—an even, out of the money finish is best. Look for an excuse in that race, such as a poorish start, bad post, classy field, undesirable racing surface, and so on. My favorite specific patterns for that last dull race include: (1) a race in which the horse was 5 to 10 lengths or more off the lead a few hundred feet out of the gate, with an even but far back race at all calls showing up in the Racing Form (a case of not breaking well from the gate), and (2) a race that was run in good time, but because of a superior field the horse ran out of the money. If no excuse for a truly dull performance can be found, the early speed angle is of dubious merit.

This next to last race angle applies almost equally as well to a solid previous race without the early speed factor. Any good next to last race with an apparently dull intervening effort will tend to remove the horse from the public's attention for its next race, at which time many of the horse's previous backers will bet another horse. Again, the last two races must have been run within about three weeks of today's race for the angle to have value.

Returning to the discussion of early speed, there are two other points to keep in mind when assessing whether a quick break by a horse can be considered positive early speed. First, post position can sometimes force a horse to run faster than it would normally do so early in a race. For instance, in a sprint, the far outside and rail positions make it difficult for anything but a true speedball to gain a commanding position, and tend to put at a disadvantage mediocre speed horses. Jockeys therefore will often push an average speed horse faster than it may wish to run to avoid being shuffled back too far by horses running to the rail. Instead of being four or five lengths behind after the first furlong, the horse may be only one or two lengths back, or even in the lead. The speed may not be evident in the Form from running position, but rather by lengths off the leader. Instead of showing the horse running first or second at the first and second call, the Form may show it running fourth or fifth but behind the leader by only a length or two. This can be considered as genuine early speed if the horse normally runs further off the pace. In this regard take particular note of horses that ran their last race from outside post positions. Because of their starting positions they often get forced into fighting for the early lead in order to attain a challenging position for the stretch drive. If hung up on the outside around a turn, these horses are required to run further as well as faster, and have a good excuse if beaten off. Their struggle is not usually obvious in the Racing Form. Always keep in mind post position when examining a horse's running line. It is very, very important.

Secondly, distance switches can exaggerate or mask an early speed indicator. A sprinter in a route will almost always flash early speed by virtue of the slower pace. The times of the fractions must be considered carefully. They should be respectable sprint fractions if the horse is now running back in a sprint. Sprints will often improve a router's quickness, resulting in a subsequent route performance in which the pace is more closely attended. I usually accept a sprint race by a router as the equivalent of an early speed performance, provided the horse kept within six or seven lengths of the pace throughout.

Mighty Wonder — Dk. b. or br. f. 4, by Poison Ivory—Winamite, by Royal Gallant
Own.—Tanrackin Farm | Br.—Waller Mrs T M (NY) | Tr.—Waller Thomas M | 117 | Lifetime 10 3 3 0 $81,480

14Jun87- 8Bel	fst	1	:46	1:11⅘	1:38⅖	3↑ⒻSHydeParkH	9	1	2hd	1½	42½	57½	Bailey J D	112	9.50	65–20	Peggy'sDream1142½LadyBeR
1Jun87- 8Bel	fst	6f	:22⅖	:46⅗	1:11⅗	3↑ⒻAlw 29000	5	2	22½	31½	43¼	66¾	Bailey J D	117	28.80	75–20	Bold Mate 1113 Rajiste 1171½
23Aug86- 2Sar	fst	7f	:21⅕	:45⅖	1:23⅘	3↑ⒻSAlw 26500	3	6	1hd	12	16	16¼	Bailey J D	112	*2.30	83–10	Mighty Wonder 1126¼TorridZ
21Jly86- 7Bel	fst	6f	:22⅘	:45⅗	1:09⅘	3↑ⒻSAlw 28000	7	1	21½	22	24	27¼	Maple E	116	2.20D	86–14	Indistinctly 1117¼ DMightyW
21Jly86-Disqualified and placed fourth																	
11Jly86- 7Bel	fst	6f	:22⅗	:46⅖	1:12	3↑ⒻSAlw 26500	9	3	41	1hd	12½	14¾	Maple E	111	3.00	82–19	MightyWondr1114¾MissNlliE
26Jun86- 7Bel	fst	7f	:23	:47	1:25⅘	3↑ⒻSAlw 26500	10	4	41	2hd	21½	66½	Maple E	112	6.70	66–17	TheZimmermnNote111hdLust
27Oct85- 6Aqu	fst	6f	:22⅘	:46⅘	1:13	ⒻSMd Sp Wt	6	3	1hd	12	16	16¾	Maple E	117	*.80	76–21	Mighty Wonder1176¾Anchor
12Oct85- 7Bel	fst	6f	:22⅘	:46⅕	1:11⅖	ⒻSN YStallion	1	1	11½	2hd	21½	23½	Maple E	113	14.30	81–18	RomnticGirl1123½MightyWor
12Oct85-Run in Divisions																	
18Sep85- 6Bel	fst	7f	:23	:46⅗	1:24⅘	ⒻSMd Sp Wt	4	8	1hd	22	213	221	MacBeth D	117	7.50	57–18	Indistinctly 11721 Mighty Wc
4Sep85- 9Bel	fst	6f	:23⅖	:48⅕	1:13⅕	ⒻSMd Sp Wt	4	9	53	52½	22½	24½	Venezia M	117	16.20	71–21	GenerlCondition1174½Mighty

LATEST WORKOUTS Jun 25 Bel T 5f fm 1:05 b (d) Jun 12 Bel tr.t 4f fst :49⅘ h Jun 8 Bel tr.t 4f fst :48⅗ h Ma

Royal Tantrum — B. f. 4, by Cornish Prince—Hannimo, by Blasting Signal
Own.—Davis A & Barbara | $25,000 | Br.—Dubick & Priest (Ky) | Tr.—Moschera Gasper S | 117 | Lifetime 19 3 5 1 $44,440

14Jun87- 3Bel	fst	1$\frac{1}{16}$	:47⅕	1:12⅗	1:44⅘	ⒻClm 25000	6	1	1½	32	720	733½	Bailey J D	b	117	*2.90	45–20	Crown Piper 1172 Wild Wom
27May87- 2Bel	fst	6f	:22⅗	:46⅕	1:11⅖	ⒻClm 25000	4	6	52¼	62¼	31½	2hd	Bailey J D	b	117	3.50	83–22	Private Iron 117hd Royal Tan
16May87- 2Bel	fst	6f	:22⅘	:46⅖	1:11⅕	ⒻClm 14000	3	1	1½	11½	12½	13¼	Bailey J D	b	117	15.10	84–18	RoyalTantrum1173¼Tar'sNtiv
19Sep86- 2Med	fst	6f	:22⅗	:46⅖	1:12⅕	ⒻClm 16000	2	5	42½	31	3½	45¾	Correa C J10	b	107	5.50	75–17	Royal Steph 1154 Mint Bonn
2Sep86- 7Med	fst	6f	:22⅕	:45⅖	1:11	ⒻClm 25000	2	7	42	43¼	45½	49	Correa C J10	b	106	8.80	78–18	Speed Out First 1154½ Holly
25Aug86- 4Sar	fst	7f	:22⅕	:45⅖	1:25⅖	ⒻClm 25000	5	5	1½	2hd	54	74¾	Maple E	b	116	5.00	70–19	Ancient Gold 112½ Turnpike I
8Aug86- 6Sar	my	6f	:22	:45⅗	1:11	ⒻClm 35000	2	4	33½	32½	37½	310	Samyn J L	b	116	15.50	75–17	Ski Bunny 1188¾ Medieval M
16Jly86- 1Bel	fst	6f	:22⅗	:45⅘	1:10⅘	ⒻClm 45000	6	4	41¼	23	26	410	Cruguet J	b	112	9.80	78–17	Grotona 1129½ Triomphe'sGlc
12Jly86- 5Bel	my	1$\frac{1}{16}$	:46⅕	1:11⅘	1:44	ⒻClm 45000	1	2	11½	21	712	721	Cruguet J		112	21.80	61–15	Triomphe's Glory 1081¾ Just
7Jly86- 5Bel	fst	6½f	:23	:46⅗	1:17⅘	ⒻClm c-32500	5	3	54¾	64½	77¾	711	Santos J A		114	2.50	76–12	Groton1163½ScyN'Clssy1092¼1

LATEST WORKOUTS May 24 Bel 4f fst :48 h May 14 Bel tr.t 4f fst :50 b May 3 Bel tr.t 4f fst :49⅖ b

Matt's Schtick — B. g. 5, by Stutz Blackhawk—Regal Shoo, by Regal and Royal
Own.—Jewel E Stable | $14,000 | Br.—Farnsworth Farm & Bern Chuck (Fla) | Tr.—Ferriola Peter | 117 | Lifetir 77 9 1 $144,1

27Nov91- 1Aqu	fst	1⅛	:483	1:132	1:521	3↑Clm 14000	(10)	3	21	1hd	32½	610¾	Toscano P R	b	117	*.90e	64–26	Fake Out1174 I
22Nov91- 1Aqu	sly	1⅛	:471	1:12	1:513	3↑Clm 17500	3	4	35	43½	55½	37¾	Toscano P R	b	117	4.60e	70–28	A.M.Swinger11
17Nov91- 3Aqu	fst	7f	:232	:464	1:244	3↑Clm 17500	8	6	64½	52½	21½	21½	Toscano P R	b	117	3.80	76–21	Scugnizzo1171
2Nov91- 1Aqu	fst	6f	:223	:453	1:094	3↑Clm 17500	2	4	42½	53	46	46¾	Toscano P R	b	117	2.70	85–12	HppyKentucki
14Oct91- 3Bel	fst	1$\frac{1}{16}$	:464	1:12	1:44	3↑Clm 25000	7	7	44	62½	75¾	710¼	Migliore R	b	117	14.00	72–22	Roman Cat119
3Oct91- 3Bel	fst	1	:473	1:12	1:37	3↑Clm 25000	4	4	3nk	41½	69½	612½	Mojica R Jr5	b	112	*1.80	72–13	BowdoinStreet
25Sep91- 6Bel	sly	7f	:224	:454	1:241	3↑Clm 25000	2	3	34	35	24	21¼	Mojica R Jr5	b	112	6.50	82–14	HppyKntckn11
12Sep91- 4Bel	fst	6f	:224	:454	1:094	3↑Clm 30000	2	5	74½	63¾	53¼	58	Mojica R Jr5	b	108	*1.70e	83–16	SlntGnrlon117
22Jly91- 5Bel	fst	7f	:223	:454	1:241	Clm 35000	8	2	93¼	62½	53	56½	Migliore R	b	117	4.20e	76–18	IKepAbrst113¾
3Jun91- 6Bel	fst	6f	:213	:443	1:094	3↑Alw 28000	6	5	69	63¾	64	62	Migliore R	b	117	8.90	89–10	TopTheRecord

Speed Index: Last Race: –10.0 3–Race Avg.: –6.0 4–Race Avg.: –8.2

LATEST WORKOUTS ●Oct 28 Aqu 3f fst :372 B

Sharp Form Factors—Fast Workout

A recent sharp work since a horse's last race is normally (but not always) a very positive sign. It usually means the horse is retaining an edge if already sharp, or has improved since the last race if its form was dull or mediocre. (In certain situations, the sharp workout is a false indicator. This is elaborated on later.)

It is difficult to give precise time standards for classifying a workout as sharp. The times depend on distance, class of horse, the horse's running style, track surface, and trainer patterns. Examples: speed style horses will normally have faster times than slow starters for shorter workouts; high-class horses will produce faster times than low-class animals, especially for longer trials. Experience suggests the following rough standards for judging sharpness from a workout:

2f: 23 3/5	4f: 49	6f: 114 4/5	1Mi: 141 3/5
3f: 36 2/5	5f: 101 4/5	7f: 128	

Sharp but short workouts do not have the same value as sharp and long works. Workouts of under four furlongs are fine for "blowout" purposes but do not indicate form and ability the way that longer works can. A sharp four, five, or six furlong workout is an excellent positive indicator of race readiness.

Workout times should be adjusted for class, speed style, surface conditions, and trainer to be meaningful. This adjustment should be a qualitative, mental thing, and not a categorization using fractional cutpoints. It should lead to feelings such as "not a bad time considering the track was slow and the horse is a slow starter" or "that's a rather slow time for a horse that normally works a second or more faster," and so on.

The trainer has a very important influence on workout times. Some trainers never let their charges run fast trials in the morning, while others insist on sharp speed. It is critical that the handicapper know the habits of the trainer when assessing the value of workouts.

A good angle for finding overlays is provided by relating workout times to the trainer. For example, a trainer who wins some races with first time starters worked in mediocre times can provide a golden betting opportunity if he is starting a horse with faster trials than usual. These faster trials do not necessarily have to be eye catching, just as long as they are significantly faster than the times he normally works some of his other successful starters.

Workouts are often the only means of assessing the ability of a young, untried horse. Sharp workouts (especially longer ones) tend to be correlated with ability but do not guarantee racing success. Lack of racing experience will nullify even the best workouts. To make up for a horse's inexperience, it should be conditioned by a first-rate trainer with a proven record of producing well-behaved young runners that can win first time out. The tricky part comes when a good trainer sends out youngsters whose work sheet record is mediocre. Many do run well in spite of lacklustre workouts, especially when competing against other relatively inexperienced runners. But I can't bet them unless a workout suggests special ability. I do, however, happily bet against first-timers that are highly expected to win but have workouts that are considered mediocre or poor in light of the trainer and his methods.

Robin's Crisis	Dk. b. or br. f. 3, by Bold Hour—Many Hills, by Manassas		Lifetime
Own.—Foxwood Stable	$32,500	Br.—Fritz R (Ky)	0 0 0 0
LATEST WORKOUTS		Tr.—Dunham Bob G	**112**
●Jun 23 Aqu 4f sly :48¾ h (d)	Jun 13 Aqu 5f fst 1:00¾ h	May 26 Aqu 6f fst 1:14½ h	●M

Sharp Form Factors—Acceleration within a Race

Horses approaching good form but not quite ready for a top effort will sometimes show brief acceleration midway through a race and then flatten out to the finish. This suggests the horse was sharp enough to overcome the pace for at least a portion of the race, leaving room for further improvement in its next race. Typically these moves are made by off-pace runners.

The move has greater value if it occurred before the stretch, because it suggests the horse will be able to move early enough in a race to get a close-up position for the stretch drive. Horses that habitually wait until deep stretch to make a gaining move have a tendency to be late.

These brief accelerations by horses (other than stretch gains) are easy to miss in the Racing Form. My experience is that a move which appears visually as an outstanding effort often gets represented in the Form as an apparent dull attempt to gain position. For example, the running line

$$7^8 \ 4^4 \ 4^5 \ 5^6$$

does not appear very exciting, but it conceals the fact that the horse may have accelerated sharply between the first and second calls. The horse did make a genuine gain if it closed ground on most horses in the first flight down the backstretch. On the other hand, if the gain was made only in respect to a single leader at the same time as several other horses were making similar gains, the move takes on much less significance. It usually indicates the leader was backing up.

How can these cases be distinguished? Watching the race carefully helps, being observant of horses moving faster or slower than the general pace set by the runners in the first flight. Reading the racing chart comments can also be useful. Races of a mile or longer have one or more extra call positions in the charts than provided in the running line for the Form, a useful fact for those willing to do the digging in the charts. The charts may also depict the pace and changes in leadership during the race. This can help determine the quality of the move. Times for the individual quarter or half mile can be calculated, if necessary, to confirm apparent acceleration.

Sunny Barbie — Dk. b. or br. f. 3(Feb), by Sunny North—Pretty Barbie, by Vertex
Own.—Chevalier Stable — $25,000 — Br.—Red Oak Farm Inc (Fla) — Tr.—Shapoff Stanley R — 118 — Lifetime 17 3 0 3 $44,280

22Nov91- 5Aqu	sly	1⅛	:47^{4}	1:12^{4}	1:51^{3}	3↑ⒻClm 35000	3	3	5^{3}	2$^{1/2}$	3^{5}	4$^{9\frac{1}{2}}$	Carr D	115	8.50	68-28 AmPossible117^{1}MyLa
— 22Nov91-Originally scheduled on turf																
7Nov91- 3Aqu	fst	1	:48	1:13^{1}	1:38^{3}	ⒻClm 25000	6	5	1^{hd}	1^{1}	1^{2}	1$^{2\frac{1}{2}}$	Pezua J M	116	7.40	69-28 Sunny Barbie116$^{2\frac{1}{2}}$ Br
20Oct91- 9Bel	fst	6f	:22	:45^{2}	1:09^{2}	ⒻClm.25000	9	10	8$^{6\frac{1}{2}}$	8$^{5\frac{1}{2}}$	8$^{9\frac{1}{2}}$	4$^{13\frac{3}{4}}$	Pezua J M	116	12.60	79-08 IrishMusic116^{13}ChfM·
4Oct91- 5Bel	fst	1	:47^{4}	1:12^{2}	1:38	ⒻClm 35000	5	4	5$^{2\frac{1}{2}}$	6$^{2\frac{1}{2}}$	5^{4}	5^{9}	Bailey J D	116	4.20	71-20 LuvToMomboJumbo1
18Sep91- 1Bel	fm	1$\frac{1}{16}$ Ⓣ	:46^{2}	1:10^{1}	1:41^{4}	ⒻClm 35000	1	5	4^{4}	4$^{2\frac{1}{2}}$	5^{2}	5$^{5\frac{3}{4}}$	Vasquez M O	116	11.30	81-12 SpyLederLdy118$^{4\frac{3}{4}}$Sss
25Aug91- 3Sar	fst	7f	:22^{3}	:46^{1}	1:23^{4}	ⒻClm 35000	5	5	5^{4}	6$^{4\frac{1}{2}}$	5$^{8\frac{1}{2}}$	4$^{15\frac{3}{4}}$	Vasquez M O	116	16.20	70-12 Inciting116^{1} Miss Red
25Aug91-Took up sharply, lost irons																
15Aug91- 5Sar	fst	6$\frac{1}{2}$f	:21^{4}	:44^{3}	1:16^{3}	ⒻClm 35000	5	9	10$^{7\frac{3}{4}}$	10$^{7\frac{3}{4}}$	5^{6}	6$^{2\frac{3}{4}}$	Vasquez M O	116	8.20	89-10 No Cost116^{no}QuickTo
2Aug91- 3Sar	fm	1⅛ Ⓣ	:46^{3}	1:11^{3}	1:50^{1}	ⒻClm 35000	9	9	8$^{7\frac{1}{2}}$	6$^{4\frac{1}{2}}$	5^{5}	4$^{6\frac{1}{2}}$	Samyn J L	116	8.90	73-14 SpyLederLdy116$^{1\frac{1}{2}}$Rec
12Jly91- 1Bel	fst	1$\frac{1}{16}$	:46^{3}	1:11^{1}	1:43^{4}	ⒻClm 25000	3	3	3$^{1\frac{1}{2}}$	1$^{1/2}$	1$^{2\frac{1}{2}}$	1^{5}	Chavez J F	116	*2.30	83-17 Sunny Barbie116^{5} Div
17Jun91- 2Bel	fm	1$\frac{1}{16}$ Ⓣ	:46^{3}	1:10^{2}	1:42^{1}	ⒻClm 35000	2	6	5$^{4\frac{1}{2}}$	7$^{4\frac{1}{2}}$	5^{5}	5$^{3\frac{3}{4}}$	Vasquez M O^{5}	111	10.10	81-08 Docent116^{nk} Lanes At

Speed Index: Last Race: -4.0 3-Race Avg.: -5.3 4-Race Avg.: -4.0
LATEST WORKOUTS Nov 15 Bel tr.t 4f fst :47^{4} H Nov 4 Bel tr.t 4f fst :48^{2} H Oct 29 Bel tr.t 4f fst :48^{4} B

Miss Angel T. — B. f. 3, by Talc—Adam's Angel, by Halo
Own.—Princeway Farms — Br.—Prince I B (NY) — Tr.—Duncan Susan — 114 — Lifetime 1 0 0 $1,440

10Jun87- 9Bel	fst	7f	:23⅕	:46⅘	1:26⅗	3↑ⒻⓈMd Sp Wt	9	11	8$^{5\frac{1}{2}}$	5$^{5\frac{1}{2}}$	4$^{3\frac{1}{2}}$	4$^{6\frac{1}{2}}$	Migliore R	114	6.90	63-17 ChristyHill114^{3}TuffPo

LATEST WORKOUTS Jun 20 Bel 4f fst :48⅗ h Jun 8 Bel 4f fst :50⅖ b Jun 2 Bel 4f fst :48⅕ h

Sharp Form Factors—Bullishness

Many horses can be intimidated by slightly tougher competition arising from a class elevation, to the extent that they back down when challenged by other horses during a race. Other horses, though, are less easily daunted and refuse to back down, giving their best even when boosted in class. The term *bullishness* refers to the characteristic of some improving horses to continue to run aggressively while moving up in class.

Bullish horses are found through examination of their last two races. To fit the pattern, the next to last race should have been a very sharp effort of recent date, and the last race should have been run in a higher classification than the previous race. The horse, while perhaps not winning its last race, performed well, or at least substantially better than its odds suggested. These horses can be counted on to repeat that aggressive performance.

Many two year olds and lightly raced three year olds normally go through a bullish phase, as do some older horses with back class. Odds on these runners tend to be higher than warranted, due to a skepticism on the part of the public regarding the ability of the horse to cope with the move up in class.

Roundwood — Ch. c. 4, by Murtaugh—Slipping Round, by Round Table
Own.—Nauset Stable — **$6,500** Br.—Panorama Farms (NY) / Tr.—White Henry — **116** — Lifetime 21 4 4 .3 $27.275

22May87- 7GS	fst	1 1/16	:48	1:12 4/5	1:45 4/5	3↑	Clm 6250	9	6	$5^{3/4}$	3^{nk}	$2^{1/2}$	$2^{2\frac{1}{2}}$	Ayarza I	b	114	11.50	76-24	Shkemker116$^{2\frac{1}{2}}$Roundwo
13May87-10GS	fst	1 1/16	:47 3/5	1:12 4/5	1:46 2/5	3↑	Clm c-5000	4	2	2^{1}	2^{1}	$3^{1\frac{1}{2}}$	2^{2}	Simoff R A^7	b	109	9.00	74-24	GoldnHoofprnts119^{2}Ronc
30Apr87- 4GS	fst	1 1/16	:47 3/5	1:13 2/5	1:46 4/5	3↑	Clm 4000	3	3	3^{1}	$1^{1/2}$	1^{1}	1no	Simoff R A^7	b	109	20.00	74-24	Roundwood 109no Shake
16Apr87- 4GS	gd	1^{70}	:48	1:13 4/5	1:45 3/5		Clm 4000	1	10	$10^{5\frac{3}{4}}$	$10^{8\frac{1}{2}}$	$8^{9\frac{3}{4}}$	$7^{9\frac{3}{4}}$	Simoff R A^7	b	112	19.70	61-25	HarrahForPag119^{1}Raised
2Apr87- 4GS	fst	1^{70}	:47 2/5	1:14 2/5	1:46 1/5		Clm 4000	2	10	8^{8}	$10^{9\frac{1}{2}}$	$8^{9\frac{1}{2}}$	$8^{9\frac{3}{4}}$	Simoff R A^7	b	112	6.60	58-29	Gotama 116$^{1\frac{1}{4}}$ Benign Cz
19Mar87- 7GS	fst	1^{70}	:47 2/5	1:14 3/5	1:46 4/5		Clm 4000	11	5	$5^{5\frac{1}{2}}$	1^{hd}	1^{hd}	$1^{1/2}$	Simoff R A^7	b	109	5.50	65-30	Roundwood 109$^{1/2}$ For Ete
26Feb87- 2GS	fst	1 1/16	:48 2/5	1:14 1/5	1:47 3/5		Clm 6500	2	4	$5^{5\frac{1}{2}}$	6^{10}	8^{12}	$8^{13\frac{1}{2}}$	Simoff R A^7	b	110	8.20	56-28	Saint Paul 116^{nk} Joe Har
25Jan87-10Pha	fst	1 1/8	:47 2/5	1:12 2/5	1:51 2/5		Clm 5000	8	4	4^{4}	$1^{1/2}$	$2^{1/2}$	2^{2}	Simoff R A^7	b	109	4.70	76-14	I. D. Silverine 115^{2} Roun
26Dec86-10Pha	fst	1 1/16	:47 4/5	1:13	1:46 2/5		Clm 5000	11	6	$7^{8\frac{1}{2}}$	5^{6}	5^{4}	$3^{4\frac{3}{4}}$	Simoff R A^5	b	110	5.80	67-24	SpekToMeLdy115$^{3/4}$Golde
21Dec86- 4Pha	fst	7f	:22 4/5	:46 3/5	1:26 2/5		Clm 4000	5	6	10^{10}	9^{11}	$4^{4\frac{1}{2}}$	3^{7}	Simoff R A^5	b	110	8.40	68-30	Reading Glasses 118^{3} Pe

Sharp Form Factors—Big Win

A win fashioned by a horse that pulled away from its competition through the stretch is a very positive sign. The best kind of big win race is the one in which the horse was on or near the lead at the stretch call. Horses well behind the leaders at the top of the stretch have a low repeat win success rate.

Summer Moment — B. g. 3(Apr), by Honest Moment—Summer Reward, by Zen
Own.—Finley Terrence P — **$7,500** Br.—Martelli Domenic (Fla) / Tr.—Stubley David M — **122** — Lifetime 9 2 0 3 $8,407

27Oct91-11Pha	fst	1^{70}	$:46^{3}$	1:13	$1:44^{2}$	3↑	Clm c-5000	4	7	$7^{6\frac{1}{4}}$	3^{2}	1^{2}	$1^{5\frac{3}{4}}$	Colton R E	L	113	*.60	74-22	SummerMomnt113$^{5\frac{3}{4}}$Fu
19Oct91- 2Pha	fst	6f	:22	$:45^{3}$	$1:12^{1}$	3↑	Clm 5000	5	8	$7^{9\frac{1}{4}}$	$5^{7\frac{1}{2}}$	$3^{4\frac{1}{2}}$	$3^{1\frac{3}{4}}$	Colton R E	L	114	*1.60	81-17	CtintheAct114$^{1\frac{1}{2}}$NetWo
15Sep91-12Del	fst	1^{70}	$:46^{1}$	$1:11^{4}$	1:43	3↑	Clm 5000	5	6	4^{2}	$4^{4\frac{1}{2}}$	3^{4}	$5^{2\frac{1}{4}}$	Taylor K T	L	108	3.60	95-15	MjstcMndr112$^{3/4}$RylKng
4Sep91- 4Med	fst	1^{70}	$:46^{2}$	$1:10^{4}$	1:41		Clm 6500	2	1	$2^{1/2}$	3^{2}	3^{3}	$3^{3\frac{1}{4}}$	Olea R E^5	L	107	34.10	90-07	Topnotchr115$^{3/4}$Wdmnn1
22Aug91- 2Atl	fst	5 1/2f	:22	:46	$1:05^{1}$	3↑	Clm 5000	2	10	$4^{1\frac{1}{4}}$	$6^{2\frac{1}{2}}$	5^{3}	3^{5}	Jocson G J^5	L	109	4.60	85-15	Huxley114$^{3\frac{1}{4}}$ Dry Puddl
2Aug91- 7Atl	fst	5 1/2f	$:22^{1}$	$:46^{1}$	$1:06^{1}$	3↑	Clm 5000	4	8	$7^{4\frac{3}{4}}$	8^{7}	$7^{5\frac{1}{4}}$	6^{2}	Jocson G J^5		112	*2.50	83-22	ChampgnePt122^{nk}LeCd
16Jly91- 3Mth	fst	6f	$:21^{2}$	$:44^{3}$	1:10		Clm 12500	5	3	$4^{5\frac{1}{2}}$	$6^{9\frac{3}{4}}$	6^{11}	6^{18}	Alligood M A		119	14.90	73-12	BerlyCoping116$^{1\frac{1}{2}}$Genui
6Jly91- 2Mth	fst	6f	$:21^{4}$	$:45^{2}$	$1:11^{4}$		Clm 16000	2	7	$6^{8\frac{1}{4}}$	5^{7}	6^{11}	6^{13}	Verge M E		116	18.20	69-16	ReveilleRock112$^{3/4}$OhWh
21Jun91- 1Mth	fst	6f	$:22^{4}$	$:46^{1}$	1:12	3↑	Md 10000	2	6	1^{hd}	1^{hd}	1^{hd}	$1^{1\frac{1}{2}}$	Bravo J		115	8.60	81-18	SmmrMnt115$^{1\frac{1}{2}}$HlfMnS

Speed Index: Last Race: –2.0 3–Race Avg.: +1.0 6–Race Avg.: –4.6
LATEST WORKOUTS Oct 11 Med 4f fst :51 B

Sharp Form Factors—Close at Stretch or Finish

Any horse that ran a race recently in which it was close to the lead at the stretch call or at the finish deserves further consideration, provided the class level of the race was not below today's class, or the final time, if accurately measurable, was within about a second (slightly more for routes) of the other contenders' times. Rule of thumb suggests two or three lengths within the leader or winner as satisfactory evidence of sharpness by this criterion.

Twenty Flags — B. f. 4, by Magic Banner—Twenty Below, by Far North — $14,000 — Br.—Calafa G (NY) — Tr.—Tufariello Frank — 117 — Lifetime 16 3 0 1 $56,340

Own.—Calafa Gerard D

24Oct91- 9Aqu	fst	1⅛	:47^3	1:12^4	1:53^1	3↑ Ⓕ Clm 14000	6	2	2½	2^{1½}	5^{1¾}	8^{4¼}	Garcia P L	b	117	8.60	66-26	Olgiata116½ Betsy Bell117^{nk} Sn	
24May91- 3Bel	fst	1⅛	:47	1:12^3	1:52^2	Ⓕ Clm 22500	5	2	2^1	4¾	5^{11}	5^{21¾}	Ramos W	b	115	17.60	45-31	WoninthSun113^{2}Foxcroft119^{hd}	
3May91- 3Aqu	fm	1⅜ Ⓣ	:50^3	1:42	2:19^3	Ⓕ Clm 45000	4	4	4^5	5^{9½}	5^{15}	5^{15¾}	Velasquez J	b	113	4.70	70-13	Badtullah113^{2½} Entrust115^{2¼} W	
26Mar91- 8Aqu	fst	1⅜	:48^3	1:38^4	2:18	Ⓕ Handicap	6	3	3^4	6^{16}	6^{31}	—	Rojas R I	o	110	10.90	— —	Bunka Bunka112^{nk} Coroly114^{nk}	
20Mar91- 7Aqu	fst	1	:46^4	1:13	1:39^2	Ⓕ Ⓢ Alw 31000	7	3	3^3	3^1	2½	1^{nk}	Arguello F A Jr^7	b	112	13.90	65-33	TwentyFlgs112^{nk}NobleMri117½	
4Mar91- 7Aqu	fst	1⅛ ⊡	:48	1:12^3	1:52^3	Ⓕ Ⓢ Alw 31000	1	2	3^{2½}	3^5	5^{8½}	6^{12}	Arguello F A Jr^7	b	115	3.70	67-19	Tap Root Dancer117¾Caribia11	
20Feb91- 5Aqu	my	1⅛ ⊡	:50^4	1:16^2	1:57	Ⓕ Ⓢ Alw 29000	4	1	1½	1½	1^3	1^{3¼}	Velazquez J R^5	o	117	1.70	57-39	Twenty Flags117^{3¼} Blessings11	
2Feb91- 1Aqu	fst	170 ⊡	:49^2	1:15	1:45^1	Ⓕ Md Sp Wt	1	1	1½	1^{1½}	1^8	1^{16}	Velazquez J R^5	b	117	7.10	79-27	TwentyFlgs117^{16}CrushOnYou1	
18Jan91- 2Aqu	fst	170 ⊡	:49^2	1:14^1	1:45^4	Ⓕ Md Sp Wt	8	3	2^{hd}	2½	4^4	6^{7½}	Guerra W A	b	122	12.30	68-23	Joyous Thoughts122½ MyTearc	
5Jan91- 3Aqu	fst	1$\frac{1}{16}$ ⊡	:47^4	1:13^3	1:49^1	Ⓕ Md 30000	9	3	3^{7½}	3^{6½}	4^3	3^{2¼}	Guerra W A	b	118	10.40	60-27	SwtVrt118¾Fnn'sThndr113^{1½}Tw	

Signs of Deteriorating Form

It is a well-known handicapping fact that horses go through form cycles, and that each race contributes something to or removes something from the horse's racing fitness and energy reserves.

Early in the cycle, competitive racing usually contributes to the horse's fitness, enabling it to improve subsequent performances. After the peak of the form cycle has been reached, each additional race tends to remove something from racing fitness, with the result that later efforts lack improvement, and in many instances, show deterioration. Horses showing this deterioration are often in need of a rest, or at least a series of easy races, after which the upleg of another fitness cycle can begin.

It is highly desirable to bet on horses on the upleg of their form cycles, and conversely, to bet against horses on the downleg of their cycles. By doing this, the player restricts bets to horses that have a good chance of running even better than their recent form indicators suggest. The major difficulty here lies in properly assessing if a form cycle has peaked and is beginning to droop. There are a number of signs that can be used as clues, some of which are discussed below.

Negative Form Factors—Failure in the Stretch

Failure to run aggressively in the stretch, with the loss of up to a few lengths in the drive during a nonwinning effort, can be a strong signal that a horse is past its form cycle peak. (Loss of many lengths is not a reliable indication of staling form but is suggestive of other problems, such as a physical ailment, poor race placement, or inability to cope with a fast pace.)

Evidence of failure in two or more successive races is a certain sign of deteriorating form.

The sign has even more strength if the horse was well bet in its last race and the final time and pace were not excessively fast. The latest race in which failure is evident should ideally be after several weeks of steady racing. A conclusion based on a fading stretch drive in a race run a short time after returning from a layoff is not usually well founded. On the contrary, failure in the stretch by a fresh horse is often a positive sign, which simply indicates that the runner was a bit short. Chronically failing stretch runners are often dropped down the class ladder by their trainers, but they usually continue to fail.

Barbara Erin — Ch. m. 5, by Sauce Boat—Never Spliced, by Silent Screen — $5,000 — Br.—Avery & Humphrey Jr (Ky) — Tr.—Forbes John H — 116 — Lifetime 14 2 2 0 $14,390
Own.—Bid Side Stable

11Jun87- 2Mth	fst	6f	:22	:44⅘	1:11⅗	3↑ⒻClm 10500	11	1	3^{nk}	$2^{3\frac{1}{2}}$	2^{4}	4^{5}	Madrid A Jr	112	8.50	78-19	FiveStarRose119²BushoginE
2Jun87- 2Mth	fst	6f	:22⅗	:45⅗	1:10⅘	3↑ⒻClm 10000	6	2	1½	2^{hd}	$2^{1\frac{1}{2}}$	2^{6}	Madrid A Jr	116	3.50	80-16	Five Star Rose 116⁶Barbara
8Apr87- 6GS	fst	6f	:22⅖	:46⅖	1:12⅖	ⒻClm 17000	2	7	$5^{3\frac{1}{2}}$	$5^{5\frac{1}{2}}$	$6^{7\frac{3}{4}}$	5^{11}	Madrid A Jr	114	9.60	69-25	Merebot 116⁴½ Devil Pleasu
28Mar87- 6GS	fst	6f	:22	:45⅘	1:12⅘	ⒻClm 18000	6	1	2^{hd}	3½	$3^{1\frac{1}{2}}$	$5^{4\frac{1}{2}}$	Madrid A Jr	119	6.80	73-23	Sing Jack Sing 112ⁿᵏ Furar
21Mar87- 6GS	fst	6f	:22⅗	:47⅖	1:14⅕	ⒻAlw 10500	2	4	1^{hd}	3½	$5^{4\frac{1}{2}}$	9^{13}	Lopez C C	116	3.50e	58-26	Marshmallow Riches 116²½
9Mar87- 5Aqu	fst	6f	⊡:22⅘	:47⅕	1:12⅖	ⒻClm 22500	5	1	$3^{1\frac{1}{2}}$	$5^{4\frac{1}{2}}$	7^{17}	9^{20}	Madrid A Jr	115	17.80	62-22	Tara's Native 112³½ Adda G
26Feb87- 9GS	fst	6f	:22⅗	:46⅘	1:13	ⒻClm 18000	1	4	1½	1^{2}	$1^{3\frac{1}{2}}$	1no	Madrid A Jr	116	3.80	77-28	Barbara Erin 116ⁿᵒ Lady Rc
19Feb87- 7GS	fst	6f	:22	:45⅘	1:12⅗	ⒻClm 22500	8	3	$2^{2\frac{1}{2}}$	2^{5}	2^{4}	$6^{9\frac{1}{2}}$	Madrid A Jr	114	12.60	70-32	Awfully Awesome119³½Char
9Dec86- 7Med	sly	6f	:22⅖	:46⅖	1:11⅘	3↑ⒻClm 25000	4	2	2^{hd}	2^{hd}	$6^{6\frac{3}{4}}$	$6^{17\frac{1}{4}}$	Madrid A Jr	116	11.10	66-19	EsterimeOrchid119¹½Crmell
26Nov86- 3Med	sly	6f	:23	:47⅖	1:13⅖	3↑ⒻMd 16000	5	3	$2^{3\frac{1}{2}}$	2½	1^{5}	1^{13}	Krone J A	122	*2.00	75-23	BarbaraErin122¹³Rolfe'sFrg

LATEST WORKOUTS May 23 Mth 6f fst 1:15 b

Negative Form Factors—Failing Speed

Speed horses that fail to gain control of a pace that is slower than they have shown an ability to handle in the past are usually tired or hurting horses. These horses tend to receive substantial betting support because of their previous successes. But the sharp handicapper should accept the failure as evidence of a form cycle downswing. Their last race must be examined carefully for genuine excuses, though, such as a poor post or poor start. The horseplayer must also be alert to changes in running style, too, since maturing speed horses sometimes learn to come from off the pace.

Say Jo Jo — Ch. f. 3(Feb), by Timeless Moment—Had My Say, by Sadair — $5,000 — Br.—White & Whitney (Ky) — Tr.—Reid Mark J — 115 — Lifetime 23 5 3 2 $38,957
Own.—T-Bird Stable

8Nov91- 1Med	fst	6f	$:22^{2}$	$:46^{4}$	$1:13^{2}$	ⒻClm 5000	9	3	$3^{2\frac{1}{2}}$	$4^{1\frac{1}{4}}$	$2^{2\frac{1}{2}}$	$5^{5\frac{1}{2}}$	Jocson G J	Lb	115	2.60	69-17	TmprStr115²¼FiryDbu
22Oct91- 4Med	fst	6f	22^{2}	$:45^{3}$	$1:11^{3}$	ⒻClm 5000	7	4	$4^{1\frac{1}{4}}$	2½	1^{hd}	2^{1}	Jocson G J	Lb	115	5.60	83-15	Fiery Debutante110¹ S
28Sep91- 7Med	fst	6f	$:22^{1}$	$:45^{1}$	$1:10^{4}$	ⒻClm 10000	5	6	4^{1}	5^{6}	8^{12}	$8^{15\frac{1}{4}}$	Jocson G J	Lb	115	4.60	73-15	PunchlinePatty113³¾S
11Sep91- 7Med	fst	6f	$:22^{3}$	$:46^{1}$	$1:12^{1}$	ⒻClm 14000	8	4	5¾	2½	4^{1}	5^{4}	Jocson G J5	Lb	106	5.60	77-17	Southbound115² Birdi
1Sep91- 7Pha	fm	5f	Ⓣ:23	$:47^{4}$	$1:00^{4}$	ⒻClm 14000	11	7	$5^{1\frac{3}{4}}$	4^{2}	$3^{1\frac{1}{2}}$	$2^{3\frac{1}{2}}$	Jocson G J5	Lb	112	4.30	— —	Pen Argyl116³½ Say Jo
14Aug91- 8Atl	fst	6f	:22	$:45^{3}$	1:11	ⒻClm 16000	8	4	3^{nk}	1^{2}	2^{2}	3^{6}	Jocson G J5	Lb	113	*1.50	80-17	Southbound115⁵¾Cour
15Jly91- 5Bel	fst	6f	$:22^{2}$	$:45^{3}$	1:11	ⒻClm 22500	6	6	3^{2}	$4^{1\frac{1}{2}}$	8^{12}	$9^{21\frac{1}{4}}$	Madrid A Jr	b	114	6.90	64-17	TripleSox116⁴¼Mogmt
5Jly91- 3Bel	sly	7f	$:22^{4}$	$:45^{4}$	1:26	ⒻClm 17500	1	5	1^{hd}	$1^{2\frac{1}{2}}$	$1^{3\frac{1}{2}}$	1^{2}	Antley C W	b	116	*2.60	74-12	Say Jo Jo116² Porcela
26Jun91- 9Pha	fst	6f	:22	$:45^{1}$	1:11	3↑ⒻAlw 14500	8	3	3^{2}	$3^{1\frac{1}{2}}$	3^{4}	4^{7}	Martinez J R Jr	Lb	114	7.70	82-10	Alln'sLf122²¾CrmCont
25May91- 1Pha	fst	6f	$:22^{3}$	$:46^{2}$	1:13	3↑ⒻAlw 13500	6	5	$2^{1\frac{1}{2}}$	1^{2}	$1^{3\frac{1}{2}}$	$1^{\frac{3}{4}}$	Vigliotti M J	Lb	109	*1.30	79-22	Say Jo Jo109¾ Voodoo

Negative Form Factors—Slow Times

A comparatively slow race time, even if a winning one, can be an indication of fatigue or physical disability. Ascertainment of this fact requires a comparison of a horse's last race running time with times from its most recent prior races. An increase of a few fifths of a second is quite excusable, but a full second or more is a suspicious signal and can indicate tiring form. Care must be used with this factor, however, because very consistent winners will often run only as hard as necessary to win. These top runners should be given the benefit of the doubt and be accepted as potential contenders.

Another cautionary note: this generalization applies mainly to sprint races. Route race times can have wide variability, meaning that a slowish time should not automatically be accepted as representing poor or staling form. And conversely, a very fast route time is not easily reproduced by a horse and therefore should not be overrated by the handicapper. This is expanded upon a few pages hence.

Mr. Jet Set					B. c. 3(May), by Tri Jet—Sea Prospector, by Mr Prospector $10,000 Br.—Hofmann Georgia E (Fla) Tr.—Jennings Joseph								Lifetime 116 12 4 3 $26,940		
Own.—Hammerslag Stable															
25Nov91- 6Med fst 6f	:222	:46	1:121		Clm 10000	7 2	2hd	2hd	1hd	33	Vargas J L	116	3.60	78-19 Silent Lou116no S
12Nov91- 6Med fst 6f	:22	:454	1:11		Clm 7500	9 1	11	11	11½	12	Sarvis D A	116	2.60	87-17 Mr. Jet Set1162Co
24Oct91- 2Med fst 6f	:221	:452	1:104		Clm 7500	1 2	2½	21½	22	23	Sarvis D A	116	*.90	85-12 Concord'sKrw116
15Oct91- 4Med sly 6f	:22	:444	1:103		Clm 10000	4 2	2½	21½	23	26	Sarvis D A	116	*1.50	83-12 Super Stutz1166 I
25Sep91- 4Med sly 6f	:221	:452	1:101		Clm 7500	5 6	2hd	2hd	12	11½	Sarvis D A	116	3.10	91-06 Mr.JetSet116¼De
21Aug91- 6Mth fst 6f	:212	:442	1:102		Clm 16000	7 1	52½	78	718	724½	Bravo J	116	2.70	65-14 YnEprss116noAnn
7Aug91- 4Mth fst 6f	:212	:443	1:114		Clm c-12500	1 6	31½	24	31½	1hd	Bravo J	116	4.30	82-13 Mr. Jet Set116hd I
21Jly91- 3Mth fst 6f	:214	:45	1:11		Clm 20000	6 1	23	21½	21	2½	Bravo J	119	2.90	85-13 OhWhtJewell116½A
2Jly91-10Mth fst 6f	:22	:46	1:13	3+	Md 35000	4 2	21½	1½	13	12	Bravo J	116	*1.20	76-19 Mr. Jet Set1162 Ti

Negative Form Factors—Failed Expectations

A horse that recently failed to run well when expected to win, under conditions that suited it well, can usually be disregarded as a strong contender. Failure in this instance is revealed by poor final time and defeat by lesser horses, with no apparent excuse.

An exception is a horse that gets beaten badly in a very uncharacteristic performance. Such a horse often has an excuse that may or may not be evident, such as a change in equipment, a temporary physical aggravation, or a problem that developed during the race (e.g., dirt in nose or eye, frightened by gate handler or jockey, slipped saddle, failure to change leads, and so on). It is not prudent to write off the horse as a loser until it runs another race. As a matter of fact, it is possible that this runner is a good prospect for a bet, provided that it is sent back to race again within a short period (this topic is discussed in more detail later).

Sling Shot — Ch. c. 4, by Stutz Blackhawk—Lady Bend Fager, by Never Bend — $10,000 — Br.—J I Racing Inc (NJ) — Tr.—Tammaro John J III — 115 — Lifetime 33 6 1 $70,480

Own.—Bantivoglio Robert T

7Nov91- 5Med	fst	1 1/16	:473	1:123	1:454	3↑Clm 12500	6	2	2½	2hd	21	35¾	Sarvis D A	Lb	117	*2.00	72-23	CidermillHill1114
18Oct91- 1Med	fst	170	:461	1:104	1:41	3↑Clm 20000	7	4	42½	31	34	59¾	Sarvis D A	Lb	115b	*1.80	83-06	Nasgme115nkLigh
18Oct91-Dead heat; Originally scheduled on turf																		
7Oct91- 2Med	fst	170	:47	1:113	1:422	3↑Clm 12500	6	4	42	21½	1hd	12	Sarvis D A	Lb	117	*2.10	86-20	Sling Shot1172 Vi
26Sep91- 4Med	fst	170	:453	1:103	1:402	3↑Clm 10000	7	4	43	1hd	13	13½	Sarvis D A	Lb	115	5.00	96-09	Sling Shot1153½ V
17Sep91- 5Med	fst	170	:461	1:111	1:413	3↑Clm 12500	7	7	74¾	42¾	31	45¼	Sarvis D A	Lb	117	8.30	85-13	SupersonicFlsh11
8Sep91- 6Mth	fst	6f	:213	:443	1:10	3↑[S]Clm 16000	3	7	46½	45¼	46	610	Sarvis D A	Lb	116	4.70	81-13	Without Contemp
18Aug91- 4Mth	fst	1	:464	1:112	1:383	3↑Clm 10000	3	3	22	1½	14	13¾	Sarvis D A	Lb	115	2.40	76-23	SlingShot1153¾Ho
31Jly91- 2Mth	fst	6f	:213	:442	1:10	3↑Clm 12500	2	9	52¾	33½	56½	59	Sarvis D A	Lb	116	7.50	82-12	ArgntnEmpror116
17Jly91- 8Mth	fst	6f	:214	:443	1:102	3↑[S]Clm 12500	7	1	33½	34½	35	35¾	Sarvis D A	Lb	116	3.70	83-18	CrftyArt1163½Witl
4Jly91- 7Mth	fst	6f	:212	:442	1:102	3↑Clm 30000	4	9	78¾	87¼	98½	99¼	Sarvis D A	Lb	112	44.50	80-15	FrozenRunwy1161

Speed Index: Last Race: –5.0 3–Race Avg.: –3.3 6–Race Avg.: –1.3

LATEST WORKOUTS Oct 29 Med 5f fst 1:01 B

Negative Form Factors—Sharp Work by Failing Horse

Naturally quick horses tend instinctively to produce fast trials. During the period when these speedsters are rounding into form (as after a layoff), the sharp works should be taken as a positive sign. Once the peak of the form cycle has been reached and the horse begins to show signs of fatigue or wear, the sharp trials are more often just signs of habitual speed rather than sharp bullish form.

Mondanite — B. g. 5, by Lyphard—Social Column, by Swoon's Son or Vaguely Noble

SCHVANEVELDT C P 119 — Br.—Gainesway Farm & Hart (Tenn) — Tr.—Gosden John H M

Own.—Juddmonte Farms — Lifetime 22 1 3 6 $40,402

1987 9 1 0 4 $26,075 — 1986 8 M 2 2 $13,075 — Turf 9 0 1 1 $6,427

31May87-7Hol	1	:444	1:094	1:362ft	6	115	21½	22½	24	35¼	Sibille R 5	Aw24000	75-18	Sum Action, Athlone, Mondanite	8
3May87-5Hol	7f	:22	:45	1:231ft	6½	115	2hd	1hd	31	34½	Sibille R 7	Aw22000	83-15	Fracoza, Baby Slewy, Mondanite	7
9Apr87-5SA	a6½f Ⓣ	:213	:434	1:142fm	*2¾	118	2½	2½	21½	34½	Sibille R 3	Aw29000	82-09	Rinnegato, Recognized, Mondanite	9
29Mar87-5SA	a6½f Ⓣ	:213	:44	1:151fm	38	116	2½	1hd	2hd	52¼	Sibille R 3	Aw33000	81-19	Danczone,FbulousSound,S'neCstle	12
22Mar87-5SA	6½f	:214	:452	1:174gd	5½	118	11½	2hd	31	54½	Toro F 10	Aw29000	76-23	City View, Starshield,MidnightIce	10
4Mar87-5SA	1 1/16	:453	1:101	1:432ft	14	117	1½	12	3½	55¼	Toro F 3	Aw30000	79-16	RidgeReview,Rafel'sDncer,Athlone	12
4Mar87—Bumped at start; checked at 1/8															
11Feb87-6SA	6½f	:22	:453	1:17 ft	*2	118	1½	11	11½	1hd	DelahoussyeE 1	M45000	85-17	Mondanite,Hpigrin,DremsDon'tDie	12
24Jan87-4SA	1 1/16	:463	1:113	1:452ft	5	120	11	2hd	31	57	Delahoussaye E 5	Mdn	67-18	‡ArcticDream,Centenary,HilTheBid	9
8Jan87-6SA	6f	:22	:454	1:112m	2¾	120	66	45½	34	36	Delahoussaye E 6	Mdn	75-30	Svnfvndchng,Dn'sIrshMldy,Mndnt	10
8Jan87—Bumped hard start															
27Dec86-6SA	6f	:22	:453	1:11 ft	7½	120	63	32	41¼	32½	Delahoussaye E 9	Mdn	80-19	General At War,Rufjan,Mondanite	12

●Jun 23 Hol 4f ft :47 h ●Jun 17 Hol 3f ft :343 h Jun 11 Hol 4f ft :49 h ●May 29 Hol 3f ft :342 h

Negative Form Factors—Close-Up Finishes by Timid Horse

It is surprising that heavy win betting is still done on horses that often finish close to the winner but rarely cross the finish line first. This fact is surprising in view of the amount that has been written in the past few years about these "sucker bets." The racing public apparently cannot resist the temptation to play them, perhaps because many people feel psychologically comfortable about betting a horse that will almost certainly be close to the winner.

Although timid horses that attract heavy betting are usually underlaid, they do win once in a while, and sometimes produce signs to indicate a forthcoming winning effort.

The second, third, or fourth race after a layoff can occasionally be a winning one for these horses. This may be due to the layoff diminishing their memory, or by renewed vigour arising from the rest.

Another indicator of a potential reversal is a display of extra tenaciousness as the horse ran through the stretch in its most recent races. If a horse that normally loses these kind of races by one or more lengths is holding on better and is only being beaten by a head or neck, it may be signalling a winning breakthrough.

One Class Ack

B. g. 3(Apr), by Ack Kerala—One Classy Lady, by Northern Jove
Br.—Labe Paul E Jr (Pa)
Tr.—Reid Mark J

Own.—Burnside Charles F

Lifetime
21 3 10
$63,864

113

20Nov91- 8Pha fst 6f	:221	:453	1:11	3↑Alw 15515	1 2	2½	2hd	11	22	Jocson G J	Lb 113	*1.20	87-20 Diligent1082OneCl
10Nov91- 8Pha fst 6f	:222	:451	1:10	3↑Alw 15515	2 2	31	3½	2½	21½	Martinez J R Jr	Lb 113	*1.00	93-13 AuntDot'sBby119¹
19Oct91-10Pha fst 6f	:222	:46	1:113	3↑Alw 15058	4 4	3½	1hd	2hd	3hd	Jocson G J	Lb 112	*2.20	86-17 VslSnl116no Sptmt
28Sep91- 6Pha fst 6f	:223	:454	1:103	3↑Alw 15515	1 2	2½	23	21½	21½	Jocson G J	Lb 111	*2.00	90-18 SrvYourTim114¹¹
17Sep91- 8Pha fst 6f	:221	:45	1:102	3↑Alw 15515	7 8	42	44	44½	65½	Jocson G J5	Lb 106	2.50	87-18 FollowMyLd-Nz¹
13Aug91- 8Pha fm *5f ①		:591	3↑Alw 15515	2 2	32	23	26	29½	Jocson G J5	Lb 111	*1.30	78-12 FiremnFive116¾10
28Jly91- 6Mth fst 6f	:213	:442	1:10	Clm 45000	5 5	64	56	33½	2hd	Verge M E	Lb 114	13.30	91-10 CleanndBold116no
29Jun91- 9Pha fst 6½f	:222	:452	1:183	⑤Peppy Addy	5 4	41½	32	1hd	2nk	Martinez J R Jr	Lb 115	3.10	85-19 DustyScrn119nkOn
15Jun91- 8Pha fst 6f	:222	:452	1:111	3↑⑤Alw 18225	3 4	31½	33	2hd	16	Martinez J R Jr	Lb 110	*.70	88-16 OneClssAck110⁶M
2Jun91- 8Pha fst 6f	:223	:462	1:113	3↑⑤Alw 18225	6 6	22	11	2hd	2hd	Colton R E	Lb 113	*.40	86-18 VctrVctr116ndOnC

Speed Index: Last Race: +7.0   3–Race Avg.: +5.3   9–Race Avg.: +4.6

LATEST WORKOUTS   ●Nov 5 Pha 4f fst :48 B   Oct 10 Pha 4f fst :491 B

Negative Form Factors—Big Win Under No Pressure

A front-running horse that has been running mediocre races sometimes lucks into a situation where it is allowed to break on top in the first few strides of a race and under no pace pressure open up a clear lead within the initial quarter mile. Such a horse will often win with little difficulty in a fast final clocking. The performance looks very impressive in the Form and can lead to heavy future betting support.

But this kind of easy race is usually not repeated, for two reasons. First, unless the horse is an outstanding, consistent speedster, it is unlikely that it will encounter two fields in succession that contain a dearth of competitive speed. Second, trainers and jockeys are usually aware of the recent speed performances of competing horses in the upcoming race and will base strategy on this likely speed. Aware that a speed horse may break away, competing jockeys will force more speed out of their own mounts to ensure against a leisurely pace set by a relaxed front runner.

Crafty's Wish B. f. 4, by Crafty Prospector—Wistoral, by Exceller
Own.—Stronach Frank $17,500 Br.—Iselin & Lippert & Pozen (NY) Tr.—Sedlacek Michael C 110^7 Lifetime 27 5 1 $85,008

20Nov91- 9Aqu	fst	6f	$:22^2$	$:45^2$	$1:11^1$	3↑ⒻClm 14000	1	1	$1^{1\frac{1}{2}}$	1^3	1^7	$1^{7\frac{1}{2}}$	Brockelbank G V^7		110	17.20	85-14	Crfty'sWsh$110^{7\frac{1}{2}}$V
31Oct91- 6Aqu	fst	6f	:23	$:46^4$	1:12	3↑ⒻClm 20000	10	1	$2^{\frac{1}{2}}$	4^3	9^{12}	$9^{18\frac{1}{4}}$	Rivera M E^{10}	b	103	51.50	63-19	Underinsured117^1
17Sep91- 3Med	fst	6f	$:22^2$	$:45^2$	$1:10^2$	3↑ⒻClm 18000	7	1	$5^{2\frac{3}{4}}$	5^5	$6^{9\frac{1}{2}}$	$6^{13\frac{1}{4}}$	Garcia L I^5	b	107	7.10	77-15	HousOfLov$107^{1\frac{1}{2}}$L
26Aug91- 2Sar	fm	$1\frac{3}{16}$	Ⓣ$:47^4$	$1:12^1$	$1:56^2$	3↑ⒻClm 35000	11	1	$1^{3\frac{1}{2}}$	$11^{1\frac{1}{2}}$	12^{13}	$12^{27\frac{3}{4}}$	Smith M E	b	117	13.40	60-10	Luiana Baby$117^{\frac{3}{4}}$
1Jly91- 1Bel	fst	6f	$:23^1$	$:46^2$	$1:11^3$	ⒻClm c-14000	3	2	$1^{\frac{1}{2}}$	$1^{\frac{1}{2}}$	$3^{\frac{1}{2}}$	$6^{6\frac{3}{4}}$	Rojas R I	b	117	6.80	75-15	FinlRod$117^{\frac{3}{4}}$OhSc
20Jun91- 3Bel	my	6f	$:22^1$	$:44^4$	$1:09^4$	ⒻClm 17500	5	2	$2^{\frac{1}{2}}$	2^2	5^6	$6^{11\frac{1}{2}}$	BrockelbnkGV^7	b	110	14.80	79-06	VlidDelt$108^{5\frac{1}{2}}$Sup
31May91- 3Bel	fst	6f	$:22^1$	$:45^2$	$1:10^1$	ⒻClm 17500	3	4	$4^{2\frac{1}{2}}$	4^1	$4^{3\frac{1}{2}}$	3^6	BrockelbnkGV^7	b	111	9.40	83-03	DmdSolil117^{nk}Bu
9May91- 3Bel	fst	6f	$:22^1$	$:45^1$	$1:10^3$	ⒻClm 17500	1	1	1^{hd}	$1^{\frac{1}{2}}$	$2^{\frac{1}{2}}$	6^5	Velasquez J	b	117	4.30	82-09	Man She's Swee
25Apr91- 1Aqu	fst	6f	$:22^2$	:46	$1:10^4$	ⒻClm 20000	3	1	$1^{1\frac{1}{2}}$	1^{hd}	$2^{2\frac{1}{2}}$	$4^{7\frac{1}{2}}$	Velasquez J	b	113	10.70	79-17	MdstGlw$117^{4\frac{3}{4}}$St
14Mar91- 3Aqu	fst	7f	$:22^3$	$:46^2$	$1:24^1$	ⒻClm 25000	4	2	$2^{\frac{1}{2}}$	2^1	6^{12}	7^{29}	Rojas R I	b	117	7.60	52-25	NorthernWilly11

Speed Index: Last Race: −1.0 3–Race Avg.: −9.0 9–Race Avg.: −11.3

LATEST WORKOUTS ●Nov 30 Aqu 3f fst $:36^2$ B Nov 15 Aqu 4f fst $:48^2$ H Nov 10 Aqu 4f fst $:47^4$ H

Negative Form Factors—Habitual Stretch Gains

A recent big stretch gain by a horse that was well behind the leader at the stretch call is often considered as a sign of impending victory; however, slow starting horses that habitually save their kick until the stretch drive have a tendency to lose races by small margins. It is important that an improving off-pace runner demonstrate the ability to be close to the lead at the head of the stretch. Come-from-behind horses that are capable of challenging at the top of the stretch have much better winning records than the stretch running horses.

An important exception applies to a horse dropping in class, for which the less demanding pace may move it into contention much earlier. Another exception applies to a horse changing distance from a short race to a significantly longer one. Again, the slower pace of the longer race will result in a closer attending of the pace. Very inexperienced two- and three-year-olds can also improve markedly after showing a good stretch gain. Their poor position at the stretch call often results only from a lack of seasoning.

Career Luck B. c. 2(May), by Lucky North—Howe Swift, by Dynastic
Own.—Atkins Steve $12,500 Br.—Franks John (Fla) Tr.—Jolin Louis F 118 Lifetime 6 0 1 $3,915

7Nov91- 1Med	fst	6f	$:23^2$	$:47^3$	1:14	Md 10000	6	7	$7^{3\frac{1}{4}}$	6^4	3^4	2no	Bravo J	b	118	2.70	72-20	Cost Fifty118^{no} C.
14Oct91- 1Med	fst	6f	$:22^4$	$:46^4$	1:13	Md 16000	6	4	$7^{7\frac{1}{4}}$	$6^{6\frac{1}{4}}$	3^7	3^5	Bravo J	b	118	*1.20	72-16	Proof'sChrger118
26Sep91-10Med	fst	1^{70}	$:46^3$	$1:11^4$	1:43	Md Sp Wt	7	9	9^{10}	8^{13}	8^{16}	$7^{15\frac{3}{4}}$	Santagata N	b	118	*2.80	67-09	LuckyFind$118^{1\frac{3}{4}}$P
4Sep91- 3Med	fst	6f	$:22^3$	$:46^1$	1:12	Md 30000	8	2	6^8	$5^{6\frac{1}{4}}$	4^5	$3^{2\frac{1}{2}}$	Santagata N	b	114	*1.80	79-10	GoodtimSunny118
27Aug91- 3Mth	fst	6f	$:22^3$	$:46^3$	$1:12^2$	Md 32000	2	8	$7^{3\frac{1}{4}}$	$6^{2\frac{3}{4}}$	$6^{1\frac{1}{4}}$	$3^{2\frac{3}{4}}$	DeCarlo C P	b	118	4.50	76-15	Espiocrat$118^{\frac{3}{4}}$ Wi
6Aug91-10Mth	fst	6f	$:22^2$	$:46^3$	$1:13^3$	Md Sp Wt	1	11	11^{10}	$10^{7\frac{3}{4}}$	$8^{8\frac{1}{4}}$	$6^{5\frac{3}{4}}$	DeCarlo C P		118	27.40	67-24	Erik'sChoice$118^{1\frac{1}{2}}$

Speed Index: Last Race: −8.0 3–Race Avg.: −10.3 5–Race Avg.: −9.8

LATEST WORKOUTS Nov 1 Med 4f fst $:48^4$ B Oct 26 Med 4f fst :50 B Oct 5 Med 4f fst :52 B

Interpreting the Signs of Good and Bad Form

This discussion of signs of positive and negative form, while generally applicable to all racehorses, pertains especially to the average horse. Very low-quality animals will regularly show positive signs but never run as well as the signs suggest. This is due mainly to physical infirmities or poor racing temperament.

On the other hand, top horses will often confound the negative signs and produce repeated outstanding efforts. This can be attributed to the fact that top horses are given more time off between races, time in which to recover from the stress of a previous race. Trainers wait longer for good horses to recover from physical ailments and only bring them back to race when completely sound. Cheap horses, on the other hand, are forced by the economics of the game to run with aches and pains.

It should be noted that at the best of times these and other fitness indicators are imperfect predictors since horse racing is filled with much random variation of performance and luck, as well as other factors beyond the horseplayer's control (e.g., track and weather conditions). To improve the predictive value of a single positive or negative sharp sign, it helps if another independent sign of improving form is present. For instance, the combination of freshened form, early speed, and recent sharp work produces a very strong feeling that a horse is improving. Combinations of signs and form patterns have much more value than single indicators.

Further Analysis

At this point in the analysis, the handicapper will have identified some horses with genuinely good form, some with apparent good-looking but negative or neutral form (pseudocontenders), and others with mediocre to poor form. About 80 percent of all race winners come from the genuinely good form group. This statistic may suggest to some that all that remains is to winnow out more losers and in the process focus in on the probable winner.

No. The purpose of further analysis is to become familiar with the relative merits and deficiencies of the contenders and pseudocontenders in order to get a feel for what they are worth in betting odds. Further analysis will often point out one or two horses with an edge over the rest of the field; but without a good idea as to their value, the selections may prove to be very poor investments in spite of reasonably high win predictability. Playing the game properly is related more to knowing value than to picking winners.

The bulk of the remainder of this chapter discusses other important handicapping factors that must be considered in order to determine these relative values. Before addressing these concerns, however, I want to present my views on the importance of race times and class analysis in the overall handicapping picture.

The Merits and Limitations of Speed Handicapping

Quickness and speed (they are not the same) are the two most important equine attributes in sprint races, particularly in races of six furlongs or less. Quickness is the ability to accelerate from a standing start; speed is the ability to run a race near full capacity throughout. Final time in sprints is largely a measure of these two qualities, since, at least in North America, jockeys habitually force a near maximum pace and very quick starts.

Routes are usually run at a slower pace, permitting horses with the greatest reserve acceleration or staying power to often prove best. Quickness and speed, therefore, play reduced roles in routes. Moreover, the wider variation in pace of routes as compared to sprints produces correspondingly wider fluctuation in final times for route races run by like horses. As a result, differences of two and three fifths of a second mean much more in a sprint than in a route. The use of speed handicapping, therefore, can be valuable for assessing contenders in sprints, but is less reliable for comparing routers, except in relatively broad terms.

There are two possible uses for speed figures: to measure general ability levels and to measure current sharpness. The application of speed handicapping is usually concerned with the latter, with selection decisions being based on the comparison of adjusted recent final-time speed ratings among contenders. To the speed players, these ratings concisely summarize much of the important handicapping information into a few easily comparable numbers. Ratings from a horse's distant past play a minor or nonexistent handicapping role for the pure speed players.

The major application of speed figures in my approach relates to the determination of a horse's basic talent, rather than to a definitive ascertainment of its recent form. While a recent race time can indeed be a most useful indicator of sharpness in many circumstances, I prefer to consider it as but one of a variety of valuable tools for judging current fitness. This preference is based on the fact that while recent-race speed methods can and do work very well at certain times, particularly for shorter distances, they do not work at all during other periods, for either sprints or routes.

For instance, the usefulness of recent-race speed handicapping increases during the summer months. Form by then is usually well established and the dirt racing surface produces consistently fast times. Final times during this period are more comparable from day to day, race to race, and horse to horse, particularly for mature sprinters, which can be relied on to run repeatedly close to previously achieved times. Speed handicapping comes into its own under these conditions. But not every summer race meeting enjoys consistently fine weather. A summer of frequent wet spells can seriously reduce the effectiveness of any pure speed method. While a variant can be used to adjust times from off tracks, the figures must be viewed with caution since many horses cannot reproduce them on other surfaces.

There are several other circumstances in which speed figures are also not very applicable. These include turf races (as discussed earlier), races during the first few months of the season, races influenced by a strong temporary bias, races in which the pace is controlled by a single front-runner, and races for two-year-olds and young three-year-olds. In these situations it is often imperative that other signs of ability, form, and improvement take precedence over final-time speed figures. What does a pure speed handicapper do then? Experienced and intelligent pure speed handicappers must either recognize the deficiencies of their method and avoid playing the game on these numerous occasions, or continue to try and use the speed figures and somehow muddle through, even though results are almost certain to be poorer than when their method is more applicable.

A complete horseplayer, on the other hand, using a flexible and comprehensive approach is able to change his tactics and assess the field using other more relevant tools when warranted. In this way he can make a more accurate evaluation of each racing field and thereby find more good betting opportunities.

Having said all that, I reiterate that speed handicapping does have an important role to play in assessing ability and form of all race contenders. The key to its usefulness is knowing when and where to apply the technique. Earlier, I described the usefulness of speed figures in assessing form. What about the use of speed figures in determining ability? The next section addresses this topic.

Assessing Sprinting Ability through Speed Analysis

As discussed earlier, the two most important factors in comparing ability levels of sprinters are quickness and speed, and that final times in sprints generally reflect maximal intensive effort on the part of the top horses. An assessment of a sprinter's talent must therefore be based mainly on its final times and its ability to run on the pace in the early stages of a race.

Routes, it was noted, are not as often run with maximum intensity as a result of pace and positioning tactics within the race carried out by the jockeys. Because of this, final times in routes are not as consistently repeatable as times in sprints, and so the ability of routers cannot be properly assessed without a comprehensive study of other important indicators. These other factors are discussed later. The present discussion, while generally applicable to all horses, relates mainly to the determination of ability of the sprinter.

For a horse displaying sharp signs, it is not critical that its last race be used to judge ability. The more recently its best ability was demonstrated, the better; but if necessary, any race run at or near today's class level can be used. This race need not be a winning one, but one in which the horse gave a solid, close-up try. If none exists, then the most recent race from which the sharp signs were demonstrated should be used. (Obviously first-time starters cannot be handled in this manner. Their chances must be guessed at using workouts, the trainer factor, and physical appearance.)

The results of this key race must be examined closely, with particular attention devoted to pace, final time, running company, apparent class, date, odds, post position, and running style. If the race was more than a month or so ago, investigate the manner in which the horse approached the good race. Were the signs of an impending good race similar to those existing today? Inspect another good race in order to hopefully confirm the apparent ability level. Were the final times (adjusted for distance and variant) comparable? If not, the single top race may have been a fluke, which resulted in a fast time due to an optimal combination of speed-conducive factors.

A time rating reflects the interaction of many factors that were in operation during a race. There are many combinations of factors that affect time in sprints by up to three or four fifths of a second, some of which are impossible to know and others that can be understood only through a careful study of the race circumstances. My view is that serious thought and effort should be given to the task of uncovering reasons to explain unusually high or low ratings, in order to intelligently guess how accurately the rating represents a horse's ability to run as well or better under the conditions presented today. Some of the many situations affecting a horse's running time by at least a few fifths of a second in sprints are described below. Corrective adjustments (if only qualitative) should be made to final time ratings when it is reasonable to assume that the horse was helped or hurt by such racing circumstances.

Factors Influencing Final Times

Final Time Influences—Post and Track Bias

Every track has a post position bias of one kind or another, even if only to a slight degree. Normally the bias is positive for inside runners (post positions one and two) and negative for far outside runners (post positions 10 and over). Some tracks are biased in the opposite manner, and others for or against both inside and outside posted horses.

The amount and type of bias is influenced by the distance from the start to the first turn, the position and shape of the crown of the track, the firmness of the racing strip, the angle of the starting gate, and the shape of the racing oval. The reasons for the bias are not as important as the recognition that one exists.

An advantage or disadvantage resulting from a bias has a greater impact in sprints than in routes, because a small edge is magnified at a short distance.

In addition to the post bias, most tracks have a bias in favor of a certain running style. Some tracks heavily favor front-runners (e.g., half-mile bull-rings), while others favor late closers (those tracks with a deep surface or long stretch). Tracks on which late closers have a pronounced edge, though, are relatively rare. This generality applies especially to sprint races. Most tracks favor speed, some dramatically so. This is because of the hard driving style of North American racing, the usual hardness of the dirt racing surface, and the freedom from interference enjoyed by front-runners. In any case, serious racing fans should be aware of the degree of post and track bias that exists for each commonly run distance at their track.

The only reliable way of knowing how much a bias means under various circumstances at any track is to do a careful study of many races run there. A compilation of statistics correlating post position with race results for frequently run distances can be invaluable. In the study, it is useful to segregate races by track surface conditions, because some fast-track biases do not hold up on wet or drying tracks. In fact, new short-term biases will often show up under these conditions. Speed tends to win most wet track races, but anything can win on a drying track. Drying tracks are the most difficult tracks to make selections for, in my experience, because the early speed is unpredictable. It often happens on a drying track that normally slow starters will show speed, and speed horses will tire or never get untracked.

When reviewing the past performances, the final times of horses that ran against a bias should be adjusted downwards slightly (provided there was some struggle to overcome the bias) and times of horses that ran with a bias adjusted upwards. One or two fifths serve as a rough guide. But be careful to give enough credit to horses that struggled hard against a bias and a fast pace and to downgrade substantially the performance of horses with running styles and post positions that, for the race in question, particularly fit the track and post bias.

Final Time Influences—Come-from-Behind Horses

Slow starters do not win many sprint races, because the distances are too short for their kick and because they must cope with traffic as they make their way to the lead. Small fields negate the latter problem with the result that off-pace runners will run to their fastest times in such races.

Consequently, a fast time clocked by a horse in a race against a small field should be discounted a few fifths if the horse is now running in a large field. In fact, a good race in a large field by a slow starter should also be viewed with a little skepticism and the time adjusted upwards, because the chances are small it can be duplicated; however, the times for slow starters that are usually pressing for or on the lead at the stretch call should never be adjusted. These horses have sufficiently strong prestretch moves to overcome most traffic problems.

Lady Dictator *NEGATIVE*
Own.—Davis Barbara & A
B. m. 6, by Mr Leader—Disrespectful, by Palestinian
$35,000 Br.—Cook R J (Ky)
Tr.—Moschera Gasper S
117
Lifetime 43 4 12 5 $107,840

10Jun87- 2Bel	fm	1⅜	Ⓣ:49⅕	1:38⅗	2:17	ⒻClm 35000	12	8	9^{13}	$6^{7\frac12}$	$3^{3\frac12}$	$2^{\frac12}$	Santos J A	b 117	*2.00	76-17	Debonairly 117½ Lady Dictat	
28May87- 1Bel	fm	1 1/16	Ⓣ:46⅖	1:10⅖	1:42⅕	ⒻClm 35000	8	6	$6^{6\frac12}$	$6^{4\frac12}$	4^{3}	2^{3}	Santos J A	b 117	*2.10	82-16	Far East 117³ Lady Dictator	
17May87- 2Bel	fm	1 1/16	[T]:48⅖	1:12⅘	1:44⅕	ⒻClm 35000	1	7	6^{8}	6^{3}	4^{3}	$2^{2\frac14}$	Santos J A	b 117	6.80	78-14	Kathy W. 117²¼ Lady Dictato	
29Oct86- 1Aqu	gd	1⅛	Ⓣ:48⅕	1:14⅖	1:54⅗	3↑ⒻClm 35000	3	4	4^{7}	$5^{3\frac14}$	5^{7}	$4^{5\frac12}$	Cruguet J	b 117	*1.90	56-38	DeauvilleLove112⁴½Diplomat'	
18Oct86- 3Bel	gd	1 1/16	Ⓣ:48⅗	1:13	1:45⅘	3↑ⒻClm 45000	8	9	$7^{4\frac12}$	$7^{5\frac12}$	$4^{5\frac12}$	4^{4}	Graell A	b 113	8.80	63-29	Tammy Jean 112¾ Jarcaz 110	
8Oct86- 4Bel	fm	1¼	[T]:49⅕	1:39⅗	2:05	3↑ⒻClm 35000	1	2	$3^{4\frac12}$	9^{9}	7^{6}	$5^{3\frac14}$	Santos J A	b 117	6.40	66-29	SweetMiranda117²½BethsSor	
28Sep86- 4Bel	sf	1⅜	[T]:49⅕	1:41⅖	2:21⅗	3↑ⒻClm 45000	6	7	$8^{8\frac12}$	$8^{7\frac12}$	7^{12}	$6^{10\frac34}$	Graell A	b 113	6.90	38-37	Miss Fleming 106²½GwenJoh	
24Sep86- 2Bel	fm	1 1/16	Ⓣ:48⅕	1:12⅘	1:43⅘	3↑ⒻClm 35000	3	7	7^{6}	$8^{7\frac12}$	6^{9}	$5^{8\frac34}$	Graell A	b 117	5.50	68-19	FigurNviden117⁵¾Diplomt'sN	
23Jly86- 2Bel	fm	1 1/16	Ⓣ:45⅖	1:10⅖	1:42⅘	ⒻClm c-35000	5	7	8^{12}	$6^{4\frac12}$	$3^{1\frac12}$	$2^{1\frac12}$	Cordero A Jr	b 117	2.90	8C-17	SweetJellyBinn117¹½LdyDict	
6Jly86- 4Bel	fm	1¼	[T]:50⅖	1:39⅘	2:04	ⒻClm 35000	4	1	3^{2}	4^{2}	3^{2}	$3^{\frac34}$	Santos J A	b 117	*.90	73-18	Queen'sGntlt117½SwtJllyBinn	

LATEST WORKOUTS Jun 7 Bel 3f fst :37⅖ b May 10 Bel 5f fst 1:03 b May 3 Bel tr.t 4f fst :51 b

Diamond Joy *POSITIVE*
Own.—Nagle K
B. g. 3, by Tri Jet—Availing Joy, by Daryl's Joy
$32,500 Br.—Dizney Donald R (Fla)
Tr.—Lake Robert P
115
Lifetime 19 4 2 4 $56,095

3Jun87- 1Bel	gd	1⅜	Ⓣ:52	1:45	2:24⅗	Clm 35000	1	9	9^{13}	$4^{1\frac12}$	2^{hd}	$2^{\frac34}$	Guerra W A	b 117	3.70	38-37	CedarCreek117¾DiamondJoy1
24May87- 1Bel	fst	1⅛	:48⅖	1:13	1:51⅘	Clm 25000	2	8	7^{6}	5^{6}	$3^{\frac12}$	$1^{\frac12}$	Guerra W A	b 117	3.10e	68-16	Diamond Joy 117½ Consiere 1
7May87- 1Bel	fst	1 1/16	:46⅗	1:11	1:44	Clm 45000	6	6	6^{17}	6^{16}	6^{11}	$5^{11\frac14}$	Davis R G	b 113	6.40	71-21	SlopMstr117³½MjsticChoc113
29Apr87- 5Aqu	gd	1⅛	:48⅖	1:12⅖	1:51⅗	Clm 32500	7	8	$8^{7\frac12}$	$7^{5\frac12}$	$4^{1\frac12}$	$3^{2\frac34}$	Migliore R	b 115	5.20	74-22	[D]Cayman 113ʰᵈ Master Gene

Final Time Influences—Pace of Race

A fast, unsustainable pace set by two or more front-runners can make the closers look good as they pass the staggering leaders in the stretch. Stretch runners often win races like this largely by default, but their performance looks great in the Form. Discount the times somewhat and discount the chance of a repeat.

Slow-paced races in which a normally slow starter takes the lead early and goes on to win can also misrepresent a horse's ability. The race looks good in the Form—a sudden reversal of style resulting in a front-running win. Chances are the pace in the horse's next race will be faster, and therefore a repeat performance is unlikely. The horse will find itself back in the pack again trying to wend its way through the field.

A very fast-paced race can easily tire a horse that fought for the lead early in a race and result in a fading performance through the stretch drive. This factor often contributes to the dismal-looking defeat of young, inexperienced horses, or of horses returning to racing after a layoff. The final times from these races should be ignored completely. Instead, compare the half-mile time with those from the other contestants' races to ascertain whether or not the fading horse is a contender. If its time at the half was faster than that of the other horses, it is a candidate to dominate the pace and win, in spite of a poor final time last race.

Hair House		Gr. g. 2(Feb), by Hatchet Man—Lightasafeather, by Spring Double				Lifetime		
		Br.—Elser Farms Corp (NY)				**118**	4 0 1	
Own.—MacGuire James		Tr.—Levine Bruce N					$8,160	
20Nov91- 6Aqu fst 1	:461 1:104 1:371	Md Sp Wt	1 3 32½ 33½ 38½ 513½	Cordero A Jr	b 118	5.70	62-30	Blare of Trumpets
26Oct91- 4Aqu fst 6f	:223 :46 1:11	⑤Md Sp Wt	8 2 21 41 31½ 31¾	Santos J A	118	2.10	84-12	Alyjandro118½ Pa;
7Oct91- 4Bel fst 6½f	:23 :47 1:18	⑤Md Sp Wt	7 3 42 41¾ 43½ 2¾	Santos J A	118	29.60	86-11	Montreal Marty118
18Sep91- 2Bel fst 6f	:222 :454 1:102	⑤Md Sp Wt	2 3 21 31 34 612½	Santos J A	118	25.10	75-15	Detox118½ Iron Gu
Speed Index: Last Race: -4.0		3-Race Avg.: -5.6			3-Race Avg.: -5.6			
LATEST WORKOUTS	●Nov 16 Aqu 5f fst 1:002 H		Nov 7 Aqu 4f fst :482 H			Oct 19 Aqu 5f fst 1:042 B		

Final Time Influences—Easy Trip

An "easy trip" is a race in which a horse had little pace pressure or interference and was able to win or finish close-up while staying near the rail all the way around the track. Horses rarely get such good fortune, but when they do, the speed figures are bound to be quite generous.

Visual observation is the best way to determine if a horse had an easy trip, but careful study of a horse's post position, start, fractions, and close-ness to pace will often provide important clues. Characteristically, easy trip horses run on or close to the pace, finishing first or second, usually clearly ahead of their next nearest rival. Off-pace runners rarely get easy trips, because they must maneuver around front-running horses to challenge for the lead. An easy trip for this sort means getting an opening along the inside when the field turns for home. Clever jockeys will watch for tiring leaders to bear out on the turn, then shoot their off-pace runners through the hole along the rail. Result chart comments or visual observation are the only ways to determine if a horse had such a trip.

Speed figures from these runners must be discounted somewhat, be-cause they are not likely to be repeated. My rule of thumb is to take two fifths off their final time, sometimes a little more if the horse had it very easy.

Class

Class is a term that simply means the natural, innate ability of a horse to carry speed over a respectable distance under the stress of a race. More of it is required at longer distances, other factors being equal. Put another way, class is a measure of the combined capacities of speed and stamina. A horse that can run 6 furlongs in 1:09 $\frac{2}{5}$ and a mile and a quarter in 2:03 has less class than one that can run 6 furlongs in 1:09 $\frac{4}{5}$ and a mile and a quarter in 2:00 $\frac{1}{5}$. A mile and a quarter in 2:00 $\frac{1}{5}$ is more impressive than 6 furlongs in 1:09 $\frac{2}{5}$, because more horses can run to the sprint time than can run such a fast mile and a quarter. Sprints post a barrier to the display of class. Better horses cannot prove they are better by running sprints because of the distance limitations of such tests. For this reason the majority of important added money races are routes. The two dimensions of abil-ity—speed and stamina—are both displayed and measured in longer races.

Confirming Class Levels

Races are graded according to, among other things, class levels. In general, purse values are correlated with ability: the larger the prize, the better or higher the class of the horse, a factor that is useful in sorting out levels of allowance grade horses.

Another obvious class designation occurs in claiming races: the higher the claiming price, the higher the class, generally speaking.

However, class levels determined by claiming prices or purse values should never be blindly accepted as evidence of the calibre of horse. The class designations need to be confirmed by race results. Corresponding pace and final time figures should be in line with the designated class level, otherwise the calibre of horses is suspect. If the significance of the fractions and final time from a race are difficult to assess because of track and race conditions (off-tracks, turf races, unusual distance), then it is often beneficial to refer back to the past performance records of one or two of the well-backed horses from that race. Have a look at their record, including race dates, final times of recently run races, money won, horses they competed with, and consistency. This examination can provide useful information on which to base a reasonable assessment of the true class of that field.

In addition, be alert for results of very recent races in which other runners from the contender's questioned race have since competed. If a horse ascertained by this method subsequently raced well in a good field, then more evidence exists that the class of the race in question was respectably high.

Another means of measuring the class of previous race fields is through the race conditions. There are many comparisons using race conditions that can be made among horses to determine if some were in more difficult or easier spots in previous races. A few useful factors are listed here.

Confirming Class—Sex

A race conditioned for males is a significantly tougher spot than one for females, other factors such as claiming price being equal.

Confirming Class—Age

Unrestricted races (as to money and races won) for three-year-olds and up, or for three- and four-year-olds are often more competitive than races for three-year-olds only, particularly in the first half of the year.

Confirming Class—Nonwinner Designations

There are a variety of restrictions used by racing secretaries to keep previous winners out of races for losers, or out of races for less frequent winners, in order to ensure competitive fields. Each racing jurisdiction has its own set of designations, and handicappers must be familiar with them.

I do not recommend the splitting of hairs when determining differences in class from race conditions. For example, a race conditioned for non-winners of three races in the past five months is not significantly different from a race conditioned for nonwinners of two races in the past three months. Broader differences in designations must exist before conclusions about real class differences can be made. For instance, losing horses from a race conditioned for nonwinners of two races lifetime will usually be of a lower calibre than losers from a race conditioned for nonwinners of three lifetime. Generalizations about the winners of those races, however, are more difficult to make.

In any case, conclusions regarding class differences from the examination of race conditions should always be confirmed by a pace and final time analysis; otherwise they are suspect.

Confirming Class—Breeding

Most American states and Canadian provinces card some races restricted to locally bred horses (primarily maiden, allowance, and added money events). Normally these races are of lower class than open races because of the smaller pool of animals available from which to draw. A horse's record may be impressive simply because it has been able to win these closed condition races. Be alert to discount the record of these horses and to boost the record of runners moving from open company to restricted races.

Confirming Class—Recent Company

Anyone who attends the races regularly acquires a feel for ability or class levels of the local horses. This is a decided advantage when comparing class among horses in a race. The regular observer can often detect differences in class between competing horses simply by knowledge of the regular company a horse keeps. The difference is not very quantifiable, i.e., it does not show up in claiming price or allowance purse level. It is simply a matter of subtle but important differences existing between groups of horses within the same claiming or allowance structure. Overlays occur as a result of these differences, rewarding the regular horseplayer at the expense of the casual punter.

Drop in Class

A respectable showing in recent race of higher class than today's is one of the best positive handicapping factors. A good performance can take several forms: early speed, a move within the race, closeness at the stretch or finish, or an even race in which other good horses trailed behind.

The higher class performance must be assessed in relation to the class level of the race. More is to be expected from a horse that ran in a slightly elevated classification than from a horse that ran in a much higher class level.

Obvious class drops are usually bet heavily by the public, which makes the angle difficult to profit by. In fact, it is often worthwhile betting against horses obviously dropping in class provided the dropping horse shows negative form signs. More on this topic later. It is important to understand that positive and potentially profitable class drops are more often found among horses making less apparent steps down the class ladder, or among horses whose recent races at higher class levels were mediocre looking but contained hidden signs of sharpness.

Captain Arthur TODAY'S CLASS: Alwd — B. c. 4, by River Knight—Kazadancoa, by Green Dancer
Own.—O'Mealia Joanne — Br.—Clay & Runnymeade Farm (Ky). — Tr.—Gorman John — **116** — Lifetime 19 4 2 4 $60,751

29May87- 8Mth	fm	1 1/16	Ⓣ:47⅘	1:10⅘	1:41⅗	+ 3↑Dave Hart	6	7	7^{14}	69¼	47	47¾	Krone J A	119	11.60	86–07	FeelingGllnt119¾ArrivoOnT
25Apr87-10GP	fm	1½	Ⓣ:48⅕	2:02⅕	2:26⅖	3↑Pan Amer H	12	13	13^{26}	139½	119¼	117¾	Terry J	111	30.00f	84–10	Iroko 112^{hd} Akabir 1132½ Gl
25Apr87-Grade I																	
5Apr87- 9GP	fm	*1 1/16	Ⓣ		1:43⅘	Alw 18000	7	6	6^7	6^3	4¾	12½	Fires E	117	4.70	87–08	CptinArthur1172½Bnfbulous
14Mar87- 8GP	gd	1 1/16	Ⓣ:47⅘	1:12⅘	1:44⅕	Alw 18000	9	11	11^{17}	11^{10}	67½	46½	Penna D	117	22.30	72–22	Val D'Enchere 119^2 Viceles
3Mar87- 7Hia	fst	1⅛	:47⅕	1:11⅕	1:49⅖	Alw 23000	3	7	7^{11}	6^{11}	6^{12}	6^{16}	Penna D	116	5.10	68–20	Full Courage 116^4 Sunny P
14Feb87- 9Hia	fm	1 1/16	Ⓣ		1:42	Alw 23000	10	12	11^{25}	11^{15}	87½	63½	Gonzalez M A	116	23.20	84–18	Wollaston 116^{hd} Single Sol
13Jan87- 9Hia	fm	*1⅛	Ⓣ		1:49⅖	Alw 19000	6	6	66½	76¼	4¾	3^2	Penna D	116	18.60	82–23	New Colony 1191½ Swallage
3Nov86- 7Aqu	fm	1⅛	Ⓣ:48⅘	1:13⅗	1:5[illegible]	3↑Alw 29000	6	9	9^{17}	9^{13}	4^9	26½	Krone J A	115	13.20	78–22	Ioskeha 1156½ Captain Arth
17Oct86-10Med	fm	1 1/16	Ⓣ:47⅘	1:12⅖	1:43⅘	Summing	1	7	7^{13}	4½	31½	31¼	Krone J A	115	5.70	82–18	Silver Comet 115no Sir Mac
25Sep86- 6Med	fm	1	Ⓣ:46⅗	1:11	1:36	Alw 17000	5	7	76¼	62¾	2^1	1¾	Krone J A	113	6.70	98–09	Captain Arthur 113¾ Make

LATEST WORKOUTS Jun 19 Mth 5f fst 1:03⅕ b — Jun 13 Mth 4f fst :48 h — May 16 GP 5f fst 1:01 h

Sport Royal TODAY'S CLASS: Md — B. c. 3, by Secretariat—Linda North, by Northern Dancer
Own.—Gleaves P A — Br.—Taylor E P (Md) — Tr.—Gleaves Philip — **114** — Lifetime 5 0 0 1 $1,690

8Jun87- 8Mth	fm	1 1/16	Ⓣ:47⅘	1:12	1:43	+ 3↑Alw 15000	7	8	8^{10}	77½	7^6	6^6	Hernandez C	109	33.60	80–14	Catch A Cold 1092½ Nantah
18Apr87- 3GP	fst	1 1/16	:48⅕	1:13	1:45⅖	Md Sp Wt	4	7	73½	9^9	9^{16}	10^{17}	Lester R N	122	6.90	57–21	Carborundum 1222½ Tap Wr
4Apr87- 4GP	fst	1 1/16	:47⅖	1:13	1:47⅖	Md Sp Wt	10	11	10^{20}	8^{12}	78¾	34½	Santos J A	122	6.90	59–23	Derby Junior 1224½ Mollifie
28Mar87- 4GP	fst	7f	:23	:46⅗	1:25⅖	Md Sp Wt	1	5	1½	1½	2^2	55¼	Guerra W A	122	5.90	72-21	WngdVctor1223½FlshUncl12
8Mar87- 4GP	fst	6f	:22⅖	:46⅕	1:12⅘	Md Sp Wt	5	10	10^{10}	11^{13}	9^{16}	917¾	Guerra W A	122	*2.10	57-25	Im All Shook Up 122^{hd} Ron

LATEST WORKOUTS Jun 21 Mth 6f fst 1:17⅕ b — Jun 16 Mth 4f fst :49⅗ b — Jun 5 Mth 5f sly 1:06⅕ b — M:

Assessing Routing Ability through Class and Pace Analysis

Assessing the ability of a route runner is a more complex task than measuring talent of a sprinter. Whereas time is the principal yardstick for the sprinter, it should only be used as a confirmatory tool with a router. The ability to cope with pace, the ability to beat or run well with better horses, the capacity to make a strong gaining move or control pace by running in front, are the principal attributes of talent among route runners. Stamina, of course, is also important. All of these factors represent "class."

Detailed comparative final time analysis is generally of limited merit in separating the top contenders in routes, because fractions of a second do not as often reflect differences in ability as is the case with sprinters. Differences in time in routes primarily represent the way the race is run, other important factors such as general class level being equal. Differences in final times attributable to pace have a much greater range of variation in routes than in sprints, because of the longer distances, making speed analysis of minor importance.

Route times can, however, be highly useful in assessing the ability of improving young horses moving quickly up the class ladder after success at lower levels, since inherent class is still being developed. Final times from route races are also useful when evaluating runners coming in from out of town tracks (other than foreign tracks), for which class designations may not be comparable. This comparison requires some knowledge of speed tendencies of North American tracks, information readily available in the handicapping literature.

The horse-to-horse comparisons between routers, with the noted exceptions, must be made largely on a qualitative basis, rather than numeric or quantitative as for sprinters. The questions to be asked in assessing each router should include: (1) Does the horse comfortably belong with today's company? (2) Can the horse run close enough to the pace, or be capable of a strong enough prestretch move, to place it on or within a few lengths of the lead at the top of the stretch? (3) Does it have the stamina required at the distance and class level and still be strong in the stretch? If the answer is yes to all of these questions and the horse is sharp, then it is a very strong contender.

Question one is best answered by a thorough familiarity with the runners on the player's race circuit. Specifically, it requires knowledge of the ability of the horse's usual competitors, as measured by their earnings, class categories, distance, and surface preferences. Time analysis is not consistently reliable for reasons discussed already, but can be used as a broad guide when the preferred information is obscure or unknown, and as confirmation of the qualitative analysis. As done for sprints, times should be roughly adjusted for a daily variant, easy trips, biases, and pace of race. Once it is determined that the horse more or less belongs at today's class level, a careful study can reveal if the horse will not weaken or be intimidated by challengers in the turn for home and through the stretch. This requires an analysis of how today's race will likely be run and what kind of pace is probable.

The first need is to find the horses that should break quickly and set the early pace. Toward this end, close attention must be given to the outside and inside post horses since there is more pressure on them to break well and get position early. Outside posted horses with only moderate speed often get forced to run fast in the early speed picture by bringing another horse or two into the fight, thereby setting up faster fractions than antici-pated. Moreover, the speed displayed by these perhaps unwilling early runners must usually be paid for at a later stage in the race through a reduction of late kick.

If one or perhaps two horses stand out at this point as being able to set a clear pace and have shown ability to run without weakening through the stretch, they must be considered as very strong candidates to win. The winner, in the case of two runners controlling the pace, is often the horse that has shown recent ability to scrap out a win. Incidentally, pairs of runners, as in this instance, provide excellent exactor or quinella bets (in both routes and sprints), because the two will often finish well ahead of the pack.

Possible pace setters can at times be difficult to find in the Form if there are no obvious speed horses in the race. When nothing stands out, use techniques described under the "early speed" sharp signs discussion to locate potential pace setters. A less obvious front-runner is still a legitimate candidate to not only set the pace but to win the race.

The picture becomes more confused if the front-runners are judged not sufficiently strong to fight off a challenge through the stretch. The type of runner to consider next is the pace runner, one that can get away in the first flight just behind the leaders. These first flight pace runners usually inherit the lead, at least for a short distance, if and when front-runners tire. Again, look for the characteristic of strength in the stretch drive so the horse can stave off late charges by others. Pace runners without a stretch drive reserve must be considered as weak candidates to win. They do however often finish second and third and receive generous betting support, providing on occasion good opportunities for counterbets.

Off-pace routers should be judged by their ability to make a strong, quick move into contention before the stretch drive. There should exist the likelihood of a reasonable pace as well, against which the move can be made. A very slow pace can harm the chances of a slow starter, because it permits the front-runners to retain an energy reserve for the latter stages of the race.

One of the major problems in route races lies in determining which horses will set the pace at various points in the race and the likely fractional times. For each route I like to have a clear mental picture of the probable position of all contenders at all stages of the race. I run this race through my mind's eye until I feel confident about how the race will be run. Only after this analysis does it become clear which horses really belong in the race and what their relative winning chances are.

When looking for a bet in a route race, I lean toward front-runners, on-pace runners, and horses able to make a rapid, powerful move prior to the stretch. Less reliable are those routers that can only achieve victory through a combination of their own grinding style and a weakening of the opposition. These plodders fill the ranks at all class levels, and while they do win races, their victories are more difficult to predict. Strong front-runners and big move horses are the most reliable routers to bet.

Unfortunately, most route races do not contain even one horse with these desirable attributes, and as a rule, the horses with the right stuff are found at higher class levels. Most of my bets in route races, therefore, are made on horses with proven ability in better class races. Because of the relative scarcity of these horses in most route races, I find fewer bets in routes than in sprints.

Consistency

Consistency of effort and consistency of character are equine attributes revered by most horseplayers. Consistency of effort implies a predictability of physical exertion as measured by finish position and final times. Consistency of character refers to the likelihood of repeating ingrained tendencies in a race, such as the desire to be in front, a preference to be near the front but not lead, the dislike of fast early effort, and so on.

A horse that consistently makes a solid effort from race to race needs to show less evidence of sharp signs than a horse that only occasionally produces good results. The form of these consistent effort horses is relatively easy to assess. As a result, it is often difficult to find overlays among horses with a high win and place consistency record. Most overlays occurring on consistent effort horses accompany some kind of elevation in class.

It is far more common to find overlays on horses that do not give their best effort every race or that win irregularly. For this reason it is unwise to avoid betting horses with mediocre win and place consistency records. The key to making reasonably accurate guesses about the likely performance of a relatively inconsistent horse is time-consuming examination of the Form. A thorough understanding of the tendencies of individual horses, particularly the less consistent ones, requires detailed study.

For example, consider the "sucker horse." While the average player will bet horses that rarely win but are often close, serious players tend to avoid them completely. The records of these horses show a high percentage of finishes in the money, but a meagre proportion of wins. A record such as 20 starts, 1 win, 4 seconds and 7 thirds, is typical of these horses. It results from a lack of determination or a lack of understanding by the horse that it should pass other horses when put down for the drive. Occasionally it results from a physical problem or from regular placement in races of class too high for the ability level of the horse.

If the horse is easily intimidated, then there is little hope the characteristic can be changed; however, skilled trainers can teach a horse to pass other horses in the drive if the problem is poor understanding; and they can correct physical ailments if they are the cause. Dropping a horse into its proper class category can also help. For these reasons, horses that for long periods exhibit "sucker horse" tendencies will sometimes reverse their habits and become consistent winners. So it is folly to summarily dismiss a horse because of a poorly weighted consistency record.

Another aspect of the study of consistency involves determining how a horse will likely react to the racing circumstances facing it. Will it back away from a speed duel? Will it try and pass other horses in the drive? Will it be bothered by an inside post position? Will a filly make a normal effort when facing males? Will a horse quit if mud is kicked back into its face? Does the horse usually react the same way to similar racing situations?

There are many quirks of equine character that the player must be aware of when judging a horse's ability to perform under a set of racing conditions. These include the horse's preferences as to surface and post position (some horses do not run well on the inside, others on the outside); its predilection for a certain frequency and competitiveness of races; how it runs in various weather conditions (certain horses come alive in cold weather); its liking for certain tracks (the term "horses for courses" definitely holds true); and its jockey and weight preferences. Equipment changes can also contribute to a horse's performance. Blinkers on or off often affect the performances of young horses, particularly at the start of a race. Even older horses, accustomed to one set of equipment, can produce dramatic form reversals when new equipment, such as a tongue strap, blinkers, or shadow roll are introduced.

There are no hard and fast means of getting answers to questions about these equine likes and dislikes, as most trainers well know. My approach is to make educated guesses about these details based on what the horse has done in the past under similar circumstances. If the horse is running inside today, I like to see in the Form a sharp previous race from the inside, or failing such evidence, feel confident about the horse's speed to break on top. Otherwise, the horse's consistency record should suggest it has the drive and character to overcome the poor post.

The same reasoning applies to off tracks, distance switches, surface switches, and so on. Has the horse shown evidence of being able to handle these conditions? If evidence is not available, does the running style and consistency record indicate a willingness to overcome stressful race situations? Consistent, winning horses generally win under under any conditions when racing at the appropriate class level.

Equipment changes are more difficult to assess in relation to performance improvement. Records of equipment changes and performances can be kept to supplement the past performances and can provide the handicapper with an edge sometimes. I do not keep such records, relying instead on inferences from the performance of a horse's most recent race, past ability, and potential for form reversal today. A horse running reasonably well should not require equipment changes. But one that has ability but is not running well lately is a candidate for improvement through an equipment change. To qualify for serious consideration at betting time, though, the horse should clearly show sharp signs, normally through workouts or early speed.

The important thing to realize is that consistency of character or style in a horse is more important to the horseplayer than considerations regarding consistency of effort. Deeply ingrained habits are repeated with more regularity than are effort patterns. The careful study of these habits can enable the player to say with some certainty whether a horse will fit well or poorly the specific conditions of today's race. This is critical to making good assessments of probabilities.

Distance

The ability of a horse to cope with a particular distance depends on several factors. (Coping in this context means handling the distance sufficiently well to be in contention at the stretch call with enough energy left to at least threaten in the drive.)

Class level, of course, is of great importance and can be a serious confounding factor in judging a horse's ability at a longer distance. A drop in class will often produce dramatic improvement in a horse's ability to run well at a previously demonstrated unsuitable distance. In particular, great care must be exercised to avoid rejecting seemingly poor but possibly legitimate contenders at a route distance because of an apparent weak previous route race at higher class. It is judicious to give the benefit of the doubt about distance ability to such a horse dropping in class, provided it showed speed for at least a part of the race or was not disgraced completely at all calls.

There are other important considerations in judging distance ability:

experience at or near the distance; the horse's running style; the way the race will likely be run; consistency of the horse; and its inherent speed and stamina. These are discussed briefly below.

Experience counts for a lot in a horse race. Thoroughbreds are naturally high-strung and skittish and often react unfavorably to new experiences. A radically new distance can upset a horse enough to make it lose concentration.

Since nearly all horses begin their racing careers in sprint races, the experience factor at short distances is of minor significance, except, of course, for horses running their first few races. The longer the sprint, the more importance the experience takes on. First-time starters rarely win at six or seven furlongs, but they do win a large share of five-furlong races even when competing against multiple race runners. Rating by the jockey comes into play at the longer distances. Young horses are difficult to rate, as a rule, and will quit trying or become upset by being forced to run slower than they want to go.

Horses running in routes should show some experience and ideally some success at two turns if they are to be considered strong contenders. Success in this context means being able to get around the second turn without losing ground before the stretch call. Inexperienced routers can win if from well-managed stables, because quality training can make up for lack of race experience. In any case, the chances of horses new to the routing game, or new to two-turn racing, are difficult to assess accurately. My usual approach is to let them run a few routes before considering them for betting. There are, however, some clues to be garnered from the form that can help build a case for or against a horse's chances at a longer distance.

The sprinters that usually run best when entered for a route are those that do not fade in the stretch of their sprints. This may seem obvious, but the fact is that more mature sprinters that have been fading in the stretch of sprints appreciate the slower pace of a distance race and can win when occasionally spotted in a route. These distance switching horses should not be expected to produce repeatedly good distance races, however. Typically the first route after a steady diet of sprints is the race that can yield a win for a horse, owing to its intensive sprint conditioning. This anaerobic conditioning wears off after one or two longer races, and these horses must then rely on their stamina reserves, which are usually relatively meagre compared to that of regular routers. Good trainers know this and will send their charges back to sprints where they belong, after one or two routes.

However, stretch-fading sprinters with limited or no experience at two-turn racing or route distances rarely perform in this manner. The fact that they fade in the stretch in sprints suggests the stress of running around the second turn in a route will weaken their drive or spirit even more, even if they do possess adequate stamina. This lack of character is often evident in the behaviour of young, immature horses. This is not to imply that it is imperative for a sprinter to show recent races in which it gained ground through the stretch, contrary to popular belief and contrary to the fact that indeed the public does bet the strong closers more heavily than pace runners when horses move from sprints to routes.

The characteristics of importance for a regular sprinter trying a route are evidence of stamina when holding a lead, and a record of high consistency. The stamina (in both a physical and character sense) possessed by a sprinter trying a route for the first time can be guessed at by (a) how the horse runs when it takes over the lead in sprints, (b) how it runs when the pace is slow, and (c) how well the horse can be rated. A horse that collapses on the lead in sprints under a slow pace will likely fail on the lead at longer distances. Collapsing under sharp fractions is not an unforgivable sin and should not be taken to mean an inability to cope when in front. A front-running sprinter can be expected to win, though, when the pace is relatively slow.

The major problem in getting a sprinter to run a distance lies in rating it sufficiently to conserve energy for the stretch drive. Consistent horses are usually tractable and can be guided intelligently around a route distance by a competent jockey. The exception to this is the hard running speed merchant that attains a degree of consistency by virtue of its raw speed and pell-mell style. These kind of sprinters usually show first at the opening call, sometimes in front by several lengths in spite of little competitive pressure. This is an obvious sign of unmanageability. These headstrong runners normally make poor routers. A consistent sprinter that has shown ability to handle a variety of situations and run in a versatile way as dictated by pace, post, and track conditions, will usually be able to handle the route distance.

So much for sprinters trying a route distance. What about routers dropping into sprints? A horse than ran its last few races in routes and is now moving to a sprint should possess a reasonable amount of natural quickness and speed; otherwise it will be far behind the leaders before the half-mile post with only a little room left to gain enough ground to be in contention at the finish. This is especially true for races at six furlongs. Seven-furlong races are more appropriate for routers trying a sprint.

A few sharp works prior to the sprint can improve the horse's chances, but in the absence of some natural speed, its prospects must still be considered rather poor. Ideally, the horse should have displayed good early foot in its last race at the route distance, with early time fractions to suggest it won't fall too far behind the leaders in the first half of the sprint. Otherwise, unless an excuse for that last race can be found, the horse can be dismissed as a serious candidate today.

Another very important consideration for judging the ability of a horse to run well at a particular distance is running style. Running styles of the race combatants, combined with likely strategies employed by trainers and jockeys, can provide important clues as to distance capabilities of contenders under today's conditions. Some horses will have improved or reduced chances according to their ability to cope with pace. A race filled with off-pace runners gives a boost to the prospects of a single speed merchant, no matter how well beaten it has been in previous races of the same distance. Speed is always very dangerous, particularly when unopposed early. There is a tendency by bettors to underbet speed horses at longer distances, even when there is little competing speed in the race. But unchallenged speed can go long distances at a slightly reduced pace. The horse must be amenable to rating, though. Look for a previous race, no matter how far back in the Form, in which the horse led all the way. Any horse that has shown a front-running victory is a talented runner and can again be productive under the right distance and pace conditions.

The presence of several natural speed runners in a race can improve the chances of the off-pace runners if their speed is expected to tire. Be aware, however, that speed horses with the capacity to be rated by the jockey do not fall into this category. Rateable speed horses often win competitive races containing a lot of front-runners. Off-pace runners stand a better chance if all the speed horses have shown a dislike of jockey rating.

Complementing the running style analysis is a study of jockey tactics. The handicapper should try and make an informed guess as to the likely tactics of the jockeys on the basis of the capabilities and usual style of their mounts. The jocks read the Form, too, and the better ones will devise a strategy based on post position, track condition, speed tendencies of their horses, and how the race will likely be set up in the early stages. The top riders get more from their mounts in this way, and by timing their moves, can sometimes turn a natural sprinter into a router and vice versa. So, any pace and running style analysis done to ascertain which horses can run the distance at today's probable pace should include a guess as to jockey strategy.

The consistency record can often be a useful guide to distance ability in the absence of more concrete evidence. A record that shows a high percentage of in the money finishes (say 75 percent) with an acceptable proportion of wins suggests that the horse is dependable, likes to run hard, can be rated, and is probably flexible enough to run well enough at the new distance. A further check on the behaviour of the horse when it encountered a new obstacle during its racing career can also be useful. How did the horse run in its first career start, or its first time at a new track, or when it encountered mud or grass? If the horse ran well, then it will not likely be timid about a new distance. Poor finishes under those circumstances, however, may indicate that it will have some difficulty in coping with a major distance change at first asking.

Excuses

A good handicapper learns with experience to distrust the obvious. Apparent form, either good or bad, is never accepted without scrutiny by a good horse picker. Close attention to detail can determine when positive-looking form will be overrated by the public and when dull-appearing form will be underrated. In this regard, awareness of the kinds of good and bad luck that can befall a horse during a race is important in properly evaluating the results of past races. The discussion here relates to bad luck and racing excuses.

There are so many racing misfortunes that can befall a racehorse that probably a good many have yet to occur! Well, a few at least. The point is that the handicapper must remain alert to new possibilities all the time. This requires original thought as well as pattern recognition. Obvious excuses do not require much digging, but, alas, they are usually apparent to the public, too, and therefore discounted. A very poor start by a natural speed horse is an example. A poor performance by a horse over an off track is generally excusable by the public, as is a poor performance in a much higher classification. These are a few of the more conspicuous excuses for a poor racing performance by a horse; however, there are many more subtle reasons for dull or poor efforts that are often missed by the public. Some are described below.

Excuses—Poor Post

A poor post position (e.g., outside posts in races with a short run to the turn, or a post with a negative bias) can be a common excuse for a bad performance.

Gracie Fling — Dk. b. or br. f. 3(Apr), by Satan's Charger—Family Fling, by Winged T — Lifetime 10 3 0 $20,550

Own.—McManus W L — $6,500 Br.—Giardina Frank (Md) Tr.—Campbell Michael J — 114

29Oct91- 3Lrl	fst	6½f	:23	:47	$1:18^3$		ⒻClm c-6500	9	4	$4^{1½}$	4^2	$8^{7¾}$	$10^{17¼}$	Prado E S	Lb	119	*1.70	67-19	P. P. Dancer114^3
15Oct91- 3Lrl	fst	6f	$:22^4$	:47	$1:12^2$		ⒻClm 6500	1	4	$6^{4½}$	$4^{1½}$	1^2	1^4	Prado E S	Lb	114	*2.20	79-20	GracieFling114^4Gi
29Sep91- 2Pim	fst	6f	$:22^4$	:46	$1:12^1$		ⒻClm 12000	2	2	2^{hd}	2^{hd}	$2^{2½}$	$5^{5¼}$	Pino M G	Lb	114	*2.40	79-17	Ameri Allen$114^{3½}$
7Sep91- 7Pim	fst	6f	$:23^1$	:47	$1:12^3$		ⒻClm 25000	6	5	2^2	5^4	$7^{9½}$	$7^{13¾}$	Fenwick CCIII^5	Lb	109	4.90	68-20	Missy's Music119
16Aug91- 7Lrl	fst	6f	$:22^1$	$:45^4$	$1:10^3$		ⒻClm 25000	7	7	8^5	$7^{4¾}$	$7^{5¾}$	$4^{4½}$	Fenwick C C III^5	L	114	7.50	83-19	Missy'sMusic114^1
28Jly91- 4Lrl	fst	6f	$:22^4$	$:46^2$	$1:12^2$		ⒻClm 20000	3	3	3^2	$4^{2½}$	2^2	$1^{¾}$	Fenwick C C III^5	L	109	2.40	79-22	GracieFling$109^{¾}$Sa
4Jly91- 4Lrl	fst	6½f	:23	$:46^3$	$1:17^4$		ⒻClm 35000	4	4	3^3	3^3	$5^{7½}$	$5^{10¾}$	Fenwick C C III^5	L	109	9.60	77-12	GrcfulLil$114^{1¾}$Mis
20Jun91- 6Pim	fst	6f	$:23^1$	$:46^2$	1:12	3↑	ⒻAlw 16500	3	5	$3^{½}$	$3^{1½}$	$5^{6½}$	6^{11}	Fenwick C C III^5	L	108	2.50	74-14	FeelingFrivolous1
8Jun91- 5Pim	fst	6f	$:22^3$	$:45^4$	$1:11^2$	3↑	ⒻMd 25000	7	6	4^4	2^3	$2^{½}$	1^3	Fenwick C C III^5	L	108	*3.20	88-16	Gracie Fling108^3 G
3May91- 7Pim	fst	6f	$:23^3$	$:47^1$	$1:12^3$	3↑	ⒻMd 25000	2	8	$1^{½}$	1^2	2^{hd}	$3^{4½}$	Fenwick C C III^5		107	3.20	77-18	Satchmo'sLdy112^4

Speed Index: Last Race: –14.0 3–Race Avg.: –6.3 10–Race Avg.: –5.2

LATEST WORKOUTS ●Nov 24 Pim 4f fst :48 H

Excuses—Poor Start

Results charts should be checked to confirm if an off-pace runner was hindered by a very poor start. As explained, a slow start by a normally fast-breaking horse is usually apparent to most Racing Form readers; however, a slow start by a horse lacking natural early speed is not normally indicated in the running line in the Form. It must often be determined from the information provided in the results charts. The value of the excuse is diminished if the horse makes a big comeback to finish close to the leaders.

Fiestero's Star — B. f. 3(Apr), by Fiestero—Joni's Trance, by In a Trance — $10,000 — Br.—Fox Meadow Farms (Va) — Tr.—Simms Debra C — 119 — Lifetime 13 2 3 $15,372
Own.—Simms Thomas E

29Oct91- 4Lrl	fst	1$\frac{1}{16}$	:47^1	1:12^3	1:45^1	ⒻClm 14000	1	5	5^{12}	6^{16}	6^{18}	6$^{34\frac{1}{4}}$	Chavez S N	120	7.80	53-18	Alanna114^4 Witch
12Oct91- 9Del	fst	1$\frac{1}{16}$	:48^1	1:13^4	1:48^1	3↑ⒻAlw 8300	3	4	4$^{2\frac{1}{2}}$	2$^{3\frac{1}{2}}$	1^1	1^4	Taylor K T	116	3.50	71-29	Fiestero'sStr116^4(
5Oct91- 4Del	fst	1^{70}	:47^2	1:13^4	1:44^1	3↑ⒻMd Sp Wt	1	5	5^7	3^4	2$^{1\frac{1}{2}}$	1$^{1\frac{1}{4}}$	Taylor K T	116	5.70	81-16	Fiestero'sStr116^1
15Sep91- 8Pim	fm	1$\frac{1}{16}$	Ⓣ:47^4	1:13^2	1:46^1	3↑ⒻMd Sp Wt	9	13	12^8	8^5	7$^{4\frac{3}{4}}$	4^3	Johnston M T	117	59.20	71-20	JustAbotDwn112^1
1Sep91- 3Pha	fm	1$\frac{1}{16}$	Ⓣ:49^1	1:15	1:49	3↑ⒻMd Sp Wt	2	10	10^{11}	9^{11}	7^{14}	6^{18}	Lloyd J S	116	11.60	44-38	FlghtLux116$^{2\frac{1}{2}}$Ms
22Aug91- 2Lrl	fm	1$\frac{1}{8}$	Ⓣ:46^4	1:12^4	1:52^2	3↑ⒻMd Sp Wt	4	11	11^{18}	10^{15}	8^{13}	4$^{8\frac{1}{4}}$	Seefeldt A J	115	35.20	69-24	FrnchRby115$^{2\frac{3}{4}}$Flg
31Jly91- 4Del	fst	1	:48^1	1:12	1:41^1	3↑ⒻMd Sp Wt	3	3	3^2	3$^{1\frac{1}{2}}$	2$^{3\frac{1}{2}}$	2$^{4\frac{1}{2}}$	Lizarzaburu P M	113	8.10	70-24	CouldBeSpecial11
23Jly91- 6Pha	fst	1^{70}	:47^1	1:13^4	1:46^3	3↑ⒻMd 7000	3	6	7$^{8\frac{1}{2}}$	6$^{7\frac{1}{2}}$	5$^{3\frac{1}{2}}$	4$^{2\frac{1}{4}}$	Winnett B G Jr	112	*2.50	61-25	Impax112^{nk}Cheerl
21Jun91- 1Del	fst	6f	:22^1	:47	1:14^2	3↑ⒻMd 7500	5	7	6^9	5$^{7\frac{1}{2}}$	3^4	2^5	Luzzi J B Jr	116	*1.90e	70-18	GreenVlleyLdy112
7Jun91- 1Del	fst	1	:47^3	1:13	1:40^3	ⒻMd 7500	7	3	3^4	3^5	2$^{3\frac{1}{2}}$	2^6	Luzzi J B Jr	122	5.50	72-25	CommdoresDrlin1

Speed Index: Last Race: –29.0 3–Race Avg.: –10.6 6–Race Avg.: –9.1

Sentimentally Sally — Dk. b. or br. f. 2(Apr), by Maudlin—Pretty Proud Sally, by Iron Ruler — Br.—Bronzine Mrs Neeyna (NY) — Tr.—Carroll Del W II — 117 — Lifetime 1 0 0
Own.—Farish W S

21Nov91- 5Aqu	fst	6f	:22^4	:46^2	1:12	ⒻMd 45000	5	12	12^{10}	10$^{9\frac{1}{4}}$	9^{11}	5$^{8\frac{1}{2}}$	Carr D	113	25.20	72-19	FrVlly117$^{5\frac{1}{4}}$TrggrM

Speed Index: Last Race: –9.0 1–Race Avg.: –9.0 1–Race Avg.: –9.0
LATEST WORKOUTS Nov 30 Bel tr.t 4f fst :50^1 B Nov 18 Bel 4f fst :48^3 H Nov 9 Bel tr.t 6f fst 1:15 B

Excuses—Female vs Male

The sex factor is perhaps an obvious excuse, but females will sometimes throw a terrible race when in against males. Ignore such races if they are racing against their own sex again. Taking this a step further, embrace a filly that ran better than expected against males. They often make wonderful overlay bets when dropping back to their own classification.

Excuses—Jockey

A change from a raw apprentice or lower quality jockey to an accomplished rider can sometimes make a big difference in a horse's performance. While it is not a good idea to simply bet jockeys, the fact is that good riders do win the majority of races. The top 20 percent of the riders at a track usually win 80 percent or so of the races. (The jockey factor is described in detail shortly.)

Excuses—Eased Slightly

A jockey will ease up slightly on a decisive winner or a horse that is clearly second, third, or fourth when there is no chance of catching the horse immediately ahead. The beaten margin can look worse than it really should because of this. Moreover, the fact that the eased horse finished much in front of the rest of the field is in itself a very positive factor.

Saintly Cheif — B. c. 4, by Noble Saint—No Powwow, by Chieftain
Own.—Vee Pee Jay Stable — $25,000 Br.—Thoro Breeding Assoc Inc (Ky) Tr.—Ferriola Peter
1125 — Lifetime 26 2 8 4 $64,500 — 1987 11 — 1986 7

23May87- 9Bel	fst	6f	:22	:45⅗	1:09⅘	Clm 25000	2	2	2^{4}	$1^{\frac{1}{2}}$	2^{2}	$2^{2\frac{1}{2}}$	Messina R	b 117	5.30	88–13	Fugie $117^{2\frac{1}{2}}$ Saintly Cheif $117^{4\frac{1}{2}}$ Craig's
11May87- 9Bel	fst	6f	:22⅖	:46	1:11	Clm 35000	3	9	$9^{5\frac{3}{4}}$	$7^{8\frac{1}{2}}$	10^{13}	11^{11}	Nuesch D5	b 112	5.50	74–22	Semaj 117^{hd} Shine Diulus $117^{1\frac{1}{2}}$ Saltine
26Apr87- 1Aqu	fst	6f	:22⅗	:45⅘	1:10⅗	Clm 45000	5	7	$3^{1\frac{1}{2}}$	$2^{1\frac{1}{2}}$	2^{2}	4^{hd}	Nuesch D5	b 110	3.50	88–21	Tis Royal 113no Sports Medicine113^{no}F
10Apr87- 7Aqu	fst	7f	:23⅕	:45⅖	1:23⅗	3↑ Alw 26000	2	3	1^{1}	1^{1}	$1^{\frac{1}{2}}$	1^{2}	Nuesch D5	b 114	6.70	83–24	Saintly Cheif 114^{2} Racer 119^{nk} Billy Wi
19Mar87- 5Aqu	fst	7f	:23⅖	:46⅖	1:25⅘	Alw 26000	1	9	—	—	—	—	Santagata N	b 117	4.20	— —	Rexson's Quill $117\frac{1}{2}$ Billy Wilbur $117\frac{1}{2}$ R
9Mar87- 7Aqu	fst	6f	⊡:23	:47	1:11⅘	Alw 26000	1	5	$2^{1\frac{1}{2}}$	$2^{\frac{1}{2}}$	$2^{1\frac{1}{2}}$	$3^{3\frac{3}{4}}$	Santagata N	b 117	1.90	81–22	Fugie $112^{2\frac{1}{4}}$ Glittering Dawn $117^{1\frac{1}{2}}$ Sain
28Feb87- 6Aqu	fst	6f	⊡:22⅖	:45⅘	1:11⅕	Alw 26000	7	3	$1^{\frac{1}{2}}$	$1^{\frac{1}{2}}$	2^{hd}	2^{hd}	Badamo J J5	b 114	10.90	88–16	Gold Crop 112^{hd} Saintly Cheif $114^{2\frac{3}{4}}$ Ke
18Feb87- 7Aqu	fst	6f	⊡:23⅕	:47	1:11⅘	Alw 26000	7	5	$3^{\frac{1}{2}}$	3^{3}	$8^{7\frac{1}{4}}$	$8^{10\frac{3}{4}}$	Ortiz E Jr5	b 114	3.20	74–23	Upper Star 112^{3} Racer $112^{3\frac{1}{4}}$ Captain V
4Feb87- 8Aqu	gd	$1\frac{1}{16}$	⊡:46⅘	1:12	1:44	Alw 27000	9	3	3^{nk}	1^{hd}	$3^{\frac{1}{2}}$	$4^{3\frac{1}{2}}$	Santagata N	b 117	11.60	86–14	Proud And Tall 117^{nk} Carodanz117^{3}Wa
28Jan87- 3Aqu	fst	6f	⊡:23	:46⅘	1:12⅗	Md Sp Wt	3	1	2^{hd}	$1^{1\frac{1}{2}}$	1^{4}	$1^{6\frac{1}{2}}$	Santagata '	b 122	*.40	81–18	Saintly Chief $122^{6\frac{1}{2}}$ Amour Moi $117^{1\frac{1}{2}}$ F

LATEST WORKOUTS May 8 Aqu 3f fst :38 b Apr 2 Aqu 3f fst :37⅘ b

Equate — Ch. f. 3, by Raja Baba—Bank On Love, by Gallant Romeo
Own.—Taylor Shirley — Br.—W Lazy T Ltd (Ky) Tr.—Whiteley David A
114 — Lifetime 6 0 1 1 $9,130 — 1987 5 — 1986 1

24May87- 4Bel	fst	1	:44⅘	1:09⅘	1:36⅕	3↑ ⒻMd Sp Wt	8	3	$3^{7\frac{1}{2}}$	3^{6}	2^{5}	$2^{5\frac{1}{2}}$	Vasquez J	115	7.40	78–16	My Heroine $113^{5\frac{1}{2}}$ Equate $115^{5\frac{1}{2}}$ Johan
7May87- 4Bel	fst	6f	:22⅗	:46⅖	1:12	ⒻMd Sp Wt	1	6	6^{7}	6^{7}	$5^{6\frac{1}{2}}$	$4^{4\frac{1}{2}}$	Vasquez J	121	*2.40	75–21	Holiday Pond$121^{1\frac{1}{4}}$Allison'sDance$121^{\frac{1}{2}}$I
21Apr87- 6GP	fst	$1\frac{1}{16}$	:48⅗	1:14⅖	1:46⅗	ⒻMd Sp Wt	4	3	$3^{1\frac{1}{2}}$	2^{hd}	$2^{\frac{1}{2}}$	$4^{11\frac{1}{2}}$	Perret C	121	*1.90	56–23	Tasma's Star $121^{10\frac{1}{2}}$ Knoll Drive 121^{1} I
1Apr87- 4GP	fst	6f	:22⅗	:47⅕	1:13⅕	ⒻMd Sp Wt	7	5	$6^{2\frac{3}{4}}$	$7^{4\frac{3}{4}}$	5^{4}	4^{nk}	Vasquez J	121	2.70	73–25	LuckyChile121^{no}VagueTribute121^{hd}Mc
19Mar87- 7GP	fst	6f	:21⅗	:45⅖	1:12⅖	ⒻMd Sp Wt	5	9	7^{11}	5^{11}	$3^{2\frac{1}{2}}$	$3^{2\frac{1}{2}}$	Vasquez J	121	3.80	74–24	Nickle Plated 121^{1} Temper Dear $121^{1\frac{1}{2}}$
2Oct86- 4Bel	fst	6f	:22⅕	:45⅕	1:10⅕	ⒻMd Sp Wt	11	14	11^{13}	12^{15}	13^{17}	$12^{13\frac{1}{4}}$	Vasquez J	117	20.20	78–09	Lost Peace $117^{5\frac{1}{2}}$ Beauty Coat $117^{1\frac{3}{4}}$ F

LATEST WORKOUTS May 23 Bel 3f fst :36⅖ b May 18 Bel 4f fst :47⅗ h May 15 Bel 4f fst :53 b May 6 Bel

Excuses—Distance Switch

An off-pace router running in a sprint is usually put there by its trainer to get a speed workout in order to enhance its ability to run on the pace in routes. A sprinter, on the other hand, is sometimes given a route race to improve stamina. The poor results from these temporary distance switches can be ignored.

Cote Nord
BECKON D — 119
Own.—J L Levesque Racing Stable

Dk. b. or br. f. 4, by Medaille D'or—La Bourrasque, by Victoria Park
Br.—Levesque J L Stables Inc (Ont-C)
Tr.—Dumas Jacques
Lifetime 39 1 7 8 $59,624

1987	6	0	0	2	$4,863
1986	15	0	3	5	$22,295
Turf	5	0	1	2	$7,343

17Jun87-9WO	7f	Ⓣ:221 :4521:213fm	15	122	1211 1114 1083/4 89	Driedger I10	Aw16700	89-06	SilentRoylty,FromSeToSe,BePlsur	12
7Jun87-5WO	1 1/16	:483 1:134 1:464ft	9 1/2	119	1415 1112 1114 11101/4	SymourDJ1	ⒻAw18400	65-20	BrgndyDncr,An'tThtWckd,VctrGrl	14
18May87-8WO	1 1/16	:491 1:144 1:482ft	4 1/2	122	871/4 741/2 653/4 321/4	SymourDJ2	ⒻAw18400	65-23	Sharp Rascal,VictoriaGirl,CoteNord	9
23Apr87-6Grd	7f	:231 :471 1:272ft	4 1/2	117	99 912 59 57	SymourDJ5	ⒻAw16700	71-21	Mri'sToy,ClicoFling,JudgeMyDsign	9
15Apr87-2Grd	7f	:232 :472 1:261ft	2 1/2	117	531/2 561/2 58 34	SymourDJ1	ⒻAw16700	80-19	TurnToTheresa,Mri'sToy,CoteNord	5
28Mar87-8Grd	4 1/2f	:224 :47 :531ft	3	117	6 67 661/2 563/4	Duffy L6	ⒻAw16700	82-10	FullofSprkl,TurnToThrs,VictoriGirl	6
10Dec86-7Grd	1	:493 1:142 1:423gd	3 1/2	112	68 561/2 571/2 351/4	Driedger I4	ⒻAw17100	61-38	Ephemeris, Apple Jetty, Cote Nord	8
20Nov86-8Grd	1	:481 1:14 1:412gd	*2 1/2	116	74 45 46 351/4	Duffy L5	ⒻAw17100	67-32	GoldnSunburst,ClicoFling,CotNord	8
3Nov86-8Grd	7f	:232 :47 1:273ft	*2 1/2	117	79 712 710 443/4	Duffy L4	ⒻAw15500	72-31	Oftentime,SharpRascal,AppleJetty	11
25Oct86-9WO	1 1/16	Ⓣ:4811:14 1:464gd	5 1/2	115	31 31/2 26 233/4	Duffy L6	ⒻAw17100	66-28	Comic Copy, CoteNord,VictoriaGirl	9

Jun 25 WO 4f ft :502 b Jun 14 WO Tr.Ⓣ 5f fm 1:023 b (d) May 31 WO 6f ft 1:154 b May 26 WO 6f ft 1:171 h

Flirtatious Flicka
KING R JR — 113
Own.—Carmichael J B W

Ch. f. 3, by Crow—Bold Grotto, by Bold Commander
Br.—Trillium Stables (Ont-C)
Tr.—Armstrong Kenneth T $32,000
Lifetime 6 1 1 0 $10,240

1987	5	1	1	0
1986	1	M	0	0
Turf	1	0	0	0

10Jun87-7WO	1 1/16	Ⓣ:46 1:1021:42 fm	14	113	1hd 11/2 510 8121/2	DosRmosRA9	Ⓕ 50000	81-06	LumberBun,MiswkiFrost,:	
21May87-6WO	6f	:223 :46 1:13 ft	5	113	11/2 11 12 2nk	DosRmosRA1	Ⓕ 32000	78-25	ClstlGlow,FlrttousFlck,Dr	
6May87-7WO	7f	:232 :463 1:264ft	44	1095	21 421/2 67 871/2	BrborDA4	ⒻⓈAw17800	67-33	NinetyNineFine,Emily'sCl	
16Apr87-8Grd	4 1/2f	:221 :462 :523ft	41	115	4 661/4 68 753/4	Grubb R4	ⒻAw16700	86-10	SnowRod,HighlndGren,Vr	
27Mar87-10Grd	4 1/2f	:224 :474 :54 ft	41	115	3 111/2 12 11	Grubb R3	ⒻM25000	85-13	FlirttiousFlick,Ptrmgnt,B	
11Oct86-5WO	6f	:224 :47 1:142ft	11	115	543/4 911 1122 11133/4	Fell J9	ⒻM25000	57-21	BePlesure,RisdProprly,Cr	

Jun 18 WO tr.t 4f ft :511 b Jun 25 WO tr.t 4f ft :524 b ●Jun 4 WO tr.t 4f ft :49 h ●Jun 3 WO Ⓣ 2f yl :

Excuses—Equipment Change

Some poor performances by horses can be attributed to experiments with equipment—tongue strap, shadow roll, or blinkers on or off. The racing program must be checked for these unsuccessful experiments with equipment.

Excuses—Interference

Results charts document the more blatant incidents of interference. But visual observation is the best way to discover traffic problems. The player who watches each race carefully through binoculars, and studies the television replays later, can obtain information about bumping, boxing-in, and positioning difficulties that can provide an occasional edge over the average fan.

Excuses—Pace Style of Race

A race may have been run in an unsuitable manner for a horse's style resulting in exaggerated failure. For example, a slow starter running against a slow initial pace may fail to gain much ground through the stretch and look bad as a consequence. Or, a front-runner competing against a lot of speed may set fractions that are too fast and fail badly in the stretch drive.

A front-runner that likes to open daylight between the next challenger has an excuse if it was pressured by others and thereby failed to get a clear lead.

Glory Train B. g. 6, by On to Glory—With a Paddle, by Water Prince — Lifetime

Own.—Jones William O — **$4,000** Br.—Clark Marci & Klucina Betty & J (Fla) — Tr.—Taylor Ronald E — **116** — 98 20 11 9 — $89,229

23Nov91- 4Pha	gd	6½f	:22^2	:45^2	1:17	3↑Clm 4000	2	2	2^{hd}	42¾	6^{12}	612¼	Luzzi J B Jr	L	116	7.20	81-09	Greenflash116^{6¼}Bstine
26Oct91- 2Pha	fst	6f	:22	:45^1	1:10^2	3↑Clm 4000	2	4	2^4	44½	78¼	612¾	Somsanith N^5	L	114	9.70	79-14	ShltrdMoon119^{6¾}Expo
12Oct91- 3Pha	my	6f	:22	:45^3	1:11^1	3↑Clm 4000	7	4	3^7	5^7	5^7	57½	Pennisi F A	L	119	5.70	80-18	ShelteredMoon116^{1½}P
23Sep91- 4Del	fst	6f	:22^1	46	1:12^4	3↑Clm 3500	9	1	1^{hd}	3½	31½	4^3	Stone C	L	118	5.60	80-14	AlwysGld115½Popsprt
30Aug91- 2Atl	fst	5½f	:22^1	46^1	1:05	3↑Clm 4000	3	2	1½	1½	1½	1¾	Amonte A F	L	122	3.30	91-15	Glory Train122¾ Belle
21Aug91-10Atl	fst	6f	:22^1	46	1:12	3↑Clm 4000	9	4	1½	1^{hd}	1^{hd}	32¼	Amonte A F	L	122	6.20	79-14	Quadroyal116^{nk} Makei
1Aug91- 4Atl	fst	6f	:22	45^4	1:11^3	3↑Clm 4000	1	4	2^{hd}	22½	2^3	21½	Amonte A F	L	122	13.60	81-17	Iroquois Indian122^{1½} (
27Jly91- 4Atl	gd	6f	:22^4	46^2	1:12	3↑Clm 4000	8	1	1½	11½	11½	1½	Amonte A F	L	116	54.80	81-21	Glory Train116½ Legal
19Jun91- 2Atl	sly	7f	:22^4	:45^3	1:26^2	3↑Clm 4000	6	1	3^2	6^{11}	8^{11}	913¾	Chapman J K	L	116	45.80	60-16	PlntyPronto116^{1½}Shck
26May91- 1GS	fst	5½f	:22^3	:46^3	1:05	3↑Clm 4000	3	2	1^{hd}	42½	5^8	512½	Picon J	L	116	21.70	74-13	GulfstremPilot116^{6}Str

Speed Index: Last Race: –10.0 3–Race Avg.: –6.3 10–Race Avg.: –6.3

LATEST WORKOUTS Nov 18 Pha 3f fst :38^1 B

Excuses—Poor Ride

The last race of a horse can look bad if the jockey forced on it a running style that did not fit. Forcing an off-pace runner to keep close to the pace, or pulling back on a speed horse are two common examples. Pushing a horse early in a futile attempt to get position for a turn can take a lot out of a horse; and saving ground just off the pace is usually ineffective if the pace is very slow. Misjudgement of pace is a common failing of jockeys; speed horses get pushed too hard, slow starters are not pushed hard enough. Trainers notice these things and usually instruct the jockey more specifically for the next race. Because of this a horse will often give a far better account next outing.

Afleet
STAHLBAUM G *SLOW PACE* 126
Own.—Kennedy R R

Ch. c. 3, by Mr Prospector—Polite Lady, by Venetian Jester
Br.—Richard R. Kennedy (Ont-C)   1987 4 3 0 0 $33,990
Tr.—England Phillip   1986 0 M 0 0
Lifetime   4 3 0 0 $33,990

21Jun87-9WO	1$\frac{1}{16}$:48^1 1:12^3 1:44 ft	*1-2 121	3^2 6$^3\frac{1}{2}$ 6^7 5^3	SthlbumG !	Marine	86-17 Duckpower,StdyPowr,Ordrofxcllnc 7
21Jun87—Grade II-C						
23May87-9WO	7f :23 :45 1:22^{4}ft	*3-4 121	3$^1\frac{1}{2}$ 3$\frac{1}{2}$ 1$^1\frac{1}{2}$ 1^4	SthlbG^9 $\boxed{S}$Queenston	95-24 Afleet,Orderofexcellence,BoldRvnu 6
23May87—Grade III-C						
9May87-9WO	6f :22^2 :45 1:09^{4}ft	*1-3 117	2$^1\frac{1}{2}$ 2^{hd} 1^{hd} 1$^1\frac{3}{4}$	SthlbumG^3 Friar Rock	94-20 Afleet, Pinecutter, Arctic Lord 4
2May87-5WO	6f :22^2 :46^1 1:11^{3}ft	*4-5 116	1^1 1$^2\frac{1}{2}$ 1^9 1^{10}	Stahlbaum G^4 Mdn	85-25 Afleet, UnbreakableCode,Cacharel 14

Jun 27 WO tr.t 4f ft :49^4 b   ● Jun 16 WO tr.t 6f ft 1:15^1 b   Jun 9 WO tr.t 4f ft :58^2 b   ● Jun 2 WO tr.t 4f gd :47^4 b

Excuses—Rail Trip

Many horses are hesitant about running along the rail if other horses are on their immediate outside. They will refuse to make bold moves normally made with ease from the outside. An inside post can relegate a horse to an inside trip all the way around if there are other horses of similar speed in the race. This can be considered an excuse for more timid horses with spotty success records but is not applicable to consistently hard runners.

Peace Peace Peace
$12,000
Own.—Garcia Jose I

Ro. g. 4, by Peace Corps—Eleanor's Melody, by List
Br.—Marcanthony A (Fla)
Tr.—Martin Carlos F
115
Lifetime
45 7 6 5
$65,677

27Nov91- 1Aqu fst 1$\frac{1}{8}$:48^3 1:13^2 1:52^1 3 ↑ Clm 14000	①4 3^2 42$\frac{1}{2}$ 42$\frac{1}{2}$ 47	Pezua J M	b 119	3.20	68-26 Fake Out1174 Numbe
18Nov91- 9Aqu fst 1$\frac{1}{8}$:48^1 1:13^1 1:52^3 3 ↑ Clm 12000	②8 107$\frac{3}{4}$ 84$\frac{1}{2}$ 42$\frac{1}{2}$ 1nk	Pezua J M	b 113	9.00	73-27 PecePecePece113nkI
9Nov91- 9Aqu fst 1 :47^3 1:13^2 1:39^1 3 ↑ Clm 14000	2 7 5^2 62$\frac{1}{2}$ 63$\frac{1}{2}$ 65$\frac{1}{2}$	Bravo J	b 117	12.60	60-25 ImpshRsnng1174$\frac{1}{4}$Gn
2Nov91- 1Aqu fst 6f :22^3 :45^3 1:09^4 3 ↑ Clm 15500	3 5 6^4 7^5 71^1 71^1	Velazquez J R	b 113	13.80	81-12 Happy Kentuckian10
26Oct91- 3Aqu fst 1$\frac{1}{8}$:46^4 1:11 1:49^2 3 ↑ Clm 20000	5 6 5^3 54$\frac{1}{2}$ 6^8 51$^2\frac{3}{4}$	Velazquez J R	b 113	17.80	76-08 Gallant Hitter115^2 U
17Oct91- 3Bel fst 7f :22^4 :46 1:24^2 3 ↑ Clm 12000	1 9 43$\frac{1}{2}$ 32$\frac{1}{2}$ 2$\frac{1}{2}$ 2^{hd}	Velazquez J R	b 113	8.20	82-19 CsetheAce113^{hd}Pece
10Oct91- 2Bel fst 1$\frac{1}{8}$:46^4 1:11^4 1:51^3 3 ↑ Clm 14000	10 12 127$\frac{1}{2}$ 114$\frac{1}{2}$ 55$\frac{1}{2}$ 54$\frac{3}{4}$	Antley C W	b 117	6.90	66-22 IrshDplmc117^{no}Arctc
30Sep91- 1Bel fst 1$\frac{1}{16}$:47^1 1:11^2 1:43^2 3 ↑ Clm 14000	2 4 32$\frac{1}{2}$ 2^2 3^5 3^5	Antley C W	b 117	*1.90	80-14 OurHomeboy108^{4}Du
26Sep91- 9Bel sly 7f :22^3 :45^4 1:24^3 3 ↑ Clm 14000	8 11 111^1 98$\frac{1}{2}$ 5^5 31$\frac{1}{2}$	Antley C W	b 117	8.80	79-16 VirginiRoudy117$\frac{1}{4}$Vc
22Sep91- 1Bel fst 1$\frac{1}{16}$:46^2 1:11 1:43^1 3 ↑ Clm 14000	1 2 1$\frac{1}{2}$ 3$\frac{1}{2}$ 52$\frac{1}{2}$ 53$\frac{3}{4}$	Vasquez M O	b 117	3.50	82-13 Rny'sChmp115$\frac{1}{4}$Irsh

Speed Index: Last Race: -6.0   3-Race Avg.: -7.0   7-Race Avg.: -8.5

Excuses—Big Field

Off-pace runners or runners shuffled back in the initial charge from the gate have a legitimate excuse if they ran in large fields of say ten or twelve or more horses. It can be intimidating as well as difficult to have to weave through a large pack of horses. This problem occurs more often in sprint races. Route races, being longer, give the slow starter a better chance of overcoming traffic problems.

Femme de Naskra — Dk. b. or br. f. 3, by Star de Naskra—Supper Show, by Knightly Manner
LAUZON J — 110 — Br.—Hall & Hillbrook Farm (Ky) — 1987 2 0 0 1 $1,837
Tr.—DePaulo Michael P — 1986 3 1 0 1 $13,345
Own.—Arosa Stable — Lifetime 5 1 0 2 $15,182

7Jun87-5WO $1\frac{1}{16}$ $:48^3$ $1:13^4$ $1:46^4$ft $6\frac{1}{4}$ 114 $5^{2\frac{3}{4}}$ 2^2 $4^{6\frac{1}{2}}$ $10^{9\frac{1}{2}}$ Lauzon JM^4 ⒻAw18400 65-20 BrgndyDncr,An'tThtWckd,VctrGrl ⑭
28May87-8WO $6\frac{1}{2}$f $:22^2$ $:45^1$ $1:17^2$ft 7 117 $6^{4\frac{3}{4}}$ $5^{4\frac{1}{2}}$ $3^{3\frac{1}{2}}$ 3^3 Lauzon JM^7 ⒻAw16700 83-20 DeltaSlew,ArtsySet,FemmedeNaskr 9
6Jly86-3WO $5\frac{1}{2}$f $:22^2$ $:46^1$ $1:06^1$ft $2\frac{3}{4}$e 120 $3^{2\frac{1}{2}}$ $3^{2\frac{1}{2}}$ 1^{hd} $1^{4\frac{1}{2}}$ Beckon D^5 ⒻMdn 86-19 FmmdNskr,AdmttoForty,SttlyTrsur 5
14Jun86-9WO 5f $:22^1$ $:46^1$:59 ft 35 114 $5^{5\frac{1}{2}}$ $5^{5\frac{1}{4}}$ $4^{5\frac{1}{2}}$ $4^{7\frac{1}{2}}$ KngRJr^7 ⒻMy Dear 83-20 Caseree,ExclusiveIslnd,ColourMein 7
14Jun86—Grade II-C; Run in divisions
4Jun86-4WO 5f $:22^2$ $:46^3$ $1:00^1$ft 38 117 $4^{3\frac{1}{2}}$ 4^5 4^6 3^2 Beckon D^1 ⒻMdn 83-27 I'mAFinLdy,ClstilGlow,FmmdNskr 11
Jun 24 WO Ⓣ 2f sf $:24^1$ b ● Jun 19 WO Tr.Ⓣ 4f fm $:46^1$ h May 22 WO 5f ft $1:01^3$ bg May 15 WO 6f gd $1:18^3$ b

Excuses—Unpreferred Surface

Off tracks and unfamiliarity with or dislike of grass or dirt can be valid reasons for dismal performances.

Warrior Country * — B. h. 5, by Chieftain—Pro Raja, by Semi-Pro
DOS RAMOS R A — 116 — Br.—Schuyler Stables (Ky) — 1987 1 0 0 0
Tr.—Hasmatali Roger $19,000 — 1986 5 1 0 0 $18,000
Own.—Four Star Racing Stable — Lifetime 30 6 5 6 $110,143 — Turf 6 0 2 1 $19,623

14Jun87-8FE 1 Ⓣ$:48^3$ $1:14^2$ $1:40^4$yl $5\frac{1}{4}$ 117 2^2 $5^{5\frac{1}{4}}$ $5^{9\frac{1}{4}}$ 7^{15} Alderson A J^2 HcpO 59-26 Mr.Bones,LuckyCucsus,TlkRonTlk 10
22Jun86-7WO 6f $:22^1$ $:45^1$ $1:10^4$ft 28 116 $7^{7\frac{1}{2}}$ $7^{6\frac{1}{4}}$ $6^{6\frac{3}{4}}$ $6^{5\frac{1}{4}}$ Penna D^5 HcpO 84-20 S.S.Entrprs,GonToGlory,NrThStrm 7
13Jun86-9WO $1\frac{1}{16}$ $:48^1$ $1:12^3$ $1:45^3$ft 32 121 $4^{2\frac{1}{2}}$ $4^{6\frac{1}{4}}$ 7^{13} 7^{12} Lauzon J M^4 Aw26400 69-27 CoolNortherner,ReglRmrk,King'sGt 7
19May86-8WO $1\frac{1}{16}$ $:47^1$ $1:12^3$ $1:46^2$sy 17 116 $3^{4\frac{1}{2}}$ 5^{11} 10^{26} 10^{23} LauzonJM^8 Eclipse 54-34 TnGoldPots,DvotdAllinc,BrWithM 10
19May86—Grade III
11May86-2WO 1^{70} $:48^1$ $1:13^2$ $1:44^3$ft 3 117 $1^{1\frac{1}{2}}$ $1^{\frac{1}{2}}$ 2^2 1^{nk} Lauzon J M^2 HcpO 80-26 WrrorContry,GnTRylty,Twgnchppy 5
3May86-8WO 7f $:23^3$ $:46^1$ $1:24^2$ft 50 111 3^{nk} $4^{1\frac{1}{2}}$ $7^{5\frac{3}{4}}$ $7^{4\frac{3}{4}}$ Swatuk B^5 Vigil H 82-24 ReglRemrk,Bnker'sJet,Let'sGoBlue 8
3May86—Grade III-C
27Nov85-9Grd 7f $:23^3$:47 1:27 sl $4\frac{1}{4}$ 114^5 3^{nk} 1^{hd} 3^2 $7^{3\frac{1}{2}}$ Sabourin RB^7 Aw18000 77-31 S.S.Enterprise,DnceCorps,TintdLov 9
13Nov85-8Grd 1 $:47^1$ $1:12^4$ 1:41 sy *9-5 119^5 $1^{1\frac{1}{2}}$ 1^3 1^2 $1^{1\frac{1}{2}}$ Sabourin RB^5 Aw20000 75-27 WrrorContry,GolLght,Twognchppy 8
27Oct85-7WO $1\frac{1}{16}$ Ⓣ$:48^2$ $1:32^1$ 1:47 gd $3\frac{1}{4}$ 112 $3^{2\frac{1}{2}}$ $2^{\frac{1}{2}}$ 3^1 $7^{6\frac{1}{4}}$ Lauzon J M^9 Aw20000 63-28 RomnStrtgy,CorncbsRylty,ArtcClr 12
13Oct85-9WO $1\frac{1}{16}$:48 1:13 $2:00^4$sy *4-5 117 2^3 $3^{3\frac{1}{2}}$ 3^{11} $3^{12\frac{1}{2}}$ HosngG^8 Mclaughln H 63-27 OldGnPowdr,RglSnow,WrrorContry 8
Jun 11 WO tr.t 4f ft $:49^3$ h May 31 WO tr.t 5f ft $1:04^4$ h May 20 WO tr.t 1 ft 1:48 b May 13 WO tr.t 5f ft $1:03^3$ h

Excuses—Poor Race Placement

Some less experienced or ignorant trainers (and/or owners) place their steed in totally unsuitable situations, trying to make something out of the horse that it can never be. Overly high class levels, wrong distances or surface, and improper sex and age groupings are some of the poor classifications to look for. When a horse that is regularly misplaced as to race is "accidently" dropped into the right spot, forget about the poor-looking form. The horse has an excellent chance to wake up.

Regal Agent
B. f. 4, by Bold Agent—Regal Miss, by Viceregal
DUFFY L — 116
Br.—Taylor E P (Ont-C) — 1987 5 0 0 3 $4,840
Tr.—Ottaway Brian — $20,000 — 1986 16 1 3 4 $21,275
Own.—Murray Stable — Lifetime 36 3 4 11 $59,594 — Turf 1 0 0 0 $435

30May87-1WO	7f	:233	:463	1:242ft	3¼	116	43½	53	45½	33	Duffy L 1	Ⓕ 20000	84-16	SvgingPrncss Mry'sMnstrl RglAgnt	6
14May87-9WO	7f	:233	:464	1:252ft	24	116	95¾	911	610	59¼	Duffy L 1	Ⓕ 32000	73-30	PrkAvenuPrls.Cmroll.SmrtlyYours	10
7May87-8WO	6½f	:231	:473	1:212ft	5¾	116	97½	94¾	66¾	32	Swatuk B 1	Ⓕ 25000	64-38	ReineCheri.StrtgicRhythm.RglAgnt	9
2May87-7WO	1 1/16	:482	1:141	1:483ft	10	117	43½	43	38½	36½	Duffy L 3	Ⓕ 25000	59-25	FastGuide.LoveVictoria.RegalAgent	7
12Apr87-9Grd	6½f	:232	:473	1:21 sy	21	116	913	811	811	67	Duffy L 4	Ⓕ 32000	74-18	Cameroll. Cailin Deas.IridiumQueen	9
27Nov86-9Grd	7f	:24	:482	1:281sl	7	115	1012	109¼	714	614¼	Pizarro J L11	Ⓕ 25000	60-35	Cmeroll.LdyRequest.DoublPurpos	11
13Nov86-8Grd	6½f	:241	:474	1:211ft	11	116	912	89½	56	32¾	Pizarro J L8	Ⓕ 32000	77-32	GentlFury.AnotnrLookRlt.RglAgnt	10
29Oct86-6Grd	1	:474	1:133	1:412gd	5¾	116	67½	54½	33	22½	Pizarro J L6	Ⓕ 20000	70-27	ChrmngSprng.RglAgnt.IllusonPlntr	8
1Oct86-6WO	7f	:233	:472	1:263sy	3¼	116	78½	77¼	57	67	Pizarro J L1	Ⓕ 25000	69-29	VictorinSilk.ReignSuprm.LdyRqust	7
12Sep86-4WO	7f	:24	:471	1:262sl	5¼	115	43½	44	36	33¼	Pizarro J L2	Ⓕ 32000	74-30	Gentle Fury. FawnLake.RegalAgent	5

Jly 1 WO tr.t 4f ft :501 b — Jun 3 WO Ⓣ 2f yl :233 b — May 25 WO tr.t 4f ft :50 h

Excuses—Wrong Distances

Early in the year, or after a layoff, a horse can run several races at unsuitable distances either for training purposes or because the optimal racing spots are not available at the time. Dramatic reversals of form can occur when the horse finally gets to run at its proper distance.

Foxy Fred
Gr. g. 4, by Wise Exchange—Regency Sweet, by Vice Regent
GRUBB R — 122
Br.—Kasper Helen (Ont-C) — 1987 11 2 2 2 $13,969
Tr.—Williams Thomas — $7,500 — 1986 12 M 2 4 $9,763
Own.—Pizzurro B — Lifetime 28 2 5 6 $26,532 — Turf 2 0 0 0

3Jly87-1WO	Ⓣ7f	:23	:464	1:264ft	13	1165	74½	74½	68	54	Gibbons D F 3	c5000	71-24	SuperDom,King'sHouse,Takeadive	13
20Jun87-2WO	1 1/16	:494	1:154	1:491ft	*8-5	119	1½	11	1hd	1½	Dittfach H 5	6000	63-22	FoxyFred,Skygain,NorthernBriartic	7
11Jun87-9WO	Ⓣ6f	:224	:47	1:134ft	4¾	122	106¼	98½	68½	65½	Dittfach H 10	6000	68-29	Bytide,‡TrckAttck,Pressmn'sRvng	11
5Jun87-2WO	1 1/16	:494	1:152	1:484ft	5¾	119	2hd	2hd	1hd	2no	Dittfach H 3	6000	65-30	King's House, Foxy Fred, Sanva	11
28May87-9WO	Ⓣ6½f	:222	:46	1:191ft	10	124	74½	84½	79½	78	Belowus J 11	6250	69-20	SwnwickLd,BenJoJo,King'sHouse	13
20May87-9WO	1 1/16	:483	1:143	1:48 ft	11	121	22	2hd	2½	34½	Belowus J 7	6250	64-28	Calanco, Dancer'sAgent,FoxyFred	10
8May87-9WO	Ⓣ6f	:224	:463	1:134ft	5¼	122	64	54½	65	65	Belowus J 9	6000	69-26	NaughtyNick,Kelly'sBid,SirBering	10

There are undoubtedly several other valid excuses to account for unexpectedly poor races, many of which can never be known by the handicapper. Physical ailments, known only to trainers, veterinarians, and handlers would certainly encompass some. Many other reasons remain mysteries.

When I encounter an unexpectedly poor race from an otherwise strong contender with no apparent or assumable excuse, I usually pass the race. Estimating a proper betting line in this instance is like trying to read a crystal ball.

Digging out excuses is educated guesswork at the best of times and often requires making reasonable assumptions. From time to time the assumptions that are part of the art of determining excuses turn out in retrospect to be wrong; however, the educated guesses regarding excuses should continue to be made even after results prove them to be erroneous. A good horseplayer needs a definitive line on race contenders, right or wrong, to compare to the public's betting pattern. A decent odds line is not possible if wishy-washy opinions are formed.

Trainers

Some noted handicappers put heavy emphasis on the trainer factor, even to the extent of making some bets on that basis alone. Specifically they place bets on unraced two-year-olds making their first start if the trainer has a high winning percentage of winners from first-time starters. The method requires the keeping of accurate past performance records for trainers.

I have always considered this kind of betting a hit or miss, hot and cold approach. It is not amenable to development of a feeling for what a proper odds line should be; however, the method can be spectacularly successful at times in view of the high mutual prices that can arise when untried two-year-olds win. I cannot argue with those who win with this approach, but it is not one that I endorse.

I do use the trainer angle, but only in conjunction with other handicapping factors, or as a means of confirming an apparent positive or negative observation. There are trainers who can bring horses back to win after layoffs through the medium of workouts and gallops alone. Combining knowledge about these trainers with handicapping facts about the horse can lend strength to an opinion of the horse's chances.

On the other hand, there are trainers who always seem to do the wrong thing. Not only are their winning percentages low, but when it appears one of their charges has a good chance to win, the horse runs poorly. These are trainers who can be counted on to produce losers from apparent good form horses. Why? Perhaps because of poor race placement, perhaps because of skulduggery, or perhaps because the trainers treat their horses in a deleterious manner for the days just prior to a race, by working them too hard or feeding them too much or upsetting their routine in some other way.

When I find a positive handicapping factor for a horse, it must be confirmed by a sense that the trainer is reasonably competent. A poor trainer reduces the predictability of a positive factor significantly. Only unmistakable signs of positive performance of a horse can be relied on for predictive purposes if associated with an incompetent trainer. In other words, the very sharp horse can win in spite of the trainer. What this means is that you must know your trainers. Studies of trainers' habits and results are time-consuming, but the knowledge gained can contribute much useful information to the overall picture of a contender's chances.

Jockey

A great many casual racegoers bet jockeys rather than horses. I know this from listening to the searing epithets and invectives vocalized by the sore losers after a race.

Jockeys are not a major part of my approach other than the requirement that I want my horse to be ridden by a reasonably competent rider. I consider a jockey to be competent if he rides regularly (minimum two mounts per day on average) and has a winning percentage of about 10 percent or higher. I downgrade the chances of a horse carrying a raw apprentice, or any jockey with a poor record and few mounts, and upgrade the chances of a horse carrying one of the top half-dozen jocks on the grounds, or any rider with a 15 percent win percentage or higher. Inexperienced riders and female jockeys in route races also give me reason to reduce my expectations for a horse. The longer the race the more a jockey's experience, strength, and judgment contribute to the outcome.

It is common to hear a bettor say he will never bet on so-and-so again because of a blunder the jockey made in a recent race. I take the opposite view. If a competent jockey makes a mistake, I like to see him back on one of my top picks, because he probably realized his error (or was told about it by the horse's trainer) and is very unlikely to make the mistake again soon. In fact, the jockey will probably try harder to make up for the error. All professional athletes operate this way or they would not be pros for long.

I strongly advise against building up negative feelings toward a particular jockey or jockeys. Granted they all blow a race now and again, and the temptation is to be unforgiving, but they are just like the rest of us—they make mistakes in their jobs. It can be very damaging to a handicapper to have to avoid betting good horses and perhaps even switch to a loser in order to accommodate a dislike for a jockey. In my view, the horse is worth a large 80 percent in the handicapping scheme of things, the trainer perhaps 12 to 15 percent, and the jockey 5 to 8 percent. The average player reverses these percentages and in so doing lets personal biases about the human element override logic and fact.

Age

The age factor is not of major importance in handicapping a race, but it can be a useful tool for verifying an opinion.

The primary use of age as a handicapping factor applies to situations in which three-year-olds are running against older horses. In a race restricted to maidens, or to nonwinners of two or three races, the age factor can substantiate the lack of ability in the older horses. Four-year-olds that have not won or only won once are usually sorely lacking in talent. They can be discounted if their form is perhaps enticing but not convincing.

Good three year olds can run with older horses when a study of the basics of form suggests they can. Three-year-olds should never be dismissed as noncontenders with older company simply because of the age difference. The fact that few three-year-olds do beat older horses, particularly during the first half of the year, is no reason to summarily reject the youngsters. The ability level of a three-year-old should be studied carefully and then rejected only if its figures, class, and racing company do not measure up to that of the older contenders.

Another consideration regarding age relates to three-year-olds racing between January and July, especially those running in maiden or nonwinners of two (or even three) races. These races are probably the most difficult in all of racing for which to produce a good mental betting line. They are filled with horses coming back to racing after layoffs, horses just learning how to run, and horses making rapid gains in physical maturity. Speed in these races tends to be unpredictable, often being displayed by horses that showed little evidence of it in previous races. Extra care must be used in assessing these races. The result can be the discovery of more potential contenders than are found for other age groups.

Old horses (age eight and older) require a little extra attention during race analysis also. While some do establish excellent, lasting form, many others do not run back to their sharp signs because physical fitness and feeling of well-being are more fleeting with age. They cannot be counted on to duplicate or improve as predictably as younger horses. Consequently, expectations for these veteran racers should be downgraded somewhat.

Sex

Fillies and mares can and do beat their male counterparts at all class levels, as European racing fans well know. The tendency in North American racing is to segregate the sexes and in the process, through purse structures and media hype, create an illusion of male dominance and superiority. There are certainly more top male racers than females, but the best fillies and mares prove regularly, when open-minded trainers permit them to compete, that they can run with the top males.

One reason for the view that females are inferior is the unequal claiming class structure for the sexes. Claiming prices for females are about 25 percent higher than for comparably talented males, attributable in the main to the additional value the female has as a broodmare prospect. The tendency then is to cursorily discount the chances of a female running against males of the same claiming price.

As a general rule, a filly or mare running for a claiming price equal to that for a male will be an inferior runner. But this should always be verified by other handicapping means. Exceptions usually occur among consistent or hard-running females, and among females with enough early speed to break away. Also, recent sharp improvement in a filly or mare can sometimes indicate a forthcoming winning effort against males.

The biggest differences between male and female thoroughbreds are their ability to recover from hard races, and the amount of work required to keep fit. Females need more recovery time between races, as a rule, and do not need as much physical work between races or when coming off a layoff. In fact, a significant number of females run their best races after a layoff of 20 days or more.

In summary, never make the mistake of downgrading the chances of a classy filly or mare running against lesser males. Treat the horse as if it were a male in the evaluation.

Recent Odds

The odds at which a horse ran its most recent races is yet another excellent aid in consolidating a handicapping opinion. The two major situations to pay close attention to are those when a horse ran clearly better or clearly worse than the public expected (as measured by the odds).

A significantly better race than expected can mean the horse improved sharply for one reason or another. It should be checked carefully, to determine whether it was a genuinely better effort, or if unusual circumstances put other more favored horses at a disadvantage. For example, the horse may have been boosted by a rapid or very slow pace, or by unusual racing surface conditions, or by dismal failure of a few top-notch, heavily bet favorites. Generally, the more forwardly the horse ran throughout, the better was the race. I tend to downgrade a come-from-far-behind performance or a spectacular front-running race at high odds. Failure at low odds can be difficult to assess for significance. Sometimes it is a clear sign of a downturn in a horse's form cycle, but other times it represents only an aberrant performance or otherwise excusable race. It may even represent an error in judgment by the public in their betting of the race.

I usually take the view that the public assigns probabalities accurately and therefore a previously well-bet horse should be considered a strong candidate today, providing that the current racing conditions are not significantly more difficult. A detailed examination of the horse's form, with emphasis placed on the last two races, is usually sufficient to form a conclusion about the horse's chances today. In the event that there is still doubt in my mind about a poorish last race at low odds, I give the horse the benefit of the doubt because of my strongly held view about public opinion, and consider it a real contender today.

Marginal contenders for today's race that went off at high odds (say >10:1) in each of their last two or three races and are not dropping into an easier spot, are definite condidates for outright rejection from further consideration. Their recent odds are very effective weeders in this instance.

Post Parade and Paddock Inspection

My opinion about the value of the paddock and post parade inspection has changed somewhat over the years. At one time I put a great deal of emphasis on how my top horse looked—if it was "on the muscle," sweating, fractious, alert, bandaged, and so on. I would closely inspect the contenders in each race and on the basis of what I saw, make a decision to bet or not bet my top horse, or perhaps to bet another horse instead.

Today I am not as convinced of the value of this information, except under special circumstances. I do not let leg bandages affect my betting unless I am looking for them to verify a view that there may be something bothering the horse, as evidenced by recent performances as shown in the form. Slight fractiousness or light sweating are factors that do not normally change my view either. Experience has taught me that accepting these mild negatives in horses does not affect long-term results significantly.

The races that prompt me to take a special look at the horses in the paddock include races early in the season, filly races, and races in which laid-off contenders are coming back to run for the first time. Additionally, I make a point of always closely examining on post parade any strongly bet favorite.

Horses laid up for a lengthy period during the season, or those coming back to racing after a winter break, also deserve a special look. It is not uncommon for a horse in these circumstances to be nervous, because the racing scene represents a distant or forgotten experience to the animal. The nervousness is usually manifested through sweating and jittery or fractious behaviour. It is best to avoid betting these horses. Sometimes it requires four or five races for a horse to get back into the racing habit, so routine post parade or paddock inspection should continue for at least a month or so after the season begins. It is also important early in the year to notice the physical condition of a horse. Look for a tight, slim girth and a leanness about the rib cage. Discount the chances of fat or fleshy horses. They probably need a few tough races to get back in shape.

Filly races also require extra special attention during post parade. My observation has been that more three-year-old fillies come to the races in an obviously uptight state than any other class of horse. An unhappy state of mind is apparent from the lather of sweat that breaks out around the neck area. Needless to say, such horses should not be bet. In fact, these situations provide a good opportunity for a counter wager if the afflicted horse is heavily bet.

With the exceptions of the above instances, it is not critically important, in my opinion, to spend time in the paddock each race to examine the horses. A quick post parade observation is sufficient. Reject for betting consideration only the relatively extreme cases of nervous and fractious behaviour. Examine the top two public favorites. They should look sharp, or, if not, there may exist an opportunity to bet against one or both.

Another such opportunity can occur in races over an off track. Mud and slop can upset some horses. While this can often be determined from the form, it may be worthwhile to watch closely the contenders as they walk through the goo for any sign of annoyance, such as the kicking back of the hind legs to shake mud off. That is a negative sign.

Occasionally a horse will give clear, unmistakable signals that it is very eager to race. Continuously pricked ears during post parade is one sign. Another is a look of eager anticipation when a horse spots the starting gate. Other signs include a tight, bouncing step on post parade and a frisky, coiled eagerness to run in the prerace warm-up.

These signs do not guarantee a win but usually mean the horse really wants to run and run hard. When paired with a couple of strong handicapping angles, these signs create a feeling of confidence about the bet.

Weight Carried

Many handicapping experts have considered the weight factor as an important one in the prediction of race outcome. Traditionally the view has been that a heavy weight load makes it difficult for a horse to run fast and is therefore bad, and a light weight load is good for the opposite reason. Weights are assigned to horses through race conditions set by racing secretaries, in an attempt to equalize the chances of competing horses having different abilities. In most cases, the higher the weight assigned, the greater the ability of the horse, and the greater penalty or handicap it must overcome.

Experience has taught me that weight carried, within the normal assignment range of 105 to 125 pounds, is usually not important as an independent handicapping factor. Rather, high weight tends to be associated with the top contenders as selected by more specific handicapping techniques, in a tautologous manner. In other words, weight assigned can be used to roughly discriminate between levels of ability of the horses in a race, but cannot be used to identify all contenders; nor is weight sensitive enough to rank the top contenders.

When is it important to consider weight? Two situations merit concern. First, weight can be significant in a race where two otherwise equal contenders are adding or dropping poundage from their recent key races. My rule of thumb is that a ten-pound weight shift is meaningful and could tip the balance toward the weight beneficiary. Second, a horse carrying a high weight (say > 120 pounds) over a long distance (any route) should show evidence that (a) it has been reasonably successful carrying high weight over a distance before, or (b) it is at the peak of its form cycle now and performing aggressively enough to overcome the additional burden.

Weighting the Factors

The handicapping factors presented in the previous section were discussed in terms of extremes (positive and negative) and as separate entities. Extremes in handicapping precepts (for example, negative and positive post bias), rather than average situations, were presented in this chapter because the public tends to err most frequently when horses show obvious bad form or obvious good form. The betting public seems to do an excellent job of assessing probabilities for "average" (common) situations, but makes significant errors when form looks very good or very bad.

The separation of handicapping factors was done as a matter of convenience and simplicity; however, a proper study of the competitive relationships existing among horses in a race cannot be made using separate, compartmentalized handicapping factors. Rather, the study must be based on the interaction of factors having importance in the specific situation as dictated by the conditions of the race. Isolated factors are of minimal importance in handicapping, and their study alone cannot possibly promote a confident feeling of the relative worth of race contenders.

The amount of weight to give the factors and their interactions depends on the race situation—distance, racing surface, track condition, number of horses, track and post bias, age and sex restrictions, time of year, size and shape of track, and so on. Unfortunately there are no clear-cut rules or formulae available to magically produce, in a wide variety of racing situations, a reasonably accurate set of comparative winning probabilities. No more than can an artist paint a masterpiece using a paint-by-numbers kit, can a horseplayer assess the comparative probabilities of competing horses by using a set of handicapping rules. The horseplayer, as does the artist, has a vast number of variables and shadings to contend with. Both must rely on a solid grounding in fundamentals, as well as experience and hard work to produce satisfactory results. The handicapping fundamentals can be acquired from informative books on the subject, or from experienced and successful players; the experience factor cannot be taught, only learned; however, one factor that can partially substitute for experience is time spent studying the Form. The more time put into that study each day, the less importance the experience factor takes on, at least to some degree.

How much study of the Form is necessary to prepare for each day at the track? It depends on the competitiveness of races, the number of horses in the races, and the amount of information available for study. The longest work sessions are connected with large fields and competitive races. The time required to do a competent job for a full card of such races would be about three hours, or about 20 to 25 minutes per race, with some races needing more time, others less. At the other extreme, some days require only an hour or so of work as a result of an abundance of small, uncompetitive fields. Races in which one horse stands out are often easily assessed in five or ten minutes of study.

Now, the work done at home on the Form may not lead to feelings of confidence as to the probable winner in more than a few races on the card. This is not necessarily something a handicapper should be striving for. Rather, the goal should be to become thoroughly knowledgeable about the relevant positive and negative factors of a horse's form as they pertain to the conditions of today's race. A sense of relative value should emerge from this work done at home on the Form. While this feel or sense may not be easily quantifiable before going to the track, it will usually become much more tangible once betting commences on the race and the odds are displayed.

The odds are, in a way, like price tags attached to the horses, and are set according to the value the public perceives the horses to be worth. The prepared handicapper will know right away if the odds line represents relative values or if it is significantly out of line. Most often (about 75 percent of the time) the feeling will be that the last minute public line is reasonable, given the available information. These races, in general, should not be bet, because overlays and underlays, if they exist, are bound to be small and unprofitable when considered over a great many races. The other 25 percent of races that are poorly bet represent the potential betting opportunities.

Finding the Bets

Finding the Bets

There is an old Russian proverb that states that things are known only by comparison. This succinctly expresses the principle behind finding profitable bets at the race track. More than just a comparison of ability and form levels among horses in a race, it is the between-horse comparisons of value and odds that really contribute to successful horseplaying.

As described in detail in chapter two, the public is generally adept at establishing odds that reflect accurately the interrelationship existing among horses in a race. It is important to appreciate, however, that certain handicapping situations do not receive the proper valuations by the public. This occurs because of confusion and because of laziness.

The public tends to be confused by similar appearing form among horses and thereby underweights significant form differences, and they also accept readily and overweight certain popular and easily discerned facts. I call this latter tendency the bandwagon principle. It results in some horses being far overbet because they have apparent form factors that are easily noticed and that appear, at first glance, to greatly outweigh the duller or more boring-looking form of the other competitors. At the same time, the public will underestimate certain positive handicapping factors if they are somewhat hidden.

Several of these overestimated and underestimated factors are described briefly below. Many of these factors have appeared earlier in the section on handicapping, but they are presented here again in order to link them to the principles of the underlay and overlay.

Form Factors Often Overbet

A good horseplayer is concerned as much with recognizing form characteristics that are overbet as in digging out factors related to a horse that are little recognized and therefore underbet. Quite often a good horse will be underbet only because the public overemphasizes an obvious positive fact of another horse's form. A comprehensive analysis of all horses' forms can reveal which factors are likely to be overrated and therefore overbet.

There are several recognisable form patterns that are often overbet by the public. Some of these are described below.

Form Factors Overbet—Hot Jockey

A large number of racegoers bet jockeys, a fact noted earlier. A racing form is not required to determine the top jockeys, because the information is published in the racing program and local newspapers; therefore, the jockey angle has wide appeal and, in many cases, results in overbetting of the horse being piloted by the leading rider.

Granted, the top jockeys win a lot of races (even as high as 25 percent or more of their mounts), but turning a profit by betting their every mount is virtually impossible. Much better results can be obtained by betting against the hot jockey when the public confuses the horse and jockey.

To make this contrariness work, be reasonably certain that your horse is at least as good now as the hot jock's horse (preferably better) and that the public has bet the two clearly out of proportion. For instance, the hot favorite might be bet at 3:2 and your selection, the second choice, at 3:1. The difference can reasonably be attributed to jockey favoritism. Bets against the hot jockey in these situations can be very profitable in the long run.

A special situation in this regard occurs when top riders from major circuits fly in to pilot mounts in added money events at the lesser tracks. My experience is that the public goes to even greater extremes when this happens and will bet a favored horse much more than warranted. In reality, the public should lay off these horses somewhat in view of the big time jock's relative inexperience with the layout of the track.

EIGHTH RACE	6 FURLONGS. (1.08) ALLOWANCE. Purse $29,000. 3–year–olds and upward. Fillies and

Belmont
JUNE 1

mares which have won three races other than Maiden, Claiming or Starter. Weights, 3–year–olds 114 lbs. Older 122 lbs. Non–winners of two races other than Maiden or Claiming since May 1 allowed 3 lbs. Of such a race since then 5 lbs.

Value of race $29,000; value to winner $17,400; second $6,380; third $3,480; fourth $1,740. Mutuel pool $56,776, OTB pool $104,890. Exacta Pool $120,721. OTB Exacta Pool $158,589.

Last Raced	Horse	Eqt.A.Wt PP St	¼	½	Str	Fin	Jockey	Odds $1
7Feb87 8Aqu8	Bold Mate	3 111 7 5	4½	4 1½	1hd	13	Santos J A	3.70
20May87 6Bel4	Rajiste	b 4 117 6 4	7	7	5hd	2 1½	Davis R G	10.90
14Apr87 9OP3	Shivering Gal	3 114 4 1	12½	11½	23	31½	Cordero A Jr	1.00
23May87 7Bel5	Fine Timing	3 113 3 3	32	2hd	3hd	4no	Lovato F Jr	7.60
16May87 7Bel1	Joyer's Zeus	b 3 102 2 7	63	62	64	5½	DeJesus I10	5.50
23Aug86 2Sar1	Mighty Wonder	4 117 5 2	2hd	3½	4½	63	Bailey J D	28.80
2Mar87 9Hia2	Dream Launch	3 109 1 6	5 1½	5hd	7	7	Samyn J L	7.10

OFF AT 4:40. Start good, Won driving. Time, :22⅖, :45⅗, 1:11⅗ Track fast.

$2 Mutuel Prices:	8–(H)–BOLD MATE	9.40	6.20	3.20
	7–(G)–RAJISTE		7.60	4.80
	4–(D)–SHIVERING GAL			2.20

$2 EXACTA 8–7 PAID $107.80.

Form Factors Overbet—Hot Form Horse

The hot form horse stands out as the obvious choice usually as a result of a recent close-up finish and the apparent lack of form of the competition, or because of seemingly good races at higher class. They are usually overbet. While they can and do win races, their share is low in relation to their odds. When I spot what I think will be an overbet form horse, I redouble my efforts in handicapping the rest of the field in order to find a suitable counter bet. Maiden races and races for nonwinners of two are the most common spots to find overbet hot form horses.

Form Factors Overbet—Top Stable

Prolific winning stables and high-class stables tend to acquire large, well-bankrolled followings, capable of dropping the odds of nearly all horses they choose to run. These stables often win a high percentage of races they enter, but again, the public is inclined to bet their horses too heavily. The handicapper should work especially hard in assessing the form of these runners and should not be influenced by stable considerations. It is necessary in this regard to ignore what is read about expectations for young, well-bred horses and the prices paid at auction for them. The only influence these factors should have relate to the potential for causing heavy over-betting.

Form Factors Overbet—Top Trainer

The best trainers quickly become well known to racing fans, much as do top jockeys and successful owners. But again, their runners tend to be overbet on many occasions, providing the astute horseplayer with opportunities to take advantage of unbalanced betting lines.

There is another class of trainer that often provides underlay opportunities. It comprises those trainers who achieve relatively modest to poor success while running fairly large stables, and whose horses receive heavy betting support from stable connections. In other words, it can be profitable to bet against betting stables with mediocre winning percentages.

Form Factors Overbet—Consistently Close but Failing Horse

Horses that make a consistently close but failing effort are often worth betting against, because the horse tends to become "programmed" to lose. The handicapper should be reasonably confident the horse is not showing improved determination, which may indicate a possible win soon (as discussed earlier). This factor is often found in combination with the "hot form" angle.

Right Jab				Ro. c. 3(Mar), by Rajab—Soon I Hope, by Peace Corps							Lifetime
Own.—Joques Farm				$35,000	Br.—Hobeau Farm Inc (Fla) Tr.—Moschera Gasper S					117	8 1 2 $20,160
31Oct91- 9Aqu fst 6f	:22⁴	:46⁴	1:12	Clm c-25000	9 1 11½ 1hd 21 31¼	Cruguet J	117	7.70	80-19 Talc's Bid115ⁿᵒ F
21Oct91- 5Bel fst 6f	:22	:45⁴	1:12	Clm 25000	3 3 2¼ 2hd 1hd 21¼	Cruguet J	117	7.10	78-17 Eagle Ave.1171¼ F
13Oct91- 3Bel fst 6f	:22³	:46	1:11	Clm 22500	3 3 12½ 2½ 1½ 2¾	Cruguet J	115	4.20	84-15 Curbex117¾ Right
31Aug91- 7Pha fst 6f	:22	:45³	1:12	3↑Alw 16335	8 3 3½ 2hd 1hd 73½	Ayarza I	112	7.10	81-17 PrThCrs117ⁿᵏAnt
18Jly91- 2Bel fst 6f	:22²	:46	1:11⁴	3↑Md 35000	10 1 1³ 1³ 12½ 1¾	Mojica R Jr⁵	111	*.80	81-20 Right Jab111¾ Ea
8Jly91- 4Bel fst 6f	:22¹	:45	1:10³	Md Sp Wt	7 2 2½ 2½ 2² 34½	McMahon H I¹⁰	112	17.90	83-13 Soigne122ⁿᵏ Bom
7Jun91- 3Bel fst 6f	:22¹	:45⁴	1:11²	3↑Md 50000	3 2 2½ 1hd 1½ 53¾	Miranda J	114	4.80	79-12 Mr. Tux1122 Silve
11May91- 4Bel fst 6f	:21⁴	:44²	1:10	Md Sp Wt	7 7 44½ 47 69¾ 817½	Toro M	122	5.50	73-13 Gaza122¾ San Ma

Speed Index: Last Race: -1.0   3-Race Avg.: -2.3   8-Race Avg.: -4.3

LATEST WORKOUTS   Oct 29 Bel tr.t 4f fst :51 B   Oct 19 Bel tr.t 4f fst :49² B   Oct 11 Bel tr.t 6f fst 1:15⁴ B

Form Factors Overbet—Sharp Last Race, but Layoff Since

A sharp race by a horse in its last outing always attracts a lot of attention. If that race took place three or more weeks ago, with few or dull workouts in the interim, the sharpness sign loses its value (exceptions: top flight horses, particularly when spotted in route races, and those horses that run well after layoffs); however, the public often overbets these horses, putting too much emphasis on the ostensible good form, and not enough on the layoff.

Durham's Dream * JUNE 26
B. f. 3, by Lord Durham—Kate's Answer, by Northern Answer
DOS RAMOS R A 113
Br.—Bruno Bros Farms Ltd (Ont-C) 1987 5 1 1 2 $15,615
Own.—Cinnamont Stable & Partner
Tr.—Cardella J $37,500 1986 10 2 2 2 $23,424
Lifetime 15 3 3 4 $38,839
30May87-10WO 7f :22 3 :45 1 1:24 1 ft 8¾ 111 1hd 1hd 1½ 1½ DosRmosRA2 Ⓕ 37500 88-16 Durhm'sDrm,Mmi'sLov,ClstilGlow 10
21May87-6WO 6f :22 3 :46 1:13 ft *6-5 114 4 2 3 2 2 2 3½ Seymour D J 3 Ⓕ 32000 77-25 ClstlGlow,FlrttousFlck,Drhm'sDrm 6
8May87-3WO 7f :23 2 :46 1 1:26 1 ft 7½ 114 1hd 1½ 2hd 2 2 Attard L 4 Ⓕ 32000 76-26 SuprRucks,Drhm'sDrm,SmsFrstGrl 6
22Apr87-8Grd 6½f :23 1 :47 1 1:21 1 ft 8 116 2 1½ 4 7 5 7 3 7½ Stahlbaum G 5 Ⓕ 32000 72-27 HolyProspct,SnnyDrhm,Drhm'sDrm 8
8Apr87-2Grd 4½f :22 3 :46 3 :53 ft 2½e 114 3 4 5 6 8½ 5 7½ Attard L 6 Ⓕ 32000 83-12 Ragos,NkedAlibi,WhosZoominWho 7
6Dec86-7Grd 6½f :24 :47 4 1:22 1 sl 8-5 115 2 1 1 2 1 3½ 1 2 Attard L 3 Ⓕ c20000 75-22 Durhm'sDrem,BigSneeze,PigonHwk 8
27Nov86-8Grd 6½f :24 :48 1 1:22 2 sl *4-5e 115 2 1 3 1 3 5½ 3 9 Attard L 4 Ⓕ 25000 65-35 GlinClico,RisdProprly,Durhm'sDrm 7
14Nov86-3Grd 7f :24 1 :48 4 1:30 ft 8¼ 114 2 1½ 2 3 2 1 2 3½ Attard L 7 Ⓕ 32000 62-35 IrshPrds,Drhm'sDrm,YongNorthmn 8
6Nov86-9Grd 7f :23 3 :48 1:28 1 ft 6¾ 115 1 1 2hd 3 5 6 7 Attard L 5 Ⓕ 40000 67-29 StrayAway,Aspenette,IrishParadise 7
28Oct86-7Grd 6½f :23 3 :47 3 1:21 3 ft 30 114 3 2 5 5½ 6 9¾ 6 14 SymourDJ 4 ⒻAw24000 64-26 ColourMeIn,DeltaSlew,ProudBeuty 7
Jun 24 WO ⓣ 2f sf :23 3 b Jun 10 WO tr.t 3f ft :37 3 b ●May 29 WO tr.t 2f ft :24 b May 7 WO tr.t 2f ft :26 4 b

Form Factors Overbet—Stale Horse

Stale horses show unmistakable signs that they have had enough racing for a while. Fading through the stretch, failure to keep a slow-paced lead, and the absence of moves when reasonably expected, are signs that, when considered with the horse's frequency of races and form cycle, indicate staleness. The public, thinking that the tired horse showing these signs will be able to suddenly revert to form, backs them out of proportion to their chances. The best underlays of this type are produced on horses that are dropping in class.

Mary T. French
Dk. b. or br. f. 4, by Pretense—Shirley's Sun, by Hill Run
TOHILL K S 122
Br.—Sanders R D (Cal) 1987 6 M 4 1 $10,550
Own.—Sanders R D
Tr.—Mahorney William 1986 2 M 0 0 $375
Lifetime 8 0 4 1 $10,925
5Jun87-6GG 1 :45 3 1:10 2 1:36 3 ft 4¼ 121 2½ 2hd 2½ 2 2 Tohill K S 8 ⒻM28000 83-18 Kng'sPot,MryT.Frnch,BlconyRmnc 8
28May87-7GG 6f :21 3 :44 1 1:10 ft 2¼ 116 3 1 3 3½ 3 7 3 7 Baze R A 5 M28000 82-11 TllWhWht,ChrmnThtch,MrTFrnch 11
13May87-6GG 1 :46 2 1:11 1:37 2 ft *9-5 120 3½ 2½ 1½ 2 3 Tohill K S 8 ⒻMdn 78-15 Con's Sister, MaryT.French,SilkFan 8
29Apr87-5GG 6f :21 4 :44 3 1:10 1 ft 15 113 2 1 2hd 1hd 2 2½ Tohill K S 6 ⓈM28000 85-18 WinterTan,MaryT.French,Nt'sRbbit 8
7Apr87-1GG 6f :22 1 :45 1 1:11 2 ft 16 120 2 1 4 3 2 1½ 2hd Tohill K S 4 ⒻM20000 82-14 FancyHitter,MryT.French,LuckyTril 9
13Mar87-1GG 6f :22 :45 3 1:11 3 gd 27 120 2hd 4 3 6 10 8 13 Tohill K S 2 ⒻMdn 68-22 MythclMd,Ktty'sEvrywhr,LftHrMrk 8
3May86-2GG 6f :22 2 :46 3 1:12 4 ft 3½ 117 5 5 8 13 9 14 9 17½ Chapman T M 8 ⒻMdn 57-21 Hertlifter,BrmbleDwn,Wndy'sSmil 10
3May86—Ducked in start
19Apr86-3GG 6f :22 :44 4 1:10 3 ft *2¼ 117 1½ 2hd 5 4½ 5 8 Castaneda M 1 ⒻMdn 78-12 Ancient Ice, Nomowho,Heartlifter 10
19Apr86—Broke slowly
Jun 24 GG ⓣ 5f fm 1:01 4 h (d) Jun 13 GG 6f ft 1:13 3 h May 21 GG 5f ft 1:02 3 h May 6 GG 5f ft 1:02 h

Form Factors Overbet—Punishing Races

One of the most difficult facets of handicapping involves the assessment of the impact of tough races on a horse's form. A single hard-driving race usually is a positive sign, often presaging another sharp race. Two hard races in a row may be positive, provided that the horse improved between those two races and/or the horse is a natural hard runner as evidenced by the consistency record. If these conditions do not hold, the horse is likely to regress to a less productive level of output next race.

Fillies and mares are especially prone to a drop in production after a couple of hard recent races. On the other hand, very consistent horses are always dangerous, no matter how many sharp races they have run.

One Judge — Own.—Marsh J D
Dk. b. or br. f. 4, by One For All—She's Dreamy, by Cyane
$12,500 Br.—Marsh J D (Va) Tr.—Tammaro John III
117 — Lifetime 8 1 3 1 $12,650

13May87- 2Pim	fst	1 1/16	:48⅕	1:13⅘	1:47⅗	ⒻClm 11500	9	6	$4^{3\frac{1}{4}}$	1^{hd}	1^{hd}	2^{nk}	Sarvis D A^{5}	112	6.20	66-22	Bashful Star 109^{nk} OneJudg
23Apr87- 6Pim	fst	1 1/16	:48⅕	1:13	1:44⅘	ⒻClm 11500	1	2	2^{1}	2^{3}	2^{5}	$2^{5\frac{1}{2}}$	Sarvis D A^{5}	114	19.50	74-21	Taking Chances $107^{5\frac{1}{2}}$ One J
8Apr87- 2Pim	gd	1 1/16	:49⅖	1:15⅖	1:48⅘	3↑ⒻMd 11500	2	2	$2^{\frac{1}{2}}$	1^{hd}	1^{hd}	$1^{\frac{1}{2}}$	Sarvis D A^{5}	119	2.70	60-28	One Judge $119^{\frac{1}{2}}$ Inflation Ki
30Mar87- 3Pim	sly	6f	:23⅗	:47⅖	1:13	3↑ⒻMd 11500	11	7	8^{10}	$7^{6\frac{1}{2}}$	$5^{6\frac{1}{2}}$	3^{7}	Sarvis D A^{5}	117	*2.70	74-21	Gay Garden 117^{4} Silver Char
19Mar87- 2Lrl	fst	1	:47⅘	1:13⅗	1:41	3↑ⒻMd 16500	4	5	$6^{5\frac{1}{2}}$	$6^{5\frac{1}{2}}$	$6^{3\frac{1}{4}}$	$4^{3\frac{3}{4}}$	Sarvis D A^{5}	b 117	6.30	63-26	ShoshoneGuide124^{1}RinbowL
24Feb87- 1Lrl	gd	6f	:23⅗	:48⅗	1:15⅖	ⒻMd 11500	2	7	$5^{3\frac{1}{2}}$	$6^{4\frac{3}{4}}$	$3^{1\frac{1}{2}}$	2no	Sarvis D A^{5}	117	2.70	66-26	Broadway Smile 117no One J
12Feb87- 2Lrl	fst	6f	:23	:47⅘	1:13⅖	Md 14500	10	7	5^{6}	5^{5}	$4^{6\frac{1}{2}}$	$5^{4\frac{3}{4}}$	Sarvis D A^{5}	112	9.10	71-26	Raise AGroom122^{1}PicnicSup
20Jun86- 9Mth	fst	6f	:23	:47⅕	1:14⅕	3↑ⒻMd 25000	7	9	$11^{9\frac{1}{2}}$	8^{11}	$7^{8\frac{3}{4}}$	$6^{3\frac{1}{2}}$	Rocco J	115	12.30	65-24	Five Star Song $115^{\frac{1}{2}}$Dancing

LATEST WORKOUTS May 27 Bow 1 fst 1:46⅘ b May 9 Bow 5f fst 1:03⅘ b

Form Factors Overbet—Slow Starters

Slow starters with a stretch kick attract much support from racing fans. Bettors love to see their choice fly through the stretch, even for a losing cause. The rationale is that at least the horse gave them a run during the exciting part of the race. These horses are often quite heavily underlaid and should be bet against if possible; however, avoid making specific counter-bets against slow starters that usually achieve a contending, close-up position by the stretch call. These kind of slow starters win frequently.

Isn't She Nice — Own.—Augustin Stable
B. f. 4, by Mr Redoy—Dianette, by Thorn
$35,000 Br.—Equine Investments (Ky) Tr.—Sheppard Jonathan E
117 — Lifetime 19 1 6 4 $46,440

5Jun87- 8Del	gd	1 1/16	(T):47⅗	1:12⅗	1:45⅖	3↑ⒻAlw 7500	3	7	7^{9}	5^{4}	3^{7}	$2^{5\frac{1}{2}}$	Fitzgerald J F	116	*.60e	71-23	FlagPoleGl$112^{5\frac{1}{2}}$Isn'tSheNice
21Jan87- 6Pha	my	1	:48⅕	1:14⅕	1:41⅕	ⒻAlw 11500	7	7	7^{13}	7^{10}	4^{4}	4^{2}	Madrid A Jr	115	2.80e	66-31	Happy April 116^{hd} Sissy Sha
2Dec86- 6Med	sly	1 70	:47	1:11⅘	1:44⅕	3↑ⒻAlw 15000	2	6	6^{28}	6^{22}	6^{15}	$4^{7\frac{1}{2}}$	Antley C W	113	*1.60	68-23	Bbyneedsnewshoes112^{nk}With
24Nov86- 9Med	my	1 1/16	:48	1:13⅖	1:46⅘	3↑ⒻAlw 16000	2	6	$5^{5\frac{3}{4}}$	$5^{4\frac{1}{2}}$	3^{5}	$3^{3\frac{3}{4}}$	Santos J A	119	*.90	65-27	Frost Cove $112^{\frac{3}{4}}$ Fairest I ra
13Nov86- 8Med	fst	1	:49⅖	1:15⅕	1:40⅖	3↑ⒻAlw 15000	5	6	7^{11}	$5^{3\frac{1}{2}}$	3^{2}	$2^{\frac{3}{4}}$	Antley C W	115	2.00	72-25	Koluctoofully $113^{\frac{3}{4}}$ Isn't She
6Nov86- 4Med	my	1 1/16	:47⅗	1:12⅗	1:46⅕	3↑ⒻAlw 18000	9	9	9^{16}	7^{12}	$4^{7\frac{1}{2}}$	$4^{5\frac{1}{2}}$	Rocco J	118	2.80	66-20	Marginal Money 113^{nk}Eight
28Oct86- 9Med	fst	1 1/16	:48	1:12⅗	1:45	3↑ⒻAlw 15000	2	8	$8^{4\frac{3}{4}}$	7^{5}	3^{1}	$2^{2\frac{1}{4}}$	Antley C W	117	6.80	76-19	Koluctoo'sRobin$113^{2\frac{1}{4}}$Isn'tS
4Oct86- 4Bel	gd	1⅜	:50⅗	1:41	2:18⅖	3↑ⒻAlw 25000	4	6	7^{7}	$7^{4\frac{1}{2}}$	$5^{5\frac{3}{4}}$	$5^{8\frac{1}{2}}$	Santos J A	119	6.40	79-14	Rosa May 117^{3} Once And Fo
25Sep86- 4Bel	fm	1¼	[T]:50⅖	1:39⅗	2:04⅗	3↑ⒻMd Sp Wt	7	9	$10^{8\frac{3}{4}}$	$6^{3\frac{3}{4}}$	3^{1}	1^{nk}	Santos J A	118	*2.90	71-20	Isn't She Nice 118^{nk} Shiitak
18Sep86- 4Med	fm	1 1/16	[T]:46⅕	1:11	1:43⅘	3↑ⒻMd Sp Wt	11	11	10^{12}	8^{11}	$4^{\frac{3}{4}}$	$2^{2\frac{1}{4}}$	Dufton E	116	4.10	82-09	AbsenceofMalice$116^{2\frac{1}{4}}$Isn'tS

LATEST WORKOUTS Jun 17 Del 5f fst 1:03 b

```
*Athlone                          B. g. 5, by Corvare—Ela Marita, by Red God
 DELAHOUSSAYE E           117     Br.—Ardenode Stud Ltd (Ire)          1987 11 0 5 3      $41,5
Own.—Burford & Folsom             Tr.—Hartstone George D               1986  4 0 0 0
                                 Lifetime  22 1 8 5  $45,774           Turf 12 1 3 2      $4,1
17Jun87-7Hol  6½f:22  :451 1:161ft   4¼ 119  810 87¼ 85½ 41½  DelhoussyeE 1Aw22000 97-15 TeddyBerHug,ANewEr,MYouAndQ.
31May87-7Hol  1  :444 1:094 1:362ft *9-5 116 76¾ 76 35½ 24    DelhoussyeE 1Aw24000 77-18 Sum Action, Athlone, Mondanite
    31May87—Wide into stretch
24Apr87-7Hol  6f :221 :452 1:091ft  *8-5 116 66¾ 55 44 24½    DelhoussyeE 5Aw22000 92-12 Superoyale, Athlone,NorthernValo
 8Apr87-7SA   6f :22  :451 1:094ft   2¼e 117 812 811 56 21½   DelhoussyeE 2Aw29000 87-22 Superb Moment,Athlone,Doonspor
    8Apr87—Broke slowly
27Mar87-7SA   1⅛:464 1:113 1:50 ft   3 117   55½ 31½ 32½ 35¼  DelhoussyeE 5Aw31000 74-23 ArcticDream,It'sNotMyJob,Athlon
    27Mar87—Bumped start
17Mar87-7SA   1 1/16:46 1:102 1:423ft 4¼ 117 912 77¼ 36½ 35½  DelhoussyeE 9Aw31000 82-16 PrinceO'Fire,It'sNotMyJob,Athlon
    17Mar87—Wide into stretch
 4Mar87-5SA   1 1/16:453 1:101 1:432ft 6¼ 117 1011 97¼ 42½ 32¼ DelhoussyeE 9Aw30000 82-16 RidgeReview,Rafei'sDncer,Athlone
18Feb87-5SA   1  :454 1:10 1:363ft   7 118   43½ 46 56 55     Solis A 4      Aw29000 80-19 Alibi Ike, Watch'n Win, Gum Fleet
 1Feb87-3SA   6f :212 :444 1:11 ft   14 118  109¾ 96¾ 64 2no  DelhoussyeE 3Aw26000 83-16 Dad's Quest, Athlone,WassiDancer
    1Feb87—Broke slowly; wide into stretch
24Jan87-5SA   a6½f ①:213 :44 1:15 fm 7 116   109½ 1112 1211 1213 DelhoussyeE 8Aw26000 71-17 River Mist, Nurely, Top Wing
    24Jan87—Wide into stretch
  Jun 13 Hol 4f ft :472 h       ●Jun 8 Hol 4f ft :474 h        May 25 Hol 5f ft 1:004 h
```

Form Factors Overbet—Back Class, Poor Form

Previously classy but presently failing horses often continue to get substantial betting support while dropping down the class ladder. The backers expect these horses to suddenly spring back to their old form; however, for that to happen the horse must begin to show fresh signs of vigour or be dropped sharply enough to dominate an easy field. Gradual class drops from one failed effort to another often attract enough betting support to produce underlays.

```
Kazbek                           B. g. 5, by Caucasus—Zambia, by Native Charger
 KING R JR                118    Br.—Taylor E P (Ont-C)                 1987  5 0 0 1      $4,355
Own.—Norcliffe Stable            Tr.—MacLean David        $40,000       1986 12 2 1 2     $75,768
                                Lifetime  27 4 1 4  $106,530            Turf 19 3 1 2     $87,271
24Jun87-8WO  1⅛①:463 1:103 1:492fm *9-5 118 54¾ 65½ 66 43½   King R Jr 5          50000 79-18 CapChat,BigBizPres,OldGunPowder 8
14Jun87-8WO  1⅛①:45 1:084 1:453fm 43 115    21½ 31 710 712¾  KingRJr 5 King Ed Cp 88 — Blue Finn, Carotene, Introspective 7
    14Jun87—Grade III-C; Run in divisions
31May87-8WO  1 1/16 Ⓣ:483 1:134 1:451gd 5½e 121 64½ 54½ 711 68½ KnRJr6 ⓈCon'ht Cup 71-16 BoulderRun,Corseque,RoylTresurr 13
    31May87—Grade III-C
23May87-8WO  1  Ⓣ:512 1:172 1:42 fm 4¼ 119  22 21 21½ 3¾     King R Jr6  ⓈAw28600 66-33 Boulder Run, Carotene, Kazbek 6
11Apr87-11GP 1  ①:464 1:111 1:35 fm 33 113  1010 914 715 511½ Penna D1            45000 83-07 Texola Joe, Onslow, NoholmesBoy 12
 5Oct86-9WO  1½:502 2:052 2:322sl  34 113    2½ 914 1026 1024¼ King RJr1 Niagara H 60-21 GoldenChoice,RoylTrsurr,DoublDn 10
    5Oct86—Grade III-C
27Sep86-8WO  1¼:493 1:392 2:061gd   7 124    513 59 514 58¾   King R Jr1      Aw26400 66-20 IBnZdoon,MstrLornzo,OldGnPowdr 6
28Aug86-8WO  1⅛:493 1:141 1:52 ft   3 124    54½ 64 56 36¾    King R Jr 6     Aw26400 73-20 I Bin Zaidoon, Vatza's Key, Kazbek 6
10Aug86-9WO  1¼①:49 1:412 2:07 gd   4 118    21 2½ 54½ 67½    King R Jr 4        HcpO 64-14 ‡Vtz'sKy,SongofDom,CoolNrthrnr 10
20Jly86-9WO  1¼①:503 1:42 2:083sf  7¼ 126   21½ 2hd 1½ 1nk   KnRJr 3 ⓈCan Maturty 64-36 Kazbek, Red's Run, S. S.Enterprise 8
    20Jly86—Grade II-C; Lost whip;handily
  Jun 27 WO 3f ft :362 h    Jun 11 WO 5f ft 1:024 h    May 23 WO 2f ft :243 b    May 17 WO Tr.① 6f fm 1:112 h
```

Form Factors Overbet—Fractious or Nervous Horse

Uptight horses, as evidenced by heavy sweating or severely quarrelsome behaviour, can be confidently bet against. When these horses are strong favorites, they provide good counterbetting opportunities.

Form Factors Overbet—Running Against a Bias

Any horse situated in a tough post position with a running style not conducive to overcoming the bias has potential to be overbet. The same goes for any well-bet horse that is running on a surface that it has never shown evidence of handling adequately.

The situations described in this list are some of the most obvious ones and provide frequent opportunities for underlays at all racetracks. There are more single factors that get overbet by the public, of course, as well as an infinite variety of combinations of factors that can also produce a strong sense that a horse is heavily overbet. The discovery of these factors requires that nothing in a horse's form be taken for granted.

Form Factors Sometimes Underbet

When is a horse underbet? It is much more difficult to tell if and by how much a horse is underbet on the basis of its past performance record and current odds than it is to determine to what degree a horse is overbet. To qualify as an underlay that can be bet against, a horse must only show a serious negative in its form pattern and be heavily bet. Finding an overlayed horse, one which is truly underbet only because of specific hidden information, usually requires (a) the discovery of an obscure but important positive fact about the horse, (b) a very close comparison with the competition, and (c) a finely tuned judgement as to relative values among contenders. The task requires much greater study, insight, and judgement than is needed to determine if a single horse is overbet.

There are no hard and fast rules to guarantee the discovery of handicapping nuggets that get ignored or undervalued by the crowd. The job demands a probing mind, one that forever questions the apparently obvious, and one that perseveres in spite of long successions of blind alleys. Results can be very rewarding and are paid out in direct proportion to the amount of time and effort put into the work.

Several methods of uncovering important but poorly valued information have been described previously. Keeping a good variant is one, an important tool that can give proper meaning to apparent times. Others include the analysis of post position, race fractions and running style, the study of results charts, knowledge of trainer tendencies, and the discovery of excuses for poor performance. Besides these, there are other handicapping situations that tend to confuse the public to the extent that real information is undervalued, and which require additional attention from the handicapper. Some are described below.

Form Factors Underbet—Recent Hard Races, Bullish Horse

A horse that has been subjected to stiff drives for a lengthy part of its last few races tends to be overlooked in the betting when competing against an apparently difficult field, particularly if moving up in class. A surprisingly high number of these horses produce yet another good effort.

It is important that the horse show some indication of improvement in its last race, whether in terms of pace, final time, class level, or overcoming a bias. Moderately high odds (nonfavorite) in the last race is a good sign, too, because it means that the horse is showing surprise improvement, more of which may well be in store today.

Lightly raced three-year-old horses frequently show this pattern once they come to hand. One additional point to note about these horses: they almost invariably have either returned from a layoff in the recent past or have shown dramatic improvement within their last half dozen races or so.

Irish Music — B. f. 3(Apr), by Stop the Music—Tom's Lass, by Tom Rolfe
Own.—Evans Edward P — $35,000 — Br.—Weber Francis X (Ky) — Tr.—Lukas D Wayne — 118
Lifetime 18 5 2 2 $74,440 — 1991 14 5 — 1990 4 M

10Nov91- 5Aqu	fst	1	:47^1	1:12	1:38^2	(F)Clm 35000	5	1	1^1	1^{hd}	1^{hd}	1no	Santos J A	b	116	*1.00	70-25	IrishMusic116^{no}AboveTheSalt112$^{6\frac{3}{4}}$Tunec
20Oct91- 9Bel	fst	6f	:22	:45^2	1:09^2	(F)Clm 25000	2	2	1$^{1\frac{1}{2}}$	1^1	1^6	1^{13}	Velazquez J R	b	116	*2.40	93-08	IrishMusic116^{13}ChifMistrss116^{no}Southrn
18Sep91- 3Bel	fst	6$\frac{1}{2}$f	:22^3	:45^3	1:17^2	(F)Clm 35000	5	1	1$\frac{1}{2}$	1^{hd}	2$\frac{1}{2}$	4$^{4\frac{1}{2}}$	Smith M E	b	116	*.70	85-15	LvToMomboJmbo112$^{2\frac{3}{4}}$RthrBScl112$^{\frac{3}{4}}$Rbb
29Aug91- 1Bel	fst	6$\frac{1}{2}$f	:22^2	:45^1	1:16^1	(F)Clm 50000	5	3	3$^{2\frac{1}{2}}$	2$\frac{1}{2}$	2$\frac{1}{2}$	3^1	Smith M E	b	116	2.70	95-10	Mrs.O'Rilly116^{nk}MjsticTrck116$^{\frac{3}{4}}$IrshMusc
26Jly91- 9Mth	sly	1	:46^2	1:12	1:39	3↑(F)Alw 20000	6	4	4^4	6^{11}	5^{20}	5$^{36\frac{1}{2}}$	Gryder A T	b	112	*.60	37-27	DremingJenie116^{2}St.Hvn116^{no}KookyAunt
26Jly91-Originally scheduled on turf																		
13Jly91- 5Mth	sly	1$\frac{1}{16}$	:47^1	1:11^4	1:45^1	3↑(F)Alw 19000	4	1	1^5	1^4	1^7	1^{15}	Gryder A T	b	112	*1.50	83-22	IrishMusic112^{15}LostScrt116$^{4\frac{3}{4}}$FshonModl
13Jly91-Originally scheduled on turf																		
22Jun91- 6Mth	fst	1	:46^1	1:11^1	1:38	3↑(F)Alw 18000	9	2	2^{hd}	1$\frac{1}{2}$	1$^{2\frac{1}{2}}$	1$^{1\frac{1}{2}}$	Gryder A T	b	112	*2.10	79-13	Irish Music112$^{1\frac{1}{2}}$ La Splash117^1 Say Vodk
1Jun91- 5Mth	fst	170	:46^3	1:12^2	1:43^3	3↑(F)Alw 17000	6	2	2$\frac{1}{2}$	1^2	2^{hd}	2$^{3\frac{1}{4}}$	Gryder A T	b	112	2.20	75-17	Long Walk113$^{3\frac{1}{4}}$ IrishMusic112$^{2\frac{1}{4}}$Vigorous
10May91- 9Bel	fst	7f	:22^4	:45^1	1:22^2	3↑(F)Md 35000	4	2	1^1	1$^{2\frac{1}{2}}$	1^3	1$^{9\frac{1}{2}}$	Smith M E	b	115	4.40	92-09	Irish Music115$^{9\frac{1}{2}}$ BossyEdna115$^{7\frac{1}{4}}$SweetAt
29Mar91- 4SA	fst	6f	:21^4	:45^1	1:10^4	(F)Md 32000	5	3	2^{hd}	3^2	4^6	7$^{10\frac{1}{4}}$	Stevens G L	Bb	117	6.90	72-14	FrontirNursing117$^{1\frac{1}{4}}$ShttrSilnc117$^{1\frac{3}{4}}$Curous

Form Factors Underbet—Only Speed Horse

The ability of a fast-breaking pace setter is sometimes underestimated by the betting public. It happens in two situations particularly.

One situation occurs when there exists little apparent speed from any of the horses. The public becomes confused about the way the race is likely to be run and tends to bet come-from-behind horses heavily. It can be highly profitable to concentrate the handicapping effort toward finding the likely pace setters. Post and pace analysis, workouts, and jockey are valuable signals in this regard.

Another good overlay opportunity occurs when the top speed horse in a race has been overmatched on speed in its last few races. The public tends to see the recent failures as a sign of poor form. A close examination of dates, pace, speed competition, and class should be made to determine if the failure was excusable. If so, and the horse has clear speed today, it could provide a genuine overlay.

Ameri Allen — Dk. b. or br. f. 3(Apr), by Allen's Prospect—Amerricoinrest, by Amerrico — Lifetime 20 6 1 $100,980

Own.—Alecci John V — $35,000 — Br.—Clagett Hal C B (Md) — Tr.—Patty Karen A — 114

19Nov91- 6Lrl	fst	6f	:22^1	:45^4	1:11^3	ⒻClm 35000	1	1	1^2	1^{hd}	2$^{1\frac{1}{2}}$	4$^{5\frac{1}{4}}$	Prado E S	Lb	114	*1.00	78-17	GrcefulLil114$^{\frac{1}{2}}$Mi
1Nov91- 8Lrl	fst	6$\frac{1}{2}$f	:22^3	:45^4	1:17^3	ⒻClm 25000	8	1	1^1	1^1	1$^{1\frac{1}{2}}$	1^4	Prado E S	Lb	114	4.90	89-19	Ameri Allen114^4
27Oct91- 4Lrl	fst	6f	:22^2	:46	1:11^1	ⒻClm 16000	3	5	1$^{1\frac{1}{2}}$	1^{hd}	1^{hd}	1$^{\frac{3}{4}}$	Prado E S	Lb	119	*2.30	85-16	Ameri Allen119$^{\frac{3}{4}}$
17Oct91- 4Lrl	sly	6$\frac{1}{2}$f	:22^4	:47^1	1:19^4	ⒻClm 16000	3	6	1^1	1$^{1\frac{1}{2}}$	1^2	1$^{2\frac{1}{2}}$	Prado E S	Lb	114	*1.50	78-27	Ameri Allen114^2
29Sep91- 2Pim	fst	6f	:22^4	:46	1:12^1	ⒻClm c-12000	1	1	1^{hd}	1^{hd}	1$^{2\frac{1}{2}}$	1$^{3\frac{1}{2}}$	Hutton G W	b	114	5.40	84-17	Ameri Allen114^3
13Sep91- 4Pim	fst	6f	:22^4	:46^2	1:12^4	ⒻClm 16000	2	1	2^{hd}	2^{hd}	4^3	6^5	Hutton G W	b	114	6.90	76-20	Betterton114$^{1\frac{1}{2}}$D
28Aug91- 6Tim	fst	4f		:23	:46	ⒻClm 15000	5	5		3^2	3$^{3\frac{1}{2}}$	3$^{4\frac{1}{4}}$	Peterson T L^5	b	109	*1.00	90-13	Dixielamb116$^{3\frac{1}{2}}$
16Aug91- 7Lrl	fst	6f	:22^1	:45^4	1:10^3	ⒻClm 25000	8	1	1^{hd}	2^{hd}	4$^{3\frac{1}{2}}$	8$^{7\frac{3}{4}}$	Hutton G W	b	114	10.80	80-19	Missy'sMusic11
4Aug91- 9Lrl	fst	6$\frac{1}{2}$f	:22^3	:46^2	1:18	ⒻClm 25000	5	3	1$^{\frac{1}{2}}$	1$^{\frac{1}{2}}$	1^{hd}	2$^{3\frac{1}{4}}$	Hutton G W	b	114	4.10	84-22	TwoEyesFrYou'
23Jly91- 4Lrl	fst	6$\frac{1}{2}$f	:23	:46^1	1:18	ⒻClm 16000	1	1	1^{hd}	1$^{\frac{1}{2}}$	1$^{2\frac{1}{2}}$	1$^{4\frac{3}{4}}$	Hutton G W	b	116	3.00	87-16	Ameri Allen116^4

Speed Index: Last Race: –5.0 3–Race Avg.: +1.3 10–Race Avg.: +1.7

Form Factors Underbet—Excuse / Easy Race

A horse with an excuse for a poor performance in its last race can frequently be underbet, because the excuse may not be known to many players.

To qualify, the horse should be coming back to race again within ten or twelve days of its last race (unless it is a top class animal) or else the validity of the excuse is suspect. Sometimes there will not exist any apparent excuse for a reduced level of effort by a highly consistent, hard-running animal. Nevertheless, the easy race can help the horse regain form for the next race. This fact is not recognized to the extent it should be by the public and tends, therefore, to be underbet. Again, the horse should be returning within a short period of its last race if the angle is to have validity.

```
Deanne's Lady *                                B. m. 5, by Dancing Champ—Zeesa Lisa, by Northern Monarch
  DAVID D                                      Br.—Detoro N M (Ont-C)                   1987  5  0  1  1      $4,286
Own.—DeToro N                           116    Tr.—DeToro N                  $10,000    1986 22  2  3  2     $24,735
                                             Lifetime  51  5  5  6   $60,528            Turf  3  0  0  0
27Jun87-4WO  1 1/16:48  1:132 1:481m  *3 1/4 114  912121911191112 1/2  Sabourin R B2 (F) 15000 55-22 CelryHrts,Mrs.Murph,IllusionPlntr 13
     27Jun87—Stumbled
 5Jun87-7WO  1 1/16:484 1:142 1:484ft  7 1/2 116  73 1/4 1hd 31 23/4      David D J7   (F) 15000 64-30 MissJean,Deanne'sLdy,PssingMoon 9
27May87-6WO  1 1/16:482 1:142 1:481sy   11 116  57 811 77 1/4 54 1/2     Skinner K3   (F) 20000 63-23 ChttyChocolte,MissJen,LdyofthIsl 10
15May87-6WO  6 1/2f :224 :462 1:183ft    6 116  107 3/4 99 1/4 68 3/4 56  Duffy L6     (F) 16000 74-25 ChttyChocolt,IllusionPlntr,MissJn 10
 9May87-5WO  6f :222 :461 1:14 ft        8 116  98 88 3/4 87 1/4 31 1/2   Duffy L5     (F) c12500 71-20 IllusionPlnter,BenKitty,Denn'sLdy 10
 5Dec86-8Grd 1 :484 1:143 1:422sl       *5 1095 52 42 42 31            O'Brien S G J1 (F) 9500 67-27 StephnieL.,BlzcPrincess,Dnn'sLdy 11
27Nov86-2Grd 7f :241 :49 1:302m       3 1/2 116  31 1/2 52 3/4 85 1/4 75 1/4  Attard L7  (F) 8000 58-35 BalzcPrincess,Unmsked,RreStrtegy 8
19Nov86-6Grd 7f :233 :48 1:284ft     *2 1/4 116  32 64 1/2 67 1/4 55 3/4   Attard L11   (F) 10000 65-32 SmrtlyYours,LittleGrt,TiffnysGold 11
10Nov86-6Grd 1 :49 1:142 1:414ft         4 117  3nk 1hd 34 1/2 33 3/4      Attard L7    (F) 12000 67-26 Miss Jean, Fly OnGo,Deanne'sLady 9
 1Nov86-2Grd 1 :492 1:144 1:414ft        5 115  32 1/2 42 1/2 34 23        Duffy L3     (F) 15000 68-27 LadyStrategy,Deanne'sLdy,MissJen 6
   Jun 20 WO 5f ft 1:021 h        Jun 13 WO 5f ft 1:014 h        Jun 3 WO 3f ft :354 h        May 23 WO 5f ft 1:023 h
```

Form Factors Underbet—Many Excuses

For a variety of reasons (e.g., ignorant trainer, poor weather conditions, venue changes) a horse may run a series of races unsuited to its style or ability, and consequently have a mediocre or poor recent record. When the horse finally gets its preferred conditions, a win at high odds can result. It is important, for this reason, to examine several races in the past performances, and not just the last one or two.

```
Vital Score                                    Ch. m. 5, by Gummo—Snowy Cape, by Snow Sporting
  DELAHOUSSAYE E                               Br.—Dryer D A (Cal)                      1987  7  1  3  1     $30,575
Own.—McAtee R & Melodie                 116    Tr.—Bernstein David           $40,000    1986 11  2  3  1     $37,350
                                             Lifetime  33  6  9  2  $117,275
23May87-3Hol 1 1/16:462 1:113 1:434ft  6 1/4 116  68 1/2 65 32 1/2 22     DelhoussyeE 3 (F) 50000 88-15 KeepHoping,VitlScore,StrightStory 6
     23May87—Broke against bit
 1May87-3Hol 1 :452 1:11 1:371ft       5 1/4 116  65 3/4 67 35 1/2 22 1/2  DelhoussyeE 3 (F) 32000 74-13 Universlly,VitlScore,CuriousPrincss 6
26Mar87-9SA  1 1/16:47 1:122 1:45 ft      4 118  43 1/2 31 1/2 31 1/2 23/4 Olivares F 8 (F) c25000 75-22 Orry'sLady,VitalScore,Anc'entLady 8
     26Mar87—Bumped start, wide 7/8
17Mar87-9SA  1 :461 1:111 1:362ft      6 1/2 118  99 1/2 77 1/2 38 38 1/2  Olivares F 3 (F) 32000 77-16 Kristin, Lotus Delight, Vital Score 10
     17Mar87—Lugged in
13Feb87-7SA  1 1/16:47 1:112 1:442sy     15 116  77 1/2 710 67 1/2 67      Olivares F 4 (F)Aw32000 72-13 Jell, Private Sorrow,PrincessOfAck 7
     13Feb87—Wide into stretch
```

Form Factors Underbet—Marked Improvement

It is sometimes necessary that a horse run a few races at a higher level of performance before the public accepts apparent, sharp improvement in a runner. Meanwhile, overlays may be available to the early believers.

A careful study of race results must be made to determine if an apparently improved performance was due to a poor race pace or class pattern (i.e., a fluke) or whether it represented a genuinely sharp, improved effort. The races indicative of real improvement are those in which the horse was near or on the lead throughout or contended for the lead early in the stretch. As confirmation of the improvements in results, the horse should show improvement in pace and final time.

Vicky's Orient Dk. b. or br. f. 4, by Far Out East—Victorious Answer, by Northern Answer
STAHLBAUM G 117 Br.—Schickedanz Gustav (Ont-C) 1987 5 1 1 0 $19,430
Tr.—Doyle Mike J 1986 13 2 0 3 $29,542
Own.—Schickedanz G Lifetime 23 4 1 3 $59,725 Turf 4 0 0 0 $1,090

21Jun87-7WO	$1\frac{1}{16}$	$:47^4$	$1{:}12^4$	$1{:}44^2$ft	$4\frac{3}{4}$	116	$5^{2\frac{1}{4}}$	$5^{2\frac{3}{4}}$	$1^{\frac{1}{2}}$	1^{hd}	SthlbumG[7]	ⒻAw23300	87-17	Vicky'sOrient,Plylist,Ain'tThtWickd	7
12Jun87-6WO	$1\frac{1}{16}$	$:47^4$	$1{:}12^3$	1:46 ft	17	119	$3^{1\frac{1}{2}}$	5^3	$2^{3\frac{1}{2}}$	$2^{2\frac{1}{2}}$	SthlbumG[4]	ⒻAw20800	76-24	StdyHop,Vcky'sOrnt,DncngOnACld	9
8May87-9GP	6f	$:22^1$	:45	$1{:}10^3$ft	24	119	5^3	5^6	$5^{7\frac{1}{2}}$	5^6	GafflioneS[8]	ⒻAw20000	80-25	NorthernMissy,Chitec,SilveredDncr	8
7Apr87-8GP	a$1\frac{1}{16}$ Ⓣ			$1{:}44^4$fm	13	117	2^4	2^1	4^3	$4^{4\frac{1}{4}}$	Penna D[6]	ⒻAw18000	78-15	ImprdntLov,LkChmpln,FltwodFncy	8
22Mar87-9GP	1 Ⓣ	:47	$1{:}11^3$	$1{:}36^4$fm	31	117	$6^{5\frac{1}{4}}$	5^6	$5^{6\frac{1}{2}}$	5^8	Maple E[2]	ⒻAw19000	78-14	TrChompon,ChrstmsDncr,TForTop	8
13Oct86-8WO	$1\frac{1}{16}$	$:49^1$	$1{:}14^1$	1:47 ft	10	111	$1^{1\frac{1}{2}}$	$3^{\frac{1}{2}}$	5^5	5^5	DsRmsRA[1]	ⒻAw21500	69-25	SwiftandBold,SharpBriar,Greyechel	7
5Oct86-7WO	7f	$:23^1$	$:46^2$	$1{:}25^2$sl	13	116	$3^{\frac{1}{2}}$	2^{hd}	1^{hd}	$3^{\frac{1}{2}}$	DsRmsRA[2]	ⒻAw19500	81-21	SmplySplshng,FoxyAlxs,Vcky'sOrnt	6
18Sep86-8WO	7f	$:23^2$	$:46^3$	1:25 ft	36	117	$6^{3\frac{1}{2}}$	$6^{4\frac{3}{4}}$	7^7	$7^{5\frac{1}{2}}$	LndryRC[2]	Ⓕ[S]Aw24000	78-26	MissTressette,DoubleBundles,Relit	8
6Sep86-9WO	1 [T]	$:48^3$	$1{:}14^1$	1:40 yl	101	112	$8^{3\frac{3}{4}}$	8^5	7^8	$6^{8\frac{1}{4}}$	LdrRC[2]	Ⓕ[S]OntCollen	69-23	MssEnchntd,Armcr,DncngOnACld	10

6Sep86 Grade II-C; Run in Divisions

●Jun 4 WO 6f ft 1:15 b   May 27 WO Ⓣ 5f yl $1{:}01^4$ b   May 21 WO 4f ft $:49^3$ b

Form Factors Underbet—Fresh Horse

The freshened horse angle is a special case of the improvement angle. Usually between the first and second, second and third, or third and fourth races after a layoff, a horse will show marked improvement. This fact is not appreciated sufficiently by average horseplayers and provides overlay opportunities. Signs of an impending victory to watch for include early speed (especially in sprints), getting progressively closer to the lead at the stretch call, change from sprints to a better-suited route race, increased willingness to do battle in the stretch, improving final times, a drop in class.

Little Paces Dk. b. or br. c. 3, by Hempaces—Little Tempest, by Trondheim
PATTON D B 111^5 Br.—E L Allee Ranch (Cal) 1987 4 1 1 0 $5,475
Tr.—Bernstein David $25,000 1986 0 M 0 0
Own.—E L Allee Ranch Lifetime 4 1 1 0 $5,475

28May87-9Hol	$6\frac{1}{2}$f	$:22^2$	$:45^1$	$1{:}17^2$ft	8	111^5	1^1	1^2	2^{hd}	$2^{2\frac{1}{2}}$	Patton D B 5		20000	90-16	Banche, Little Paces, Glory Quest	8
31Mar87-7GG	6f	$:21^3$	$:44^3$	$1{:}09^2$ft	41	122	2^1	$4^{2\frac{1}{2}}$	$5^{9\frac{1}{2}}$	$7^{15\frac{3}{4}}$	SchnldtCP 1	[S]Aw17000	76-20	Agn'sBlgr,OlmpcL.A.,H'sADncngMn	8
3Mar87-7GG	6f	$:21^3$	$:44^1$	$1{:}09^2$ft	33	120	2^{hd}	2^{hd}	2^1	$4^{5\frac{1}{2}}$	CampbellBC 2	Aw17000	86-10	FleetSudan,GreatEmperor,Tm'sWy	9
8Feb87-1AC	6f	$:22^3$	:45	$1{:}09^4$ft	9-5	119	1^1	1^{hd}	1^{hd}	1^{nk}	Lopez A D[7]	AlwM	90-13	Little Paces, Silverstep, Tarraco	7

Jun 20 Hol 5f ft $1{:}00^4$ h   Jun 14 Hol 4f ft $:48^1$ h   May 21 Hol 7f ft 1:29 h   May 14 Hol 6f ft $1{:}14^4$ h

Form Factors Underbet—Also Eligibles

This is not exactly a four-star professional handicapping secret, but once in a while, when a horse whose record is buried in the also-eligibles list in the Form breaks into a field as a result of a scratch, the public will underestimate its chances. This may happen because of some confusion in finding the horse's past performance record or perhaps because "also-eligible" implies to some unsophisticated fans a feeling of "substitute" or "spare." In any case, it can occasionally be profitable, particularly in situations where an outside post is beneficial.

From Factors Underbet—Good Performance in Large Field

Any in-the-money finish by a horse looks good in the Form. But this can be deceiving. If the horse finished third out of four, five, or six horses, the performance is not the same as finishing a good third or fourth in a field of 12 or more horses. The public tends to weigh an in-the-money performance regardless of field size; however, a close-up second, third, or fourth in a large field is usually much more positive than the same finish in a small field, because more horses finished up the track.

```
Autumn Lyric                        Ch. f. 3, by Gain—Mineral Springs, by No Parande
                                    Br.—Massey R J (Ont-C)                    1987 10  1  1  0          $7,327
   SWATUK B                111      Tr.—Smithers Andrew G       $15,000        1986  3  M  0  0            $60
Own.—Memory Lane Stable                                          Lifetime  13  1  1  0    $7,387      Turf  2  0  0  0          $240
21Jun87-5WO   6f :223 :463 1:122ft     5½ 113   3½  3½  2²  2³    Swatuk B⁵    ⑧ 12500 78-17 SunshnSolo,AtmnLyrc,Slton'sPlsr ⑭
4Jun87-6WO    1¹⁄₁₆:484 1:141 1:482ft  5 111   1½  54½ 711 716    Kelly J⁴    ⑧ 24000 51-27 On the Avon, Gizike, Pigeon Hawk  7
16May87-7WO   6f :23  .47 1:13 ft      6½ 113   85½ 66  55½ 45    Kelly J⁵    ⑧ 20000 73-23 SnnyDrhm,LovConncton,TrstorBty  9
30Apr87-10GP  a1 ⑦        1:392fm     15 112   8¹⁴ 8¹³ 7¹² 710½   Kelly J⁵    ⑧ 35000 73-16 CptvtngAppl,Chrmn'Wn,Rck'sDlvry  9
1Apr87-1GP    6f :23  .47 1:131ft      9¼ 116  31½ 12½ 15 110½   Kelly J⁸    ⑧ 10000 73-25 AutumnLyric,UpClose,BingoMarth 11
21Mar87-1GP   6f :222 .46 1:121ft     35 112  63½ 34  57  47½    Kelly J⁶    ⑧ 10500 70-22 FullMoonPul,MissDnZro,KnocNKr 11
18Feb87-6Hia  7f :231 .47 1:26 ft     53 111  62½12⁸²12¹⁹ 92²    Kelly J 11   ⑧ 18000 51-24 Amberlyjean,SmrtGinny,SmilingFy 12
30Jan87-10Hia a1⅛⑦       1:494fm     50 110  10¹² 9¹¹ 915 918½   Kelly J10    ⑧ 28000 63-11 Dawndeh,CptivtingAppel,Amplest  10
13Jan87-3Hia  7f :234 .472 1:262ft    24 111  73½107  88½ 516½   Kelly J10    ⑧ 18000 55-22 Minibreva,Joanie'sDouble,Amplest 12
7Jan87-1Crc   6f :22  .47 1:14 ft     43 118  75½ 48  3⁸ 45½     Kelly J12    ⑦M17000 75-18 OxfordsJet,Cecily'sJde,SimplyRed 12
   May 31 WO tr.t 4f ft :512 b        May 25 WO tr.t 4f ft :512 b        May 13 WO tr.t 4f ft :502 b
```

Form Factors Underbet—Unexpected Early Speed

Human distance runners use speed drills as part of their training regimens to improve their ability to run extra quickly when required during a race. Speed training enhances their ability to cope with a fast pace and to make a sharp kick at the end. Horses can be trained for the same purposes. An early speed effort by a horse that normally runs off the pace can markedly improve its form for a subsequent race. To be effective, the speed should not have been carried for more than three quarters of the race, with a fading finish out of the money to remove the horse from the public eye.

Exclusive Partner B. h. 5, by Exclusive Ribot—Floral Blossom, by Diplomat Way

Exclusive Partner		Br.—Farnsworth Farms (Fla)	1987	3	0	1	0	$25,125
MCCARRON C J	117	Tr.—Mandella Richard	1986	10	2	2	3	$182,524
Own.—Hubbard R D		Lifetime 29 7 3 5 $361,957	Turf	23	6	3	5	$352,957

26Apr87-8Hol	$1\frac{1}{16}$ Ⓣ:47^{1}1:11 1:41^{1}fm	8	116	2½	2^{1½}	4^{1¾}	4^{4½}	McCrrCJ^3	Prmr H	83-13	CleverSong,AlMmoon,LeBelvedere	5
26Apr87—Grade III												
18Apr87-9SA	a6½f Ⓣ:21^3 :43^{4}1:13^{3}fm	10	117	6^4	6^4	5^5	4^{4¼}	McHrDG^6	Sn Smn H	87-16	BolderThnBold,PrincBobbyB.,Lichi	9
18Apr87—Grade III												
21Mar87-8SA	a6½f Ⓣ:21 :44 1:14^{4}gd	9	117	5^7	5^{6½}	3^{3½}	2^{5½}	McCrrCJ^4	Sra Md H	75-15	PrncBbbyB.,EclsvPrtnr,GrndAllgnc	7
21Mar87—Grade III												
3Nov86-8SA	1¼ Ⓣ:47 1:36 2:01^{1}fm	19	116	3^3	3½	10^6	10^{8¼}	VlsquzJ^{10}	C F Brk H	73-9	Louis Le Grand,Schiller,Silveyville	10
3Nov86—Grade I												
16Oct86-8Bel	1 Ⓣ:47 1:12^{4}1:38^{1}sf	*1	117	4^{1¼}	1½	1^3	1^{3¼}	Antley C W^3	HcpO	74-28	ExclusivePrtnr,FlingGlint,Wollston	7
7Sep86-8Bel	1¼ 🅃:50^{2}1:38^{4}2:02^{3}gd	10	115	5^2	4^{2½}	3^{2½}	3^{3¼}	AntlyCW^2	Mnhtn H	78-23	Dngr'sHour,PrmrMstr,ExclusvPrtnr	8

Form Factors Underbet—Shipper from Slow Track

A horse shipping from a track that produces relatively slow running times, to one that produces fast times, is often overlooked by the public because the horse may appear to be a plodder. Times from races run at tracks such as the Aqueduct inner, Hazel Park, the Meadowlands, Calder, Detroit, Garden State, Pimlico, Florida Downs, Laurel, and Thistledown are considerably slower than the times reproducible by the same horses at tracks such as Gulfstream, Atlantic City, Woodbine, Saratoga, or any of the major West Coast tracks, and many more.

If shipping of horses is a common occurrence at a player's track, he should either get to know the speed and idiosyncracies of the commonly shipped-from tracks or buy one of the several books or magazines that rate them for speed. A shipper from a slow track does not automatically qualify as a bet, of course. In fact, shippers do not win an especially high percentage of races. The point is that slow times almost always get rejected out of hand by the public, a fact to be used to advantage by astute horseplayers when further analysis suggests the horse is a contender.

How to Take Advantage of Underlays and Overlays

The examples of the form factors that are often underlaid and overlaid have been kept separate up until now, for reasons of presentation and simplicity. But in reality, both must exist in a race if a bet with long-run profit potential is to be made. When a heavily bet horse is underlaid, some other horse or horses must be overlaid in the same race. And, when a specific overlay exists, then at least one other horse must be underlaid. How can a hand-icapper keep these ideas straight and profit from them? There are basically two approaches that I use: one for betting against clear underlays, the other for betting apparent specific overlays.

Betting Against Heavy Underlays

An underlay, to summarize, is a well-bet horse (rule of thumb odds 7:2 or less) that has little chance of winning the race under consideration. The lower the odds, the bigger the underlay.

When I spot what in my opinion is a sizeable underlay, I will bet against it if I have a selection, provided that the odds are reasonable. If the favorite is the underlay, I usually assume that my choice to win, if I have one, is the horse that is underbet at the expense of the favorite. Often in these situations, my own selection ends up as the second choice in the betting.

When more than one horse is heavily underlaid (for example both the favorite and second choice) and I have a counterbet selected, then this comprises for me a best-bet situation. These horses have a high probability of winning and usually go to post at generous odds, often 4:1 and higher. They occur infrequently, because normally when the favorite is overbet the second choice is the horse that is most underbet.

If I do not have another specific counterbet in mind, then I will con-fidently bet the second choice against a heavily underlaid favorite if no other horse appears better. And I will normally bet the favorite if the second choice is heavily underlaid, provided the favorite meets my handicapping criteria and no other horse is a strong threat to win. In the rare instance where the first two choices are obvious underlays, the bet goes on the third choice.

These low choices are bet because the underlay-overlay relationship usually is strongest among low odds horses and because of their high win-ning probabilities. If a favorite is overbet, the most underbet horse is usually the second choice; and if a second choice is overbet, the most underbet horse is logically the favorite, and so on.

Are there any price guidelines that can distinguish a betting imbalance among the low-priced choices? As one might expect, there are no absolute numbers or cutpoints for distinguishing when an overwhelming choice is overbet or conversely when another strong favorite or high choice is un-derbet. Determining value is mainly a matter of feel, which comes only through experience. There are, however, some general guidelines that I have developed to reduce the difficulty.

When I simply bet against a favorite, I like to see it bet down to at least 3:2, preferably even money or less. I must also have a very strong feeling that the favorite cannot win today, for one or more of the reasons discussed previously. The low odds requirement for favorites provides room for error on two counts. First, the favorite may indeed be ready to win today, and second, my choice to beat the favorite may not be the best horse; therefore, I demand the favorite be overbet in my view by a wide margin.

A rough estimate of the expected percentage profit from bets against favorites of this type can be obtained from the table 3. It gives the percentage of total win pool money bet on a horse according to its win odds. odds.

For example, at 1:1 a horse has 50 percent of the total money bet (after the track take is subtracted from the pool); at 2:1 it has 33 percent; at 9:1 it has 10 percent, and so on. My procedure, when I find a favorite that I think will almost certainly lose, is to assign it mental odds of about 6:1, or worth 14 percent of the money bet. The difference between the money percentage corresponding to the public odds and 14 percent represents my expected profit. For example, if the overbet favorite goes postward at 1:1, and my own choice at 3:1, then the percentage overlay, based on the false favorite is $(50\% - 14\%)/25\% \times 100 = 144\%$, where the 25 percent figure is the percentage corresponding to the 3:1 odds on my own choice. The same calculation can be applied to any other underlay-overlay situation.

Betting Favorites

When is a favorite a good bet? When it is the best horse in the race, when it provides odds of even money or more, and when the second choice is bet heavily (odds of roughly 3:1 or lower) but has very little chance of winning. If the third betting choice is also heavily bet and has a poor chance, then the overlay on the favorite will be even greater. Usually such overbet second and third choices have form that looks on the surface to be quite good, but a comprehensive analysis shows them up as inferior in some very important way or ways. When I bet a favorite, I insist that the second choice be clearly inferior to the favorite, much more so than suggested by the odds spread between the two. In doing so I am assured of an overlay to some degree. Further, I prefer that the third choice be overbet, too, although this requirement is not critical since the third betting choice does not contribute as much to the potential overlay as does the second choice.

Table 3
Percentage of Total Win Pool Money Bet
Corresponding to Odds Values

Tote Board Odds	% of Win Pool*
1:5	83%
2:5	71%
1:2	67%
3:5	63%
4:5	56%
1:1	50%
6:5	46%
7:5	42%
3:2	40%
8:5	38%
9:5	36%
2:1	33%
5:2	29%
3:1	25%
7:2	22%
4:1	20%
9:2	18%
5:1	17%
6:1	14%
7:1	13%
8:1	11%
9:1	10%
10:1	9%
20:1	5%
50:1	2%

*After removal of track take from win pool.

Finding the Classic Overlay

Locating straight overlays without reference to specific underlays is trickier in view of (a) the potential for finding many seeming overlays among the less well-bet horses, and (b) the considerable competition usually provided by the well-bet public choices. Winning percentages are therefore lower, requiring a moderately high odds level on any bet. My rule of thumb for bets I consider as straight overlays (i.e., any selection that is third public choice or higher) is an odds requirement of 5:1 or higher for large fields (10 horses or more) and somewhat less for smaller fields (down to 3:1 for five or six horse fields). These high odds levels compensate for the lower percentage of winners than attainable when betting first and second public choices.

Finding real overlays and judging their worth are, in my experience, very difficult tasks for even the most seasoned professional. For one thing, genuine overlays at odds of 5:1 are quite rare, contrary to popular opinion. In spite of the fact that every day horses do win at high odds, they are not usually overlaid. On the contrary, in many cases they are heavily overbet. Long run betting on these types would show a serious loss.

Secondly, betting suspected overlays requires courage enough to declare that the public's judgement is grossly in error, something that is not a common occurrence in view of their relatively accurate odds estimates. For this reason I try to keep as objective as possible my opinion about a horse, no matter how exciting or enticing a piece of apparently hidden information culled from my analysis may be. I also redouble my efforts in looking around for another horse that may be better. As an additional precaution I require that any overlay candidate have undisputed signs of sharp form (although not necessarily obvious sharp-looking form), or have a significant class edge. Apparent poor form is common among these horses, and there are usually some questions regarding distance, surface, class ability, or some other factor, or they would not be overlayed.

A fine-touch judgement is required to distinguish the real overlays from the fool's gold. It is a skill developed only by study, practice, and experience. Interestingly, I find that very often the selections made at home that I expect to go off at high prices end up being among the top two choices in the betting, and rather than overlaid are properly bet or occasionally underlaid. This kind of betting action constantly reaffirms my belief in the expertness of the public and at the same time gives me confidence that my ability to analyse a race is well developed.

I realize that many horseplayers must feel that my respect for the public's unknowing ability to sort out the complexities of a horse race is perhaps misguided. But I also once felt that the racing public was to be sneered at because the top choices only won a meagre 33 percent of all races, and 67 percent lost. When I came to realize, however, that no other expert was able to (a) match the winning percentage of favorites over thousands of unselected races or (b) produce a consistently good odds line, then my outlook changed and so, too, gradually, did my results.

Because I use the public's betting line in nearly every race to make a judgement about the potential profitability of a bet, and because most of my bets are at odds of less than 5:1 with a healthy smattering of favorites and second choices, my winning percentage is high enough to keep unnerving losing streaks or periods to a minimum.

There is no doubt that this kind of betting requires a good deal of intestinal fortitude and flexibility. It is not an easy thing for most players to bet against overwhelming choices, when warranted, and then to switch hats and declare that a well-supported favorite is underbet and therefore worth a wager. Handicappers tend to lean consistently one way or the other: playing favorites and other low choices, or betting higher-priced horses. To achieve maximum profits in the shortest time, it is imperative the horseplayer strive for balance.

Stepping Up to the Betting Window

Ideally, when sizing up a potential bet, there should exist a feeling of conviction that it is clearly a profitable situation, i.e., that win or lose, the bet would be a good one. I love to step up, without hesitation, and bet under these circumstances, because there is no second guessing involved. Unfortunately many bets are not so clear-cut and instead involve considerable second guessing.

However, the results from the wavering decision bets, while not as good as from the strong conviction bets, can be (for me at least) still profitable. A few years ago, when I realized that these bets were profitable, I developed a strategy designed to keep second guessing to a minimum. I made it a rule to bet all situations that forced me, because of uncertainties, to last minute decision making. In other words, a bet was made on a horse that was tabbed early in the betting period as a potential bet, if I could not clearly reject it for a fundamental reason well before post time. If my mind repeatedly returned to the situation for futher consideration during the last five minutes, then the strategy required a bet be made. The procedure was designed to reduce the large number of last-second decisions and to minimize the psychological pain that was associated with erroneous decisions made under duress.

I have found the method to be of benefit in reducing stress and in

improving overall results. Results have improved because previously I had
a tendency to be too restrictive in my betting, waiting patiently for perfect
situations. It turned out that these perfect situations existed only in my
imagination since the subsequent increase in the number of less-than-perfect
bets, while reducing profit percentage, actually increased absolute or total
profits. Psychologically, this betting approach has helped to improve my
attitude after losing bets, because, instead of relying on a last-second im-
pulse to bet or not bet, the decision is based on much broader, less frenetic
reasoning.

Probabilities

On a strictly professional basis, a bet should be made only when there exists
an expectation of reasonable profit from a long series of similar bets. Hopes,
wishes, and expectations about the specific bet being considered at the
moment should never be allowed to influence a decision to bet or not.
There is a strong, almost overwhelming tendency by the average race fan
to believe that what is required to make money at the track is to win the
next bet and many others. There is little consideration given to underlay-
overlay concepts, or to the large part played by random elements in the
determination of the outcome of a race. The large random factor necessitates
a mental approach geared toward low expectations for any one bet or short
series.

   In fact, even a series as large as 50 bets can have a wide range of
winners and losers simply as a result of random factors at work. For an
expected winning percentage of, say 30 percent, then on the average in
five out of every hundred series of 50 bets the winning percentage will be
less than 18 percent or greater than 42 percent. Longer series of bets have
a narrower expected range, but the range containing the true 30 percent
figure for thousand-bet samples is still a surprisingly wide 27 to 33 percent,
i.e., 5 percent of all series of one thousand bets could show a winning
percentage outside this range. A table of these confidence ranges based on
various sized series of bets, for this and other winning percentages, is shown
below. (These ranges are calculated on the basis of statistical probability
theory, which need not concern the reader.)

   The same probability theory suggests that in any series of 50 bets, for
an approach that on average achieves 40 percent winners, a range of winning percentages which would encompass 95 out of 100 such 50-bet series
would be 26 to 54 percent winners. For an approach that garners 20 percent
winners (a long shot method) the comparable range would be 10 to 30
percent. These ranges decrease in width as the size of the series increases.

Table 4
Confidence Ranges* for Winning Percentages
by Size of Bet Sample

True Winning Percentage	Size of Bet Sample				
	20	50	100	500	1000
20%	2–38%	10–30%	12–28%	16–24%	18–22%
25%	6–44%	13–37%	17–33%	21–29%	22–28%
30%	10–50%	18–42%	21–39%	26–34%	27–33%
35%	14–56%	22–48%	26–44%	31–39%	32–38%
40%	19–61%	26–54%	30–50%	36–44%	37–43%
45%	23–67%	31–59%	35–55%	41–49%	42–48%
50%	28–72%	36–64%	40–60%	46–54%	47–54%

*Encompasses 95% of all winning percentages from similar sized samples.

For 500 bets, the range for 40 percent winning percentage is 36 to 44 percent; for a 20 percent winning percentage, 16 to 24 percent. It should be clear from this discussion and the data displayed in the table that at least 500 bets are needed to confidently establish a winning percentage. Smaller series simply exhibit too much random variation from sample to sample to be reasonably assured that a trial can be duplicated.

These statistics have other important implications for horseplayers. First, the low winning percentages arising from long shot systems have more relative variability than the winning percentage from, for instance, favorite systems.

For example, with the 50-bet series, the expected low end of the range for the 40 percent winning average is 26 percent, a reduction of 14 percentage points or 35 percent (14/40×100). For the 20 percent winning average the comparable figure is 50 percent; thus, a temporary drop in winning percentage over a modest number of bets has greater impact on profitability for a long shot player than a lower odds player. Not only that, but the loss of one high-priced winner has a greater effect on profits for a long shot player than two low-priced winners for a favorite player. On the other hand, a temporarily high winning percentage favours the long shot system.

The point, however, is that variability in winning percentage and monetary returns is greater for a long shot player. A system or approach with a 20 percent winning percentage that produces two plays per day over a 250-day season may be profitable over samples of 1000 or more races, but can suffer some single years when the bottom line looks anemic. A profitable lower odds system with a high winning percentage is less likely to suffer poor years. I believe that for the average player or professional who has a profitable approach, the psychological aggravation of a bleak year (to say nothing of the financial hardship) cannot be compensated for by the occasional spectacularly profitable year.

Summing Up

These last two chapters have covered a lot of ground. The volume and nature of the information presented may be somewhat overwhelming for the less experienced horseplayer, and for them I recommend a couple of readings. In the process of repeated readings, the important principles should eventually filter through.

It is tempting to try and lay out a structured set of rules or steps to quickly guide the horseplayer through a race in a manner similar to a mechanical system. Such a summary must be quite general, by definition, and would therefore be of limited use in addressing the myriad specific race-to-race situations that arise. This deficiency underlines the catch-22 nature of horse racing instructional material. A horseplayer with wide experience and proper understanding of race-betting principles doesn't need a guide; but for those who do need a guide, none exist that can possibly be specific enough to deal with the complexities of the game!

The critical thing to realize is that there exists no system or set of rules or calculator or computer program that can duplicate results possible by consistently applying the logical handicapping and betting principles at the track.

In any case, it may be beneficial to describe in quick point-form the most frequently applicable and important points covered in the past two chapters, as an overview. It may also be useful to briefly relate many of my own highly personal observations and preferences in regard to handicapping and betting. They reflect my own experiences over the past 20 years.

Preparation and Procedures

- I read the Form twice—once the night before, then more thoroughly the next morning. It is surprising how effective the second read is in sobering judgment.
- It takes me 3 to 4 hours to complete this work.
- I look for races where *at most* 3 or 4 horses have a real edge in current race readiness.
- I also look for races where 1 or 2 horses have potential for heavy overbetting.
- About 60 to 70 percent of all races are too close (several horses could win), too confusing (many unknowns), or too obvious (little or no possibility for an overlay).
- An average day will yield 2 to 4 races with the potential to lead to a bet later at the track.
- Of the 2 to 4 potential races, about half result in a bet.
- Where there is only one real contender, I will bet it if another horse is bet heavily (favorite or second choice), or if two or three other horses are bet below about 5:1.
- Where there are clearly two almost equal contenders, I will bet one if its odds are significantly higher than odds on the other (e.g., 3:1 versus 7:5 or lower).
- In the above situation, I will sometimes bet both horses if another noncontending horse is bet down to favoritism.
- Where one or two noncontenders are bet as favorites, and I don't have a specific counterbet, I will bet the next highest choice or make an occasional hunch bet.
- A straight overlay (a horse that has hidden form and an edge in basic talent) is bet if odds are 5:1 or more in large fields (10 horses or more) and at least 3:1 in smaller fields.
- When I bet extactas or trifectas, I bet combinations with the underbet horse(s) on top; I never put an overbet horse on top.

Favorite Types of Form Patterns—Individual Horses

- Horse that won last race with character (i.e., in a tough drive or with good acceleration);
- Proven front-running speed horse, beaten lately by competing speed, runs against a field without matching speed;
- Close-up second place finish last race, well ahead of third place horse (2 or more lengths);

- Young, improving, bullish horse that won or fought hard through stretch last race;
- Solid accelerating move, close to lead at top of stretch last race (two or three lengths), horse coming to hand;
- Multiple respectable finishes against better horses recently;
- Out of the money last race, drop in class today, signs of improving form;
- Two-point speed rating margin over opposition in character race, improving or maintaining form;
- Difficult post position last race, finished in top quarter of field, ran better than odds suggested;
- Last race finish in top three in a very large field;
- Sharp longer workout (at least 5 furlongs);
- Sharp and positive early speed last race, drops in class today;
- Horse that has won at least 20 percent of its races.

Situation Preferences (Approximate Proportions)

- Sprints over routes, 70 to 30 percent;
- Older horses over 2 years old, 80 to 20 percent;
- Male races over female races, 75 to 25 percent;
- Claiming races 50 percent, allowance/stakes 50 percent;
- Races for winners over races for maidens 85 to 15 percent;
- Smaller fields (9 horses or fewer) over large fields, 70 to 30 percent;
- Fast or nearly fast and sloppy tracks over drying tracks, 95 to 5 percent;
- Dirt over turf races 70 to 30 percent;
- Most bets in March, April, July to December, fewest in May and June (too many new horses);
- Top dozen jockeys at track, 80 percent;
- Competent and respected trainers, 90 percent; desperate trainers 0 percent;

Your Own Approach

A final thought about horse race handicapping: There is simply no single clearly best method or approach to use to beat the game; and there are no perfect handicapping rules or precepts that can be used to distinguish between desirable and undesirable equine attributes. Handicapping rules of thumb can be valuable as rough yardsticks, but the inches and feet for the yardsticks must be judged, not measured.

A handicapping method that works for one person will not necessarily work for another. This is so because everyone has unique mental biases that must be accommodated, just as every athlete or performer has unique gifts and style that must be allowed free expression. Inexperienced horseplayers sometimes begin a serious long-term dedication to the game by adopting a method passed on by word of mouth or through a book on the subject. But these methods are usually temporary, to be discarded or abstracted when they are found to be wanting or unsuitable for the player's temperament.

The handicapping and betting principles described in this book are the ones that I have developed for my own use; and because they have been formulated and tailored over many years, for my own approach, they may not be wholly useful for other horseplayers. I urge those interested in serious pursuit of handicapping excellence to develop their own flexible approach, based on a thorough understanding and application of the useful techniques available for recognizing ability and form differences (and their degrees) among horses and a cultivated feel for value with regard to odds.

A Few Examples

The concepts and principles presented here may better be understood by actual examples. I have selected three California races for this purpose, deliberately avoiding races from New York and other eastern tracks. This was done to reduce the complexity of presentation. A handicapper on the tough eastern circuit is faced with coping with the significance of track-to-track variation, because many horses move from venue to venue during the racing season. While this is not as daunting as it may seem, it is certainly a factor that complicates the analysis. The purpose of these examples is merely illustration.

Of course, three examples cannot begin to present the wide range of handicapping factors required to analyse the situations encountered during a racing season; nor can three races represent the spectrum of betting opportunities and unplayable races arising during a year. However, the analyses are useful in demonstrating the application of the theory and concepts described in this book.

Two of the example races present what I consider to be good betting opportunities. The other race was chosen as representative of the most common type of race—one which is competitive and reasonably properly bet by the public.

Really good bets, such as the two illustrated here, are relatively rare. I would estimate that bets with similar characteristics, including at least a 50 percent chance of winning and a 50 percent overlay potential, occur only once in every three days of racing. Many horseplayers would scoff at this figure and claim that they find at least one or two good bets every day. This is silly. While it may be true that on some days it is possible to find more than one or two outstanding bets, most days at the track are void of high-quality bets. The failure of many horseplayers to recognize this fact is one of the major reasons why even good handicappers do not make money.

How many bets, then, can an expert horseplayer expect to find at the track? I would estimate that, in every 100 races, about 40 are usually too close in a competitive sense, and too well bet by the public for any player to have even a slight hope of making profits from. Another 30 races are somewhat more predictable, but predictable to the public also, with the true probabilities so accurately estimated that little or no advantage exists. Marginal profitability exists in perhaps another 15 races, leaving roughly 15 as representing truly profitable opportunities. In terms of daily totals, one or maybe two profitable bets can be expected on an *average* day, and perhaps one other marginally profitable opportunity. While my tendency is to also bet the marginal opportunities, I would like to develop enough patience to wait for and bet only the really profitable situations, such as the two presented here. Let's take a look at those bets now.

Hollywood, July 3 —9th Race

12 DAILY RACING FORM, FRIDAY, JULY 3

9th Hollywood

TURF COURSE
1 1/16 MILES
HOLLYWOOD PARK
START FINISH

1 1/16 MILES. (Turf). (1.38⅘) ALLOWANCE. (Stretch Start) Purse $24,000. 3-year-olds. Non-winners of $3,000 other than maiden or claiming. Weight, 120 lbs. Non-winners of a race other than claiming at a mile or over since May 15 allowed 3 lbs.; such a race any distance since then, 6 lbs.

Coupled—Ponderable and Mountain Camellia.

Boo Boo's Buckaroo — B. g. 3, by Kris S—Merry Graustark, by Graustark
GRYDER A T — 109⁵ — Br.—Meadowbrook Farms Inc (Fla) — Tr.—Palma Hector O
Own.—Vicki-Beth Stables Inc — Lifetime 15 3 1 4 $47,575

1987	9	3	0	2	$38,250
1986	6	M	1	2	$9,325
Turf	1	0	0	1	$3,600

20Jun87-9Hol	1 1/16 (T)	:46 3	1:10 4	1:41 2 fm	14	104 5	3 2	3 2	3 2 1/4	3 3 1/2	Gryder A T 2	Aw24000	83-13	FvDddyFv,Istorto,BooBoo'sBckroo	9
20Jun87—Lugged out 7/8															
10Jun87-3Hol	6f	:22 3	:46	1:11 ft	5 1/2	116	6 7	6 5 3/4	6 7 1/2	5 11	DelahoussayeE 1	40000	77-16	Silk Vail, DelVolante,HeadlineNews	6
1May87-9Hol	1 1/16	:46 1	1:10 4	1:43 3 ft	*3	119	4 4	4 4 1/2	5 5	5 3 3/4	Pedroza M A 3	40000	87-13	GrtNgotitor,SomHittr,LovDn'sGtwy	8
22Apr87-5Hol	1	:45 2	1:10 2	1:36 ft	3	115	4 3	4 1 1/2	4 4 1/2	3 8 1/2	Pedroza M A 1	45000	74-18	NvrMssT.V.,SprActon,BooBo'sBckr	5
27Mar87-5SA	1	:46 4	1:11 4	1:37 4 ft	19	114	5 3 1/4	4 2	4 3	1 1/2	Pedroza M A 4	45000	79-23	BooBoo'sBuckroo,Drion,BeucoupJ'	9
27Feb87-1SA	6f	:21 4	:45 2	1:11 2 ft	5	118	8 9	6 5 1/2	4 3	1 nk	Sibille R 6	c25000	81-16	BooB'sBckr,Mr.Edlwss,PrmCncrd	10
22Feb87-9SA	1	:46 3	1:11 2	1:36 4 ft	25	113	9 5 3/4	9 6 1/2	8 8 1/4	8 10 1/2	Douglas R R 2	Aw29000	73-14	FlyingFlags,BoldArchon,Ponderble	9
22Feb87—Broke in a tangle															
15Jan87-2SA	6f	:22 1	:46	1:11 4 ft	2 1/2	118	8 4 1/4	4 2	2 1	1 3	Sibille R 11	M32000	79-25	BB'sBckr,ImprssvRsn,FrnchBrgdr	12
3Jan87-6SA	1 1/16	:47 2	1:11 3	1:44 2 ft	19	117	7 9	10 14	9 16	9 18	Sibille R 9	Mdn	61-16	SvorFire,NstyNskr,FmousForever	11
26Dec86-6SA	6f	:21 3	:44 4	1:09 4 ft	20	117	9 6 3/4	7 5 1/4	6 4 3/4	5 5 1/4	Sibille R 2	Mdn	84-13	Barb'sRelic,ChartTheStars,Chinati	12

Jun 28 Hol 5f ft 1:00 1 h   May 31 Hol 5f ft 1:01 2 h   May 20 Hol 5f ft 1:01 2 h

Auto Focus

B. g. 3, by Somethingfabulous—Soft Focus, by Deck Hand
OLIVARES F — 114
Br.—Bachecki-Block-Law (Cal) — 1987 7 1 0 0 $11,500
Tr.—Stein Roger — 1986 1 M 0 0
Own.—Nikki Stable — Lifetime 8 1 0 0 $11,500

26Jun87-2Hol 6½f :22 :451 1:17 ft 8 116 129¼ 129½ 1114 1013¼ Olivares F 5 [S] 25000 82-11 LittlePaces,RoyalAgori,NomadBoi 12
12Apr87-3SA 1 :461 1:12 1:391ft 7 116 43 77¾ 714 719¾ Olivares F 5 [S]Aw31000 52-18 WindwoodLne,‡OleDveWll,PetNwll 7
27Mar87-5SA 1 :464 1:114 1:374ft *2 116 86¼ 911 916 925 Meza R Q 1 c50000 54-23 BooBoo'sBuckroo,Drion,BeucoupJt 9
27Mar87—Stumbled start
14Mar87-8GG 1 :453 1:113 1:39 m 23 116 1112 1116 1123 1026½ Kaenel J L 12 Lfyette 46-23 Momentus,MountLgun,FlyingFlgs 12
22Feb87-9SA 1 :463 1:112 1:364ft 5½ 113 11 11½ 1hd 44 Meza R Q 2 Aw29000 80-14 FlyingFlags,BoldArchon,Ponderble 9
13Feb87-4SA 1 :46 1:11 1:364gd *2½ 117 11½ 12½ 16 110 Meza R Q 4 [S]M40000 84-20 Auto Focus,KingClyde,PeteNewell 10
21Jan87-6SA 6f :214 :45 1:101ft 24 117 63¾ 78¼ 69 511¼ Meza R Q3 [S]Mdn 75-19 NoDoblDl,Prsdnt'sPort,ExcptnlTlnt 7
21Jan87—Wide into stretch
26Dec86-4SA 6½f :213 :441 1:162ft 34 117 44 1013 1013 917 Black C A1 [S]Mdn 71-13 WindwoodLne,Clvinist,PsDeGuerr 10
Jun 13 Hol 3f ft :353 h   May 19 Hol 4f ft :483 h

Ponderable

Dk. b. or br. c. 3, by Vaguely Noble—Sissy's Time, by Villamor
SHOEMAKER W — 114
Br.—Bluegrass Farm (Ky) — 1987 5 0 0 1 $6,675
Tr.—Lukas D Wayne — 1986 4 1 0 0 $13,800
Own.—Hunt N B — Lifetime 9 1 0 1 $20,475 — Turf 2 0 0 0

22Apr87-7Hol 1 (T):464 1:113 1:363fm *2½e 114 2½ 21½ 43 66 Meza R Q5 Aw24000 78-16 DvidsSmile,Gunburst,TeddyBrHug 10
15Apr87-8SA 1⅛ (T):46 1:11 1:471fm 6½e 115 33½ 64¾ 65½ 78¼ Sibille R5 [R]La Puente 83-11 ThMdic,ChmTm,BustYourButtons 10
15Apr87—Steadied at 3/16, bumped late
4Apr87-9SA 1 1/16 :452 1:101 1:432ft *2¾ 117 99 88 611 713¼ Pincay L Jr8 Aw31000 71-17 Jamoke, Laguna Native, The Medic 9
4Apr87—Bumped break
21Mar87-3SA 1 1/16 :454 1:101 1:422sy *8-5 117 43 34 37 412 Pincay L Jr3 Aw31000 77-16 NoMrker,TelphonCnyon,KpluQuick 6
22Feb87-9SA 1 :463 1:112 1:364ft 9¾ 117 42 32 3½ 3½ ShoemkerW4 Aw29000 83-14 FlyingFlags,BoldArchon,Ponderble 9
4Nov86-4Aqu 1 :461 1:124 1:393ft 3 118 31 2hd 12½ 15¾ Day P3 Mdn 68-22 Ponderable,BarristerBob,Machismo 8
27Sep86-3Bel 1 1/16 :46 1:114 1:454sy 13 118 21 2½ 48 514¼ Stevens G L6 Mdn 59-17 PalaceMarch,SirBemis,BeMyVictim 8
27Jly86-6Bel 6f :221 :454 1:121sy 15 118 89¼ 713 716 718¾ Cordero A Jr3 Mdn 62-25 FlyingGrnville,LeoCstelli,JmesOscr 9
2Jun86-4Bel 5f :23 :46 :573ft 13 118 2½ 3½ 56 512¾ Vasquez J7 Mdn 86-13 Gulch, Flying Granville,JamesOscar 7
Jly 2 Hol 3f ft :352 h   Jun 27 Hol 1 ft 1:414 h   ● Jun 22 Hol 7f ft 1:26 h   Jun 17 Hol 6f ft 1:132 h

Bradlee Bo

B. c. 3, by Native Charger—Beaucala, by Beau Brummel
PATTON D B — 1125
Br.—Fredericks F L (Ky) — 1987 3 1 1 0 $4,600
Tr.—Stepp William T — 1986 1 M 0 0 $66
Own.—Fredericks F L — Lifetime 4 1 1 0 $4,666

25Jun87-3Hol 6f :221 :453 1:113ft 4½ 119 65¼ 55 43 21 Stevens G L4 16000 84-14 Bold Royale, BradleeBo,AndyRandy 7
25Jun87—Bumped start
17Jun87-2Hol 6f :22 :453 1:112ft 30 119 89¼ 98¾ 76½ 76¾ Stevens G L1 20000 79-15 Pete Newell,ProvingSpark,Tarland 12
17Jun87—Bumped 1/4
17May87-5TuP 6½f :222 :451 1:17 ft 5½ 115 61¾ 63¾ 34 11 Noda R H9 Mdn 86-15 Bradlee Bo, Compared, Kaleko 12
3Aug86-7SFe 6f :224 :471 1:163m 10 119 67 56 53½ 56 O'Neill E S6 Mdn 56-32 IsleSuprem,Jssi'sRun,ClssicScout 12
Jun 23 Hol 3f ft :353 h   Jun 14 Hol 4f ft :492 h   May 14 TuP 3f ft :362 h   May 8 TuP 6f ft 1:15 h

Calmo

B. c. 3, by Meneval—Cumaware, by Delaware Chief
VERGARA O — 114
Br.—Cole Sheila (Cal) — 1987 12 3 1 2 $13,955
Tr.—Nettles Kenneth — 1986 6 M 0 0 $710
Own.—Olson L — Lifetime 18 3 1 2 $14,665

21Jun87-4Hol 1 :453 1:11 1:371ft 20 116 53½ 31 3½ 33½ Vergara O 4 20000 73-14 Splendor Catch, Glory Quest,Calmo 8
21Jun87—Broke stride 1/16
31May87-1Hol 1 :453 1:112 1:382ft 111 1115 36¼ 35 44½ 46 Iammarino MP 4 25000 65-18 LicensedToWin,Rimmou,Troposphr 9
20May87-5Hol 7f :222 :46 1:243ft 45 1105 107¼ 119¼ 97 811½ Iammarino MP 1 18000 69-17 Glory Quest, Banche, Martorell 11
20May87—Broke slowly
29Apr87-2Hol 1 :453 1:112 1:37 ft 41 116 85½ 119¾ 109¼ 911½ Castanon A L 8 25000 64-13 RcBook,You'rGlorous,StrdstFolly 12
19Apr87-2SA 1 :454 1:121 1:384ft 31 115 76¼ 94¾ 75¾ 55¼ Castanon A L 6 30000 69-17 ShrewdStev,GrndVizir,J.B.R.'sDrm 10
19Apr87—Took up 1/4
2Apr87-4GG 1 1/16 :472 1:113 1:442ft 9½ 116 52¼ 33 33 22¼ Hummel C R 4 16000 78-18 Sablikla, Calmo, Biff McGuire 6
2Apr87—Bobbled start
24Mar87-2GG 1 1/16 :472 1:123 1:46 ft 4 116 31½ 2½ 2½ 1no Hummel C R 3 10000 73-20 Calmo, ToB.ARuler,SleepyBrigadier 7
24Mar87—Ducked in start
12Mar87-7GG 1 1/16 :464 1:123 1:484sy 26 116 1111 78½ 87¾ 46¼ Hummel C R 12 12500 52-28 Pappoos Boy, Table Fun, Sablikla 12
12Mar87—Broke slowly
5Mar87-9GG 1 1/16 :46 1:104 1:443sy 22 115 712 815 — — Hummel C R 7 22500 — — PddyMuldoon,ElAncon,GoldenShng 8
5Mar87—Eased
1Feb87-9PM 6f :23 :464 1:123gd *2 117 31½ 2½ 2hd 1hd Knapp K R 7 12500 84-17 Calmo, Ha Ha Hanson, NightWriter 7
Jun 30 SA 3f ft :363 h   Jun 18 SA 4f ft :473 h   Jun 12 SA 4f ft :474 h   May 16 SA 5f ft 1:004 h

Don'tsingtheblues

Ch. g. 3, by Stop the Music—Bluer Than Blue, by What Luck

SIBILLE R — 120

Br.—Rutherford M G (Ky) — 1987 4 1 0 0 $12,425

Tr.—Mayberry Brian A — 1986 0 M 0 0

Own.—Siegel M-Jan & Samantha — Lifetime 4 1 0 0 $12,425

13Jun87-5Hol 1 :451 1:093 1:343ft 16 120 1010 99¾ 812 819 Sibille R 3 Aw24000 71-11 ErnYorStrps,McKnzPrnc,JstBbby 10
24May87-6Hol 1 :452 1:103 1:362ft 7 115 1½ 11½ 11½ 1no Sibille R 4 Mdn 81-13 Don'tsingtheblus,MgnPlus,ProudCt 7
9May87-6Hol 6½f :221 :452 1:164ft 47 115 64¾ 53¾ 44½ 45½ Sibille R8 Mdn 91-10 Crystal Run, MarkChip,SharpPort 11
14Mar87-6SA 6f :213 :444 1:09 ft 22 118 96¾1114112411131½ Douglas R R9 Mdn 62-16 Looknforthbgon,Pnsco,ChstntFrz 12

Jun 26 Hol 5f ft 1:003 h   Jun 7 Hol 4f ft :492 h   May 3 Hol 6f ft 1:16 h

Contact Game

Dk. b. or br. c. 3, by Tri Jet—Miami Game, by Crozier

MCCARRON C J — 114

Br.—Hooper F W (Fla) — 1987 8 0 3 3 $30,400

Tr.—Russell John W — 1986 6 1 0 0 $9,125

Own.—Hooper F W — Lifetime 14 1 3 3 $39,525 — Turf 2 0 1 1 $8,400

19Jun87-5Hol 1⅛ Ⓣ:46 1:0941:403fm*8-5 109 64½ 53 34 33 ShoemkerW4 Aw24000 88-09 Forlaway,TableGlow,ContactGame 10
19Jun87—Crowded, bumped start; again into stretch
4Jun87-7Hol 1⅛ :454 1:102 1:423ft *8-5 115 53½ 42 21 21½ McCarronCJ3 Aw24000 94-13 CrystalRun,ContctGme,Ack'sReply 8
13May87-8Hol 1⅛ Ⓣ:4711:1121:412fm 6 114 25 23½ 21½ 2hd McCarronCJ4 Aw24000 87-13 LgunNtive,ContctGm,Mountincmlli 8
26Apr87-3Hol 6f :214 :451 1:091ft 9-5 115 64½ 43½ 44½ 36 McCarronCJ6 Aw22000 91-09 W. D.Jacks,ANewEra,ContactGame 6
3Apr87-7SA 6f :214 :45 1:10 ft 11 116 74 52 32½ 23 Solis A8 Aw29000 85-17 HonkyTnkDncr,CntctGm,WndwdLn 8
8Mar87-6SA 6f :211 :442 1:094ft 9½ 115 77½ 64½ 43 43½ Solis A6 Aw28000 86-15 War, Candi's Gold, Laguna Native 8
8Mar87—Checked at break
21Feb87-3SA 6f :22 :45 1:094ft 9 115 52½ 41½ 42 34¾ Stevens G L3 Aw27000 84-14 SimplyMajestic,Blanco,ContctGme 8
21Feb87—Steadied 1/8
6Feb87-3SA 6f :211 :433 1:084ft 19 114 66½ 56 34 44¾ Stevens G L3 Aw26000 89-15 MountLagun,SweetwterSprings,Wr 7
6Nov86-6Hol 6f :221 :454 1:112ft *2½ 118 42½ 32 31 1hd Solis A5 M50000 86-17 ContctGm,WstrlyWind,WsdomDncr 9
19Oct86-6SA 6f :22 :452 1:11 ft 16 118 95½ 54¾ 44½ 47 Solis A11 Mdn 76-18 Jamoke,SavorFire,BrigntineDncer 12
19Oct86—Lugged in late

Jun 28 Hol 6f ft 1:182 h   ●Jun 13 Hol 5f ft :591 h   May 31 Hol 6f ft 1:134 h   May 23 Hol 5f ft 1:011 h

Mountaincamellia

B. c. 3, by Sham—Crimson Prey, by Crimson Satan

DELAHOUSSAYE E — 114

Br.—Bluegrass Farm (Ky) — 1987 8 1 0 1 $24,925

Tr.—Whittingham Charles — 1986 1 M 0 0

Own.—Hunt N B — Lifetime 9 1 0 1 $24,925 — Turf 3 0 0 1 $9,900

4Jun87-7Hol 1⅛ :454 1:102 1:423ft 9½ 116 86½ 64 63½ 46 DelhoussyeE 2 Aw24000 90-13 CrystalRun,ContctGme,Ack'sReply 8
13May87-8Hol 1⅛ Ⓣ:4711:1121:412fm 2¾ 115 57 55½ 33½ 34 Toro F 8 Aw24000 83-13 LgunNtive,ContctGm,Mountincmlli 8
22Apr87-7Hol 1 Ⓣ:4641:1131:363fm *2½e 116 96½ 94¾ 54 44¼ DelhoussyeE 6 Aw24000 89-16 DvidsSmile,Gunburst,TeddyBrHug 10
22Apr87—Wide final 3/8
15Apr87-8SA 1⅛ Ⓣ:46 1:11 1:471fm 6½e 116 75½ 53½ 55½ 46½ DlhssyE 7 Ⓢ La Puente 84-11 ThMdic,ChmTm,BustYourButtons 10
15Apr87—Bumped start, at 1/8
21Mar87-7SA 1⅛ :47 1:114 1:434sy 6¾ 118 66 55½ 611 611½ ShoemkerW 2 Aw31000 70-16 Candi's Gold, Reland, Rakaposhi 6
21Mar87—Lugged out
8Mar87-9SA 1⅛ :464 1:112 1:43 ft 10 118 89½ 87¾ 710 711½ DelhoussyeE4 Aw30000 74-15 Barb's Relic, Blanco, Rakaposhi 9
8Mar87—Wide into, through stretch
22Feb87-6SA 1⅛ :463 1:12 1:442ft 2½e 117 55½ 21 23 1½ Delahoussaye E5 Mdn 79-14 Mountncmll,ErnYourStrps,ExtPoll 11
22Feb87—Wide 3/8 turn
8Feb87-4SA 1⅛ :463 1:12 1:44 ft 11 117 78¾ 64½ 58 58½ Cordero A Jr3 Mdn 72-14 NoMrker,NstyNskr,RichesToRiches 8
8Feb87—Lugged out, took up 5/16
29Nov86-5Hol 6f :22 :453 1:113ft 50 118 10131013 710 611 Solis A2 Mdn 79-12 OrchardSong,SocilDimond,Dirmid 10
29Nov86—Lugged out

Jly 1 Hol 3f ft :353 h   Jun 26 Hol 5f ft 1:00 h   Jun 16 Hol 5f ft 1:003 h   Jun 11 Hol 3f ft :353 h

Table Glow

B. g. 3, by Never Tabled—Radiant Glow, by Northern Dancer

STEVENS G L — 114

Br.—Sarkowsky S H (Cal) — 1987 4 1 1 1 $12,650

Tr.—Mandella Richard — 1986 1 M 0 0

Own.—Sarkowsky H — Lifetime 5 1 1 1 $12,650 — Turf 1 0 1 0 $4,800

19Jun87-5Hol 1⅛ Ⓣ:46 1:0941:403fm 19 114 1½ 1½ 1½ 2hd Stevens G L 1 Aw24000 91-09 Forlaway,TableGlow,ContactGame 10
12Jun87-6Hol 6f :221 :453 1:112ft 2¾ 115 21 2hd 1hd 11½ Stevens GL 3 Ⓢ M32000 86-16 TbleGlow,BrothersSteve,L.W.Kidd 11
23May87-4Hol 6f :213 :45 1:111ft *6-5 115 41½ 32½ 65 75¼ Stevens G L 6 M40000 81-15 Peppy'sConsul,PolynsinChif,Trlnd 10
13May87-6Hol 6f :213 :443 1:104ft 2¾ 115 22 24 23½ 32¾ Stevens G L 2 M40000 87-15 OlympcProspct,CmnBmbn,TblGlw 11
30Aug86-4Dmr 6f :22 :452 1:102ft 5½ 118 52½ 54 710 711¾ Toro F 1 Ⓢ Mdn 74-10 ASignOfLuck,AtTheRitz,NstyNskr 10
30Aug86—Veered in start

Jun 29 Hol 3f ft :37 h   Jun 8 Hol 3f ft :394 h   May 21 Hol 3f ft :35 h   May 11 Hol 3f ft :362 hg

This race was an allowance race conditioned for three-year-olds at a distance of a mile and one-sixteenth on the turf course.

Boo Boo's Buckaroo ran on the grass for the first time in his last start, finishing a solid third while moving up in class. He ran better than expected (at 14:1 odds), and it appears that he may appreciate grass racing. The 40-day layoff before his next to last race, plus the relatively good recent workout have set him up for a sharp try today. This gelding has won three races since January and can win here if the competition is not outstanding.

Auto Focus is obviously not a contender.

Ponderable, the better half of an entry, is returning to the races after a 70-day layoff. His works are good and he has run well after previous layoffs. On the other hand, his turf and distance abilities are not clearly demonstrated. Ponderable could run well here, though, and will be heavily bet because of jockey Shoemaker and trainer Lukas.

Bradlee Bo is moving up sharply in class, is trying a route distance and the grass for the first time. In addition, the colt's speed ratings are mediocre and his manner of running do not suggest an aggressive performance here. No factor.

Calmo's record is mediocre. The colt was dropped in class last race and failed to run well through the stretch. He moves up again today and tries the turf for the first time. It would be a surprise if he won.

Don'tsingtheblues broke his maiden in his next to last race. His last race shows a poor start and a fading finish. Even though he produced a respectable workout since, this gelding may be hurting. No factor.

Contact Game has been well supported recently, but failed to win. The running line for the last race suggests an excuse—bumping and crowding. But bumping and crowding is a part of most races and is usually overcome by good horses and jockeys. This factor may be overrated by the public today. Contact Game's consistency record suggests a close-up finish but not likely a win here. His most recent workout was very slow, which could indicate a problem. McCarron has the mount, which should also contribute to a degree of overbetting.

Mountaincamellia lends support to his entry mate, Ponderable. The two ran together on April 27, were well bet, but finished out of the money. Mountaincamellia shows very mediocre form and consistency but has been working regularly. It appears this colt should be running at a lower class level.

Table Glow is very sharp. Moving up in class and onto the grass last race, Table Glow just missed winning after setting the fractions throughout the race. In that race, Table Glow finished three lengths in front of Contact Game. Table Glow has enough speed to overcome the disadvantaged post position. This is a bullish horse with a good chance to win.

The real contenders are Boo Boo's Buckaroo, Ponderable, and Table Glow. Contact Game is also a possibility. The public made Contact Game a solid favorite at 8:5 on the strength of McCarron, and "excuse" last race, and recent close-up finishes. Table Glow and Ponderable went to post at 5:2 and Boo Boo's Buckaroo at 6:1.

Contact Game was overbet. My own line on this race would have been: Table Glow 2:1, Ponderable 3:1, Boo Boo's Buckaroo 7:2, and Contact Game 7:2. Table Glow was my choice to win the race, but did not benefit sufficiently from the overbetting of Contact Game to warrant a bet. In my view, it was a case of two contenders receiving somewhat less betting than warranted, but not enough to profit significantly from.

NINTH RACE
Hollywood
JULY 3

1 $\frac{1}{16}$ MILES.(Turf). (1.38$\frac{4}{5}$) ALLOWANCE. (Stretch Start) Purse $24,000. 3–year–olds. Non–winners of $3,000 other than maiden or claiming. Weight, 120 lbs. Non–winners of a race other than claiming at a mile or over since May 15 allowed 3 lbs.; such a race any distance since then, 6 lbs.

Value of race $24,000; value to winner $13,200; second $4,800; third $3,600; fourth $1,800; fifth $600. Mutuel pool $294,300. Exacta pool $429,744.

Last Raced	Horse	Eqt.	A.Wt	PP	St	¼	½	¾	Str	Fin	Jockey	Odds $1
20Jun87 ^{9}Hol^{3}	Boo Boo's Buckaroo	b	3 109	1	1	$3^{2\frac{1}{2}}$	$3^{\frac{1}{2}}$	$3^{\frac{1}{2}}$	2^{hd}	1^{nk}	Gryder A T^{5}	6.50
19Jun87 ^{5}Hol^{2}	Table Glow	b	3 114	9	2	$1^{1\frac{1}{2}}$	$1^{1\frac{1}{2}}$	$1^{1\frac{1}{2}}$	$1^{1\frac{1}{2}}$	$2^{\frac{1}{2}}$	Stevens G L	2.70
22Apr87 ^{7}Hol^{6}	Ponderable		3 114	3	3	2^{hd}	$2^{\frac{1}{2}}$	$2^{\frac{1}{2}}$	$3^{1\frac{1}{2}}$	$3^{3\frac{1}{2}}$	Shoemaker W	a-2.60
19Jun87 ^{5}Hol^{3}	Contact Game		3 114	7	5	$5^{\frac{1}{2}}$	5^{4}	4^{hd}	$4^{2\frac{1}{2}}$	$4^{2\frac{1}{2}}$	McCarron C J	1.60
21Jun87 ^{4}Hol^{3}	Calmo	b	3 116	5	9	9	9	7^{hd}	$5^{1\frac{1}{2}}$	$5^{1\frac{3}{4}}$	Vergara O	72.00
25Jun87 ^{3}Hol^{2}	Bradlee Bo		3 112	4	6	7^{1}	7^{hd}	8^{4}	$6^{1\frac{1}{2}}$	6^{6}	Patton D B^{5}	54.90
26Jun87 ^{2}Hol^{10}	Auto Focus	b	3 114	2	7	$8^{2\frac{1}{2}}$	$8^{\frac{1}{2}}$	9	9	$7^{\frac{1}{2}}$	Olivares F	40.00
4Jun87 ^{7}Hol^{4}	Mountaincamellia	b	3 116	8	8	$4^{\frac{1}{2}}$	$4^{1\frac{1}{2}}$	5^{3}	7^{2}	8^{1}	Delahoussaye E	a-2.60
13Jun87 ^{5}Hol^{8}	Don'tsingtheblues	b	3 120	6	4	6^{2}	6^{2}	$6^{\frac{1}{2}}$	8^{1}	9	Sibille R	11.00

a–Coupled: Ponderable and Mountaincamellia.

OFF AT 5:50. Start good. Won driving. Time, :23$\frac{3}{5}$, :46$\frac{3}{5}$, 1:10$\frac{3}{5}$, 1:35$\frac{1}{5}$, 1:41$\frac{4}{5}$ Course firm.

$2 Mutuel Prices:

2–BOO BOO'S BUCKAROO	15.00	6.00	3.40
9–TABLE GLOW		4.20	3.00
1–PONDERABLE (a–entry)			2.60

$2 EXACTA 2–9 PAID $71.80.

Races of this type are common—several contenders who could win, and a betting line that is close to being accurate or out of proportion by an amount that is difficult to profit by. Such races are tempting to bet but a bit too confusing. Better to wait for a more clear-cut situation, such as where one or two horses are overbet and there remains only one other contender.

Golden Gate, June 27 —Third Race

3rd Golden Gate

1 MILE. (1.33⅗) CLAIMING. Purse $10,000. 4-year-olds and upward. Weight, 122 lbs. Non-winners of two races at a mile or over since April 15 allowed 3 lbs.; such a race since then, 6 lbs. Claiming price $12,500; if for $10,500 allowed 2 lbs. (Races when entered for $10,000 or less not considered.)

Hasty Paster

JUDICE J C **116**
Own.—Quinn & Battle

B. g. 4, by Flying Paster—Elizabeth T, by Ruffinal
Br.—Cardiff Stud Farm (Cal) 1987 7 2 1 0 $13,700
Tr.—Offield Duane **$12,500** 1986 11 2 1 0 $9,873
Lifetime 18 4 2 0 $23,573

7Jun87-7GG	6f	$:21^1$	$:43^2$	$1:09^1$ft	24	117	8^7	7^5	$8^{7\frac{1}{4}}$	$6^{5\frac{3}{4}}$	Maple S 5	16000	87-10	Cool'nScndlous,RnCogrRn,HotMtl	10
22Apr87-4GG	6f	:22	$:44^4$	$1:11^1$ft	14	117	5^6	$5^{5\frac{1}{4}}$	$3^{2\frac{1}{2}}$	$1^{1\frac{1}{2}}$	Maple S 1	12500	83-20	HastyPaster,StockNTrde,Muskogee	9
1Apr87-7GG	6f	$:21^4$	$:44^3$	$1:10^4$ft	3¼	117	$5^{6\frac{1}{2}}$	$4^{6\frac{1}{2}}$	$7^{8\frac{1}{2}}$	8^7	Baze R A 3	16000	78-18	StrckngFury,CptnO'Dsy,GrtlmnDon	9
1Apr87—Broke out start															
19Mar87-7GG	6f	:22	$:44^4$	$1:09^3$ft	21	117	$5^{6\frac{1}{2}}$	4^7	$4^{6\frac{1}{2}}$	$4^{7\frac{3}{4}}$	SchvneveldtCP 1	20000	83-16	MYoAndQ.,FrgtThMny,IntrpdGmm	7
19Mar87—Stumbled start															
27Feb87-5GG	6f	:22	$:44^3$	$1:09^2$ft	6½	117	$8^{5\frac{3}{4}}$	$7^{4\frac{3}{4}}$	5^3	2^4	Baze R A 3	12500	88-14	ZarMoro,HstyPster,ClipperSkipper	9
27Feb87—Forced wide drive															
7Feb87-9BM	6f	$:22^3$	$:45^4$	$1:10^3$ft	7	114	$6^{6\frac{1}{4}}$	$6^{6\frac{1}{2}}$	$6^{6\frac{1}{2}}$	$4^{5\frac{1}{4}}$	Judice J C 4	16000	81-19	GentlemanDon,VientoDeOro,Zcbee	6
1Jan87-10BM	6f	$:22^1$	:46	$1:12^1$ft	6½	114	6^6	$6^{3\frac{3}{4}}$	$3^{1\frac{1}{2}}$	1^{nk}	Judice J C 1	10000	78-30	HstyPstr,TmpstDTmpo,RstlssRmpg	8
1Jan87—Drifted out 1/8															
17Dec86-5BM	6f	:23	$:46^3$	$1:12^1$sl	14	114	$8^{6\frac{1}{4}}$	$5^{5\frac{1}{2}}$	$4^{3\frac{1}{2}}$	$1^{1\frac{1}{2}}$	Judice J C 6	Ⓢ 8000	78-36	Hasty Paster,LotaPrice,Muskogee	12
27Nov86-7BM	1 1/16	:47	$1:11^2$	1:44 ft	7½	115	$4^{1\frac{1}{4}}$	$7^{4\frac{1}{2}}$	8^{12}	$8^{18\frac{3}{4}}$	Hansen R D 7	10000	53-23	Trajet, Finalized, Ziad's Scuvenir	11
30Oct86-2BM	1 1/16	$:46^3$	$1:11^1$	$1:44^2$ft	9½	114	$7^{9\frac{1}{2}}$	7^{11}	$5^{7\frac{3}{4}}$	$4^{6\frac{1}{4}}$	Lamance C 4	Ⓢ 10000	64-24	ShnesBest,ALittleGoodNws,ScrtGn	9
30Oct86—Bumped start; steadied 1/8															

May 28 BM 5f ft $:59^3$ h **May 20 BM 4f ft :46 h**

Sauternes

CAMPBELL B C **116**
Own.—Fumano J

Dk. b. or br. g. 5, by Pay Tribute—State Song, by Stop the Music
Br.—Elmendorf Farm (Ky) 1987 9 0 2 3 $9,650
Tr.—Fumano Jack **$12,500** 1986 7 0 1 0 $4,445
Lifetime 37 7 5 4 $60,245

6Jun87-10GG	1 1/16	$:44^3$	$1:09^3$	$1:42^3$ft	6½	116	9^{20}	$9^{9\frac{1}{4}}$	$6^{3\frac{1}{2}}$	4^4	Maple S9	10000	86-07	Fulger,StarRoute,MatineeAtSeven	11
25May87-6GG	1	$:45^1$	$1:10^2$	$1:37^2$ft	8	116	$7^{7\frac{1}{4}}$	6^4	3^2	$3^{1\frac{3}{4}}$	Maple S7	12500	79-13	I Heard A Voice, Khaleff,Sauternes	8
25Apr87-1GG	1	:45	$1:09^2$	$1:36^1$ft	9	117	7^{14}	6^{10}	5^4	$3^{2\frac{1}{4}}$	Maple S3	12500	85-10	VrietyExpress,GetUpAmeric,Sutrns	7
11Apr87-3GG	1	$:45^2$	$1:09^4$	$1:36^3$ft	19	116	7^{11}	6^5	$4^{4\frac{1}{2}}$	$2^{3\frac{1}{2}}$	Maple S3	10000	81-14	Star Route, Sauternes, Promptness	8
11Apr87—Broke slowly															
28Mar87-6GG	1 1/16	$:46^2$	$1:11^3$	$1:43^2$ft	13	116	8^{14}	$9^{7\frac{3}{4}}$	8^{13}	$7^{9\frac{1}{4}}$	Doocy T T5	10000	77-14	Bob'sIntnt,CptnPckrng,RnbwRdg	10
17Mar87-9GG	1	$:46^2$	$1:11^2$	$1:38^1$ft	5¾	116	$8^{9\frac{1}{2}}$	$8^{9\frac{3}{4}}$	$4^{5\frac{1}{2}}$	$4^{5\frac{1}{2}}$	Doocy T T3	10000	71-21	Miss A Bid, Coach Conway,Otrebor	9
8Feb87-10BM	1 1/16	$:46^3$	$1:11^2$	1:44 ft	7½	115	$6^{7\frac{1}{2}}$	$5^{5\frac{1}{2}}$	4^2	2^2	Doocy T T2	10000	70-22	CageyDescent,Sauternes,Irnenough	8
25Jan87-10BM	1 1/16	$:46^1$	$1:11^3$	$1:45^1$gd	3¾	115	6^{12}	$6^{7\frac{1}{4}}$	4^9	$3^{10\frac{1}{2}}$	Doocy T T3	10000	55-25	Otrebor, Toru, Sauternes	6
17Jan87-5BM	6f	$:22^4$	$:46^3$	1:11 ft	22	115	$6^{9\frac{1}{2}}$	$6^{8\frac{1}{2}}$	6^{12}	$5^{7\frac{1}{2}}$	Doocy T T3	10000	76-19	Che, Barely Noble, Pensar	10
18May86-10GG	1 1/16	$:46^2$	1:10	$1:42^3$ft	21	109^5	7^7	8^{10}	$6^{9\frac{1}{2}}$	6^8	Yamamoto T J8	16000	82-12	Frivolissimo,GetMEvn,ShdowWtch	9

May 23 BM 3f ft :37 h **●May 16 BM tr.t 4f ft $:49^4$ h** **May 9 BM tr.t 4f ft $:50^4$ h**

Lisa's Prince

CASTANEDA M **116**
Own.—Dante C T–M V–T C

B. g. 4, by Gold Prince—Lisa Again, by New Policy
Br.—Dante T (Cal) 1987 2 1 0 0 $3,900
Tr.—Retherford N J **$12,500** 1986 0 M 0 0
Lifetime 2 1 0 0 $3,900

18Jun87-4GG	6f	$:21^4$	:45	$1:10^4$ft	5	119	$4^{2\frac{1}{4}}$	$4^{1\frac{3}{4}}$	$3^{1\frac{1}{2}}$	4^4	Gonzalez R M1	10000	81-17	NoblePsser,CloudBuster,Muskogee	8
18Jun87—Broke slowly															
5Jun87-1GG	6f	$:21^3$	$:44^3$	1:11 ft	4	120	$7^{3\frac{1}{4}}$	$7^{6\frac{1}{2}}$	3^3	1^3	GonzalezRM5	ⓈM12500	84-18	Ls'sPrnc,Alld'sBloomng,TrblsLck	11
5Jun87—Broke slowly; steadied into drive															

May 20 GG 4f ft $:47^3$ hg **May 13 GG 4f ft :49 h** **May 7 GG 3f ft $:35^1$ h**

Coul Lover

B. g. 5, by Coulee Man—Thine Lovely, by Bobby Dorene
MARTINEZ E 116 Br.—Mole-Richardson Farm (Cal) 1986 13 2 0 3 $9,988
Tr.—Mortensen Dee $12,500 1985 13 M 3 1 $7,687
Own.—Martinez Elisabeth Lifetime 26 2 3 4 $17,675 Turf 1 0 0 0

26Jly86-6SR 1 1/16 :464 1:11 1:421ft 14 115 33½ 43 56½ 510¼ Martinez E 3 12500 83-08 HezaDavid,PlesntonRidge,KoolKev 6
26Jly86—Pinched at start
13Jly86-10Sol 1 :462 1:112 1:374ft 20 115 77 66 54½ 51¾ Martinez E 1 12500 83-13 PleasntonRidge,HezDvid,Scrunchy 10
29Jun86-10Pln 170 :463 1:11 1:411ft 12 115 42 1hd 1hd 1no Martinez E 3 [S] 8000 88-15 CoulLover,ALovelyTrrc,SmrtChrgr 10
21Jun86-10GG 1 1/16 ⓣ:4641:1141:441fm 23 114 1013 89¼ 710 66¾ Martinez E 4 10000 74-14 Run Cougar Run,Ayaabi,Vorlaufer 11
24May86-3GG 1 1/16 :461 1:102 1:433ft 13 114 813 611 55½ 33½ Martinez E 2 [S] 6250 81-12 Heza David, Imaenough, CoulLover 8
24May86—Ducked in start
10May86-10GG 1 1/16 :47 1:122 1:453ft 50 116 13 13 1½ 42½ Martinez E 4 6250 72-22 Addend,CremeDelCrow,Imaenough 12
26Apr86-10GG 1 1/16 :463 1:112 1:433ft 89 118 64¾ 43½ 67½ 812 Martinez E 4 8000 73-12 ‡BigBeuty,CsoSerio,RfflesEsquire 12
12Apr86-10GG 1 1/16 :462 1:113 1:45 ft 58 117 89½ 88 68 63¼ Martinez E 11 8000 75-17 TypiclPro,NtiveExplorr,WhtADiug 12
29Mar86-10GG 1 1/16 :464 1:104 1:431ft 43 117 55½ 89½ 813 812 Martinez E 7 12500 75-12 FlyingBob,‡Bini'sDncr,Vronic'sMrk 9
7Mar86-1GG 1 1/16 :483 1:131 1:47 sy 11 119 31½ 13 13 14 Ochoa A 5 [S]M12500 68-21 CoulLovr,OilRobbr,ConnvngOrphn 10
Jun 21 GG 5f ft 1:00 hg Jun 15 GG 1 ft 1:40 h Jun 8 GG 1 ft 1:424 h May 30 GG 7f ft 1:283 h

*Manerly

Dk. b. or br. g. 6, by Mansingh—Vaguely Hopeful, by Fortino II
SCHVANEVELDT C P 116 Br.—Redford I (Eng) 1987 7 1 1 0 $10,575
Tr.—Martin R L $12,500 1986 18 4 5 2 $25,485
Own.—Turman E Lifetime 48 8 8 4 $57,573 Turf 9 1 0 0 $2,743

20Jun87-7GG 1 :452 1:10 1:354ft 11 116 74½ 53 47 43¾ SchvneveldtCP 3 16000 85-12 Nordic Light, Stabilized, Finalized 10
4Jun87-9GG 1 :463 1:104 1:361ft 4½ 116 32 52½ 53½ 62½ Baze R A 1 16000 84-17 VrietyExpress,Stbilized,SpringStret 9
25May87-6GG 1 :451 1:102 1:372ft *2½ 119 67 74½ 52½ 42¾ Campbell B C 5 c12500 78-13 I Heard A Voice, Khaleff,Sauternes 8
9May87-4GG 1 1/16 :461 1:094 1:42 ft 13 119 77½ 66 32½ 22 Campbell B C 8 12500 91-11 Midford, Manerly, Miss A Bid 8
25Apr87-1GG 1 :45 1:092 1:361ft 5 119 412 711 77½ 65 Castaneda M 2 12500 82-10 VrietyExpress,GetUpAmeric,Sutrns 7
27Mar87-3GG 1 :463 1:114 1:372ft 8½ 116 46 42½ 11½ 12 Castaneda M 4 12500 81-16 Manerly, Excess Profit, Miss A Bid 7
14Mar87-2GG 6f :222 :461 1:121sy 14 117 77½ 63½ 44 43½ Davidson J R 7 c10000 74-23 LghtnngSprt,NoontmJzz,SndyBrgn 8
13Dec86-2BM 1 1/16 :471 1:12 1:44 ft *6-5e 115 67 74½ 77 88½ Hansen R D 4 16000 64-19 BrginStndrd,Her'sThBlz,Bob'sIntnt 9
13Dec86—Steadied early
29Nov86-10BM 1 1/16 :453 1:102 1:433ft 7½ 114 717 48 34 38 Aragon V A 2 16000 66-17 Never-Rust,TheAyesHaveI,Mnerly 8
18Oct86-10BM 1 1/16 :462 1:11 1:423ft 2¾ 114 43½ 43 57½ 49 Chapman T M 3 c16000 70-16 New Storm,Frivolissimo,OurNordic 8
Jun 14 GG 5f ft 1:024 h May 21 GG 4f ft :482 h May 3 GG 4f ft :481 h

Fulger

Ch. g. 5, by Dancing Champ—Nashville Trucker, by Nashville
DIAZ A L 116 Br.—Payne L H (Alb-C) 1987 8 2 2 2 $16,035
Tr.—Morey William J Jr $12,500 1986 19 1 6 3 $1[illegible]
Own.—Heller Mr or Mrs B D Lifetime 51 6 12 7 $53,339

6Jun87-10GG 1 1/16 :443 1:093 1:423ft *8-5 116 1129 1114 42½ 11½ Baze R A 11 10000 90-07 Fulger,StarRoute,MatineeAtSeven 11
25May87-5GG 1 :453 1:103 1:37 ft *3½ 116 914 97¾ 35½ 21 Baze R A 9 8000 82-13 Finalized, Fulger, Noble Passer 9
17Mar87-7GG 1⅛ :471 1:114 1:511ft *2½ 116 1117 1114 911 43½ Baze R A 6 [R]HcpO 73-21 Buc'sInfront,AffirmedNtiv,Mt.Elb 12
7Mar87-9GG 1 1/16 :462 1:11 1:431ft 13 1115 912 98¾ 43 2nk Pineda G R 1 16000 87-16 Bedouin, Fulger, Ever Brilliant 9
8Feb87-10BM 1 1/16 :463 1:112 1:44 ft 4 115 816 811 54 54 Lamance C 6 c10000 68-22 CageyDescent,Sauternes,Imenough 8
18Jan87-10BM 1 1/16 :47 1:113 1:443ft 8¾ 115 1119 99¾ 64½ 1hd Baze R A 1 8000 69-26 Fulger, Imaenough, Borrego Sun 12
10Jan87-10BM 1 1/16 :491 1:141 1:473sl 3 115 1111 1113 78½ 32 Baze R A 4 c6250 52-34 Off To Reno, Plenty Brown,Fulger 12
4Jan87-1BM 1⅛ :472 1:122 1:521m 18 116 714 78¾ 52 3¾ Hansen R D 2 8000 69-30 Lyon'sShdow,SprtnConquest,Fulgr 7
7Dec86-10BM 1⅛ :472 1:122 1:531sl 17 114 1022 1019 714 714¼ Johnson B G 1 8000 51-38 LondonExprss,HighChrmr,Mr.H.H. 10
7Dec86—Placed sixth through disqualification
29Nov86-9BM 6f :221 :444 1:102ft 63 115 1017 1024 1021 1012 Schrick D E 1 12500 74-17 Dnzg'sRturn,BlzngZulu,JustTrnLft 10
Jun 24 GG 3f ft :354 h Jun 14 GG 4f ft :502 h Jun 3 GG 3f ft :354 h May 22 GG 3f ft :353 h

United Victory

B. g. 6, by British Battle—Ike's Lady, by Ike's Glory
MAPLE S 116 Br.—Burch Audrey J (Cal) 1987 8 4 1 1 $22,795
Tr.—Molinaro Kent $12,500 1986 9 3 3 1 $14,220
Own.—Molinaro K R Lifetime 37 11 9 6 $70,898 Turf 1 0 0 0 $1,710

7Jun87-9GG 6f :212 :433 1:09 ft *3-2 117 42½ 21½ 22½ 22½ SchvneveldtCP 3 10000 91-10 AlwysQuick,UnitdVictory,FmlyFox 10
7Jun87—Bumped start
27May87-7GG 6f :213 :44 1:092ft 3½ 117 33½ 33 43½ 34½ SchvneveldtCP 6 12500 88-18 HotMetl,PowderPck,UnitedVictory 8
18Apr87-1GG 6f :214 :444 1:092ft *3 116 33 32½ 32 42¾ SchvneveldtCP 5 16000 89-08 CloudBuster,TheBrginHurtr,HjjiBb 8
31Mar87-3GG 6f :222 :452 1:104ft 2½ 116 31½ 31½ 1hd 11 SchvneveldtCP 6 12500 85-20 UntdVctory,Wll'sPowr,ThBrgnHntr 6
16Feb87-6GG 6f :214 :444 1:101ft *6-5 115 3nk 1hd 1hd 1½ Doocy T T 5 10000 88-17 UnitedVictory,ZrMoro,NoontimJzz 7
8Feb87-9BM 6f :222 :452 1:10 ft *3-2 115 33½ 32 1½ 12 Doocy T T 4 8000 89-22 UntdVctory,LghtnngSprt,RnCgrRn 6
28Jan87-2BM 6f :224 :461 1:113m *2½ 115 53½ 32 11½ 12½ Doocy T T 2 [S] 6250 81-24 UnitedVictory,KuKanak,Erin'sGlory 9
11Jan87-5BM 6f :23 :47 1:122gd *2½ 115 21 43 32½ 43¾ Baze R A 1 8000 73-27 Pro Am, Pensar, Fleet Waver 10
11Jan87—Lugged out
15Nov86-7BM 6f :223 :453 1:104ft 3½ 114 67 65 68 56 SchvnevldtCP 2 c12500 79-21 Magnatice,ShdowWtch,BlzingZulu 11
1Nov86-9BM 6f :223 :453 1:101ft 7 115 3½ 3½ 22 23 SchvneveldtCP 1 12500 85-21 Pensr,UnitedVictory,PlentyBrown 12
Jun 25 GG 4f ft :51 h Jun 19 GG 5f ft 1:01 h May 22 GG 5f ft 1:02 h May 9 GG 4f ft :473 h

Matinee At Seven *
HUMMEL C R **116**
Own.—Corcos L F

B. g. 6, by Advisedly—Matinee Girl, by Hy Swaps
Br.—Watarida F (Cal)
Tr.—Buc John R **$12,500**
Lifetime 54 6 4 6 $32,724

1987	5	1	0	1	$5,950
1986	17	3	0	2	$12,220
Turf	5	0	0	0	

14Jun87-10GG	1 3/8 Ⓣ	:49	1:38^{3}	2:17^{1}fm	28	114	7$^{5\frac{1}{4}}$	9^{6}	7$^{9\frac{3}{4}}$	8$^{9\frac{1}{4}}$	Gonzalez R M^{7}	22500	70-26	ITkeTheFifth,Surpris·;ll,IHrdAVoic	9
6Jun87-10GG	1 1/16	:44^{3}	1:09^{3}	1:42^{3}ft	14	116	5^{12}	5^{4}	5^{3}	3^{3}	Hummel C R^{1}	10000	87-07	Fulger,StarRoute,MatirerAtSeven	11
25Apr87-10GG	1 1/16 Ⓣ	:46^{1}	1:11^{2}	1:44^{2}fm	56	119	10^{18}	8$^{9\frac{1}{2}}$	6^{9}	6$^{5\frac{1}{2}}$	HummelCR^{10}	Aw18000	74-17	Snstorm,ArtOfDwn,Rton!Approch	12
9Apr87-1GG	1	:47	1:12^{2}	1:39 ft	9 3/4	116	5$^{5\frac{1}{2}}$	5^{3}	6^{4}	5^{2}	Hummel C R^{2}	12500	71-23	OurNordic,Bob'sIntent,GetUpAmric	7
12Mar87-2GG	6f	:21^{4}	:44^{4}	1:10^{4}gd	22	117	6^{7}	6$^{6\frac{1}{2}}$	4^{2}	1^{nk}	Hummel C R^{3}	8000	85-13	MtineeAtSeven,Leguehittr,StrRout	9
23Oct86-9BM	1	:46^{2}	1:11	1:38 ft	9	114	8^{11}	5$^{8\frac{1}{2}}$	5^{5}	1$^{\frac{3}{4}}$	Campbell B C^{9}	c6250	78-21	MtineeAtSvn,PocktHir,TwoBuddys	9
23Oct86—Lost whip 5/16															
11Oct86-5BM	1 1/16	:47^{1}	1:11^{2}	1:43^{2}ft	12	114	6$^{8\frac{1}{2}}$	7$^{9\frac{1}{2}}$	8$^{9\frac{1}{2}}$	8^{8}	Gomez R^{9}	8000	67-18	SpecilDollr,NickelNssu,PocketHeir	9
17Sep86-5BM	6f	:23^{1}	:46^{3}	1:12^{2}gd	18	117	8$^{7\frac{1}{2}}$	5$^{6\frac{1}{2}}$	5^{7}	3^{4}	Gomez R^{5}	6250	73-31	IrishCst,SuperGelic,MtineeAtSevn	11
1Sep86-8Sac	1 1/16	:46^{3}	1:10^{4}	1:42^{1}ft	4	114	7^{12}	6^{7}	3^{1}	1^{nk}	Gomez R^{3}	6250	92-09	MtineAtSvn,TotlRqust,Prir[illegible]go	11
2Aug86-13SR	1 1/16	:46^{2}	1:11	1:42^{3}ft	15	110^{5}	9^{11}	9$^{5\frac{3}{4}}$	9$^{6\frac{3}{4}}$	6^{7}	Barton J^{6}	6250	84-11	Eldordo'sGold,TrsDon,SprtnCnqst	10
2Aug86—Wide															

May 17 GG 5f ft 1:00 h **May 9 GG 5f ft 1:01^{4} h**

This was a one-mile claiming race for $12,500 conditioned for four-year-olds and upward.

Hasty Paster has not been racing with regularity. Based on this factor and the lack of work in the past 20 days and during the recent layoff, this gelding's chances must be deemed very poor.

Sauternes ran reasonably well in his last three starts, showing nice moves between the middle two calls. The stretch drives have been lacking, however. This lack of finish has shown up in Sauternes's win, place, and show record over the last two seasons. This horse should get some misinformed betting support based on recent races, which may contribute to an overlay on another contender.

Lisa's Prince made a nice move to win a maiden race on June 5. He was the beneficiary of a fast, unsustainable pace in that race. He was not able to repeat that performance when facing tougher horses on June 18. This gelding moves up again today and is faced with two turns for the first time. Prospects are poor.

Coul Lover has chosen a difficult spot to open the 1987 season. While the horse is working well, he has yet to prove he belongs at this class level.

Mannerly demonstrates several positive features: dropping in class one notch; ran better than expected last race; good speed ratings, familiarity with distance; excellent racing dates. Negative features: has been well bet on five occasions in previous races and failed; has run well when poorly bet in past. Mannerly will be strongly bet today, and should run reasonably well. But because of Mannerly's lack of reliability, the heavy betting may set up an overlay on another contender.

Fulger overcame a tough post position last race and rocketed to win from far off the pace. He moves up to a class level at which he should also be comfortable; however, the one-mile distance is shorter than optimal for this late closer. The big off-pace move last race should result in heavy betting today. Fulger should be close at the finish but will not likely win at this distance and class.

United Victory shows a number of positive features: consistent winning record; consistently higher speed ratings; ability to hold a lead; good turn of speed. The only negative is no demonstrated ability to run more than six furlongs; however, the consistency record and ability to hold a lead suggest that the distance will not be a problem. This horse is a strong contender, and should be well supported.

Matinee At Seven was beaten by Fulger in the June 6th race. The past performances suggest the $12,500 level is too high a class for this horse. No real threat.

The main contenders are Sauternes, Mannerly, Fulger, and United Victory. Sauternes has demonstrated recent failure in the stretch; Mannerly is unreliable; Fulgar is at a distance disadvantage. United Victory looks clean except for the distance question. But wait: There is no other speed in this race. United Victory should be able to set his own pace, relax, and have enough left for the stretch drive. If another horse is heavily bet in this race, United Victory can be bet.

As expected, Mannerly and Fulger were well bet and set up a nice overlay on United Victory. In the race, he set slow early fractions and breezed to an easy win in fast time.

Three-to-one odds may not have seemed like an overlay, but when compared with 2:1 on Mannerly and 3:1 on Fulger, the price was generous. Everything is known by comparison.

THIRD RACE

Golden Gate

JUNE 27

1 MILE. (1.33½) CLAIMING. Purse $10,000. 4-year-olds and upward. Weight, 122 lbs. Non-winners of two races at a mile or over since April 15 allowed 3 lbs.; such a race since then, 6 lbs. Claiming price $12,500; if for $10,500 allowed 2 lbs. (Races when entered for $10,000 or less not considered.)

Value of race $10,000; value to winner $5,500; second $2,000; third $1,500; fourth $750; fifth $250. Mutuel pool $155,217. Exacta pool $206,776.

Last Raced	Horse	Eqt.A.Wt	PP	St	¼	½	¾	Str	Fin	Jockey	Cl'g Pr	Odds $1
7Jun87 9GG2	United Victory	b 6 117	7	2	1½	1½	1½	15	15	Maple S	12500	3.00
20Jun87 7GG4	Manerly	b 6 116	5	3	2¹	2¹½	2²	3²	2¹	SchvneveldtCP	12500	2.00
6Jun87 10GG4	Sauternes	5 116	2	4	5¼	5½	5²	5⁵	3½	Campbell B C	12500	7.10
14Jun87 10GG8	Matinee At Seven	6 116	8	5	4³	4⁴	3hd	4¹	4³	Hummel C R	12500	11.10
7Jun87 7GG8	Hasty Paster	b 4 116	1	1	3²	3hd	4³	3hd	5½	Judice J C	12500	13.00
6Jun87 10GG1	Fulger	b 5 116	6	7	8	8	8	6¹	6⁴	Diaz A L	12500	3.30
26Jly86 6SR5	Coul Lover	b .5 116	4	6	6³	6⁵	6¹	7³	7⁸	Tohill K S	12500	30.10
18Jun87 4GG4	Lisa's Prince	4 116	3	8	7⁵	7⁶	7⁵	8	8	Castaneda M	12500	14.50

OFF AT 2:02. Start Good for all but COUL LOVER. Won Handily. Time, :23, :48, 1:00%, 1:21%, 1:34% Track fast.

$2 Mutuel Prices:	7–UNITED VICTORY	8.00	4.00	3.20
	5–MANERLY		3.20	2.80
	2–SAUTERNES			3.40
	$2 EXACTA 7–5 PAID $26.20.			

Hollywood, June 27 —Seventh Race

7th Hollywood

1 1-16 MILES
HOLLYWOOD PARK

1 1/16 MILES. (1.41⅘) ALLOWANCE. Purse $24,000. 3-year-olds and upward which have not won $3,000 other than maiden, claiming or starter. Weights, 3-year-olds, 114 lbs.; older, 122 lbs. Non-winners of a race other than claiming at a mile or over since May 1 allowed 3 lbs.; such a race since April 1, 5 lbs.

Mark Chip
PINCAY L JR **117**
Own.—Millard or Rous Mmes
B. c. 4, by Our Blue Chip—Markwind, by Windsor Ruler
Br.—Rous & Millard (Cal) 1987 3 1 1 0 $14,800
Tr.—Sadler John W 1986 4 M 0 4 $11,400
Lifetime 7 1 1 4 $26,200

5Jun87-7Hol 6f :213 :444 1:094ft 2 121 42 32½ 42 53½ Stevens G L 3 Aw22000 91-15 SunnyReson,BoldAndGren,MgicLdr 5
20May87-4Hol 6½f:224 :462 1:171ft *1 123 21½ 2½ 1hd 13½ Stevens G L 1 Mdn 94-17 Mark Chip, John's Retreat,Robigus 6
9May87-6Hol 6½f:221 :452 1:164ft 7½ 123 3½ 3nk 32 22¾ Stevens G L 10 Mdn 93-10 Crystal Run, MarkChip,SharpPort 11
23May86-3Hol 6f :222 :461 1:101ft 14 115 65 53½ 35½ 38¼ Stevens G L 10 [S]Mdn 85-23 BoldBrawley,PrinceOFire,MrkChip 12
23May86—Bumped start
21Apr86-4SA 6½f:213 :441 1:152ft 6 117 84 57 69¼ 314½ Pincay L Jr 4 [S]Mdn 78-16 IdealQulity,Mrvin'sPolicy,MrkChip 10
21Apr86—Veered in, bumped start
9Apr86-6SA 6f :213 :451 1:101ft *2½ 118 64½ 63½ 54 36 Pincay L Jr3 [S]Mdn 81-18 Rinnegato,Marvin'sPolicy,MrkChip 8
26Mar86-6SA 6f :212 :451 1:11 ft 4½ 117 75¼ 54½ 54½ 32½ Pincay L Jr7 [S]Mdn 80-17 DvilsBrigd,Mrvin'sPolicy,MrkChip 11
26Mar86—Hopped in air
Jun 21 Hol 7f ft 1:262 h Jun 15 Hol 6f ft 1:131 h May 31 Hol 4f ft :472 h May 6 Hol 5f ft 1:004 hg

***Athlone**
DELAHOUSSAYE E **117**
Own.—Burford & Folsom
B. g. 5, by Corvaro—Ela Marita, by Red God
Br.—Ardenode Stud Ltd (Ire) 1987 11 0 5 3 $41,575
Tr.—Hartstone George D 1986 4 0 0 0
Lifetime 22 1 8 5 $45,774 Turf 12 1 3 2 $4,199

17Jun87-7Hol 6½f:22 :451 1:161ft 4¼ 119 810 87¼ 85½ 41½ DelhoussyeE 1Aw22000 97-15 TeddyBerHug,ANewEr,MYouAndQ. 8
31May87-7Hol 1 :444 1:094 1:362ft *9-5 116 76¾ 76 35½ 24 DelhoussyeE 1Aw24000 77-18 Sum Action, Athlone, Mondanite 8
31May87—Wide into stretch
24Apr87-7Hol 6f :221 :452 1:091ft *8-5 116 66¾ 55 44 24½ DelhoussyeE 5Aw22000 92-12 Superoyale, Athlone,NorthernValor 6
8Apr87-7SA 6f :22 :451 1:094ft 2½e 117 812 811 56 21½ DelhoussyeE 2Aw29000 87-22 Superb Moment,Athlone,Doonsport 8
8Apr87—Broke slowly
27Mar87-7SA 1⅛:464 1:113 1:50 ft 3 117 55½ 31½ 32½ 35¼ DelhoussyeE 5Aw31000 74-23 ArcticDream,It'sNotMyJob,Athlone 7
27Mar87—Bumped start
17Mar87-7SA 1 1/16:46 1:102 1:423ft 4¼ 117 912 77¼ 36½ 35½ DelhoussyeE 9Aw31000 82-16 PrinceO'Fire,It'sNotMyJob,Athlone 9
17Mar87—Wide into stretch
4Mar87-5SA 1 1/16:453 1:101 1:432ft 8½ 117 1011 97¼ 42½ 32¼ Delhoussyef. 8Aw30000 82-16 RidgeReview,Rafel'sDncer,Athlone 12
18Feb87-5SA 1 :454 1:10 1:363ft 7 118 43½ 46 56 55 Solis A 4 Aw29000 80-19 Alibi Ike, Watch'n Win, Gum Fleet 9
1Feb87-3SA 6f :212 :444 1:11 ft 14 118 109¾ 96¾ 64 2no DelhoussyeE 3Aw26000 83-16 Dad's Quest, Athlone,WassIDancer 1:
1Feb87—Broke slowly; wide into stretch
24Jan87-5SA a6½f ⓣ:213 :44 1:15 fm 7 118 109¼ 1112 1211 1213 DelhoussyeE 8Aw26000 71-17 River Mist, Nurely, Top Wing 12
24Jan87—Wide into stretch
Jun 13 Hol 4f ft :472 h ● Jun 8 Hol 4f ft :474 h May 25 Hol 5f ft 1:004 h

Lord Turk
MCCARRON C J **114**
Own.—Saron Stable
Ch. c. 3, by His Majesty—Taba, by Table Play
Br.—Robertson C J (Ky) 1987 6 1 1 1 $19,400
Tr.—Jones Gary 1986 0 M 0 0
Lifetime 6 1 1 1 $19,400

23May87-9Hol 1 1/16:473 1:123 1:43 ft *1 120 2½ 2hd 1½ 2no McCarronCJ 2Aw24000 94-15 Be Scenic, Lord Turk, Bold Archon 6
23May87—Steadied 3/16
10May87-4Hol 1⅛:47 1:113 1:492ft *6-5 115 22 1½ 11½ 18½ McCarron C J 3 Mdn 90-17 Lord Turk, All Cat, Black Wing 8
26Apr87-6Hol 1 1/16:46 1:11 1:434ft 10 115 812 86¾ 65½ 31 McCarron C J 8 Mdn 89-09 Exit Poll, Endorse, Lord Turk 11
15Mar87-6SA 1 1/16:464 1:121 1:452ft 20 117 51½ 54 67 56¾ Stevens G L 9 Mdn 67-20 Affstar, Exit Poll, All Cat 9
22Feb87-6SA 1 1/16:463 1:12 1:442ft 13 117 910 119 914 815¾ Solis A 7 Mdn 63-14 Mountncmll,ErnYourStrps,ExtPoll 11
22Feb87—Bumped start; steadied 3/8, wide into stretch
31Jan87-6SA 6½f:213 :443 1:163ft 5 118 88¾ 810 77 67½ Stevens G L 8 Mdn 79-15 Blanco, Exit Poll, Grey Aloha 9
Jun 20 Hol 6f ft 1:123 h Jun 14 Hol 6f ft 1:123 h Jun 9 Hol 4f ft :492 h May 17 Hol 4f ft :51 h

Danski — B. c. 4, by Danzig—Pago Queen, by Pago Pago
STEVENS G L — 119 — Br.—Peters & Port (Ky) — Tr.—Drysdale Neil
Own.—Salman F — Lifetime 13 1 9 2 $52,731
1987 5 1 3 1 $36,237
1986 3 M 2 0 $9,708
Turf 9 0 7 1 $21,294

22May87-6Spt 1 :48 1:123 1:39 ft 6-5 110 22 1½ 2hd 36 OrtgLE4 Bud Brd C H 79-23 Blue Buckaroo, Ruben's Art,Danski 7
10May87-7Hol 1 :444 1:093 1:353ft *2-3 121 41½ 1½ 2hd 2hd Stevens G L4 Aw24000 85-17 Recognized, Danski, Magic Leader 7
25Apr87-9Hol 1 1/16 Ⓣ:4631:11 1:422fm*1-2 121 41½ 1hd 1hd 21¼ Stevens G L6 Aw24000 81-14 Cannon Bar, Danski, First Dibs 7
3Apr87-6SA 1 1/16 :461 1:103 1.43 ft *4-5 120 2hd 13 18 110 Stevens G L7 Mdn 86-17 Dnski,RescuePckgeII,Drco1icRwrd 7
3Apr87—Stumbled start
13Mar87-6SA 6f :214 :443 1:102ft 3 118 21 2½ 21½ 2no Stevens G L2 Mdn 86-21 Decore, Danski, Kebaba 12
14Jun86◆5York(Eng) 1 1:372gd 6 126 Ⓣ 21½ RbsP OaklyVaughn(Mdn) Majaahed, Danski, Severs 12
5Jun86◆6Epsom(Eng) 1¼ 2:073gd *1 126 Ⓣ 45¾ Quinn T Nitngall(Mdn) Sultan Mohamed,Picea,FestivalCity 9
2May86◆3Newmarket(Eng) 1¼ 2:08 gd 16 117 Ⓣ 21½ Quinn T Corl Nwmrkt Verd Antique, Danski, HelloErnani 10
28Oct85◆8Lingfield(Eng) 7f 1:214gd 2¼ 126 Ⓣ 21 WldrnP Willow(Mdn) Santella Mac, Danski, Enzeliya 13
18Sep85◆1Brighton(Eng) 7f 1:214fm*7-5 126 Ⓣ 23 Quinn T Coldean(Mdn) Picatrix, Danski,InnishmoreIsland 16
Jun 22 Hol 6f ft 1:144 h Jun 17 Hol 6f ft 1:131 h Jun 12 Hol 4f ft :512 h Jun 7 Hol 4f ft :51 h

Patient King — Ch. g. 3, by King of Kings—Sigh No More, by Old Mose
SHOEMAKER W — 109 — Br.—Pascoe III & Wais (Cal) — Tr.—Robbins Jay M
Own.—Chrys C E — Lifetime 3 2 0 0 $17,600
1987 3 2 0 0 $17,600
1986 0 M 0 0

6Jun87-5Hol 1 1/16 :473 1:124 1:463ft 8¾ 116 63 62¼ 31 13½ Meza R Q5 50000 76-17 Patient King, Darion, Some Hitter 6
6Jun87—Blocked into 2nd turn to stretch
28May87-2Hol 1 :453 1:112 1:37 ft 16 115 31½ 1hd 13 18½ Meza R Q8 ⓈM32000 78-16 PtntKng,CrtnlyTogh,IfNotThsWht 11
7May87-2Hol 6f :221 :454 1:104ft 17 115 75½ 67 710 614½ Meza R Q11 M32000 75-13 Ack'sRply,ChoosyFrind,SuprJmmy 11
Jun 23 Hol 5f ft 1:022 h Jun 17 Hol 5f ft 1:022 h May 24 Hol 5f ft 1:01 h May 18 Hol 5f ft 1:004 h

Bigbadandmean — Dk. b. or br. c. 4, by O Big Al—Go Ahead Barbara, by Extemporaneous
GRYDER A T — 1125 — Br.—Casmari Bloodstock Ltd (Cal) — Tr.—Hemmerick Anthony J
Own.—Stamatakis A — Lifetime 34 5 5 5 $28,382
1987 9 1 2 1 $16,675
1986 17 4 2 4 $10,646

10Jun87-9Hol 1⅛ :463 1:113 1:51 ft 9¾ 116 1½ 3½ 31 44¾ Stevens G L2 32000 77-16 Valiant George,LeCid,DoubleSheng 8
17May87-6Hol 1⅛ :47 1:121 1:522ft 28 115 2hd 1hd 1hd 2¾ Fernandez A L6 20000 74-15 Jrll'sGuy,Bigbdndmn,Plum5Strght 11
2May87-2Hol 1 1/16 :464 1:114 1:434ft 37 116 2hd 2hd 31 48 Fernandez A L5 20000 82-13 Bedouin, New Storm, Item Two 11
18Apr87-10SA 6½f :22 :45 1:163ft 10 115 64½ 77 79½ 711½ Patterson A5 20000 75-18 NightSwope,CoursingEagle,SaroStr 8
17Mar87-2SA 1 1/16 :463 1:112 1:434ft 17 116 21 1hd 3½ 35¼ Sibille R6 16000 77-16 Trento, Chagrining,Bigbadandmean 8
28Feb87-1SA 1⅛ :462 1:114 1:521ft 28 115 1hd 1½ 11½ 1hd Fernandez A L2 10000 68-17 Bigbdndmen,QuickSwep,Nvr-Rust 11
11Feb87-2SA 1 1/16 :461 1:11 1:442ft 98 115 21 33 34 75¼ Fernandez A L7 12500 74-17 Amorous II, Son Of Raja, TioNino 11
29Jan87-9SA 1 1/16 :471 1:12 1:453ft 30 116 63¼ 86¾ 810 915 McHargue D G3 12500 58-27 SonOfRaja,GreyMissile,Navegante 12
10Jan87-9AC 1 :472 1:14 1:41gd 2½ 114 2hd 21½ 22 22½ Barsallo E J5 Aw5000 62-30 LordLucio,Bigbadandmean,Penchnt 6
30Nov86-5AC 1 1/16 :464 1:112 1:431ft 5¼ 108 1½ 11 13 11 Hernandez M5 6250 89-15 Bigbdndmen,OldPet,ElectricMomnt 6
Jun 22 Hol 4f ft :481 h

Magna Plus — B. c. 3, by Graustark—Sleep Till Noon, by Ambiorix
MEZA R Q — 114 — Br.—Sturgill Peggy B (Ky) — Tr.—Gregson Edwin
Own.—Hand E J — Lifetime 3 1 1 0 $15,575
1987 3 1 1 0 $15,575
1986 0 M 0 0

7Jun87-4Hol 1 1/16 :47 1:121 1:444ft *3-5 115 42½ 3½ 12½ 19 Meza R Q 4 Mdn 85-17 MagnaPlus,ProudCat,ChintBridge 8
24May87-6Hol 1 :452 1:103 1:362ft *4-5 116 42 31½ 21½ 2no Delahoussaye E 1 Mdn 81-13 Don'tsingtheblus,MgnPlus,ProudCt 7
11Apr87-6SA 6f :214 :45 1:113ft 26 118 1215 1111 88½ 52¾ Meza R Q 9 Mdn 77-16 TddyBrHug,HlCommndr,DmscsLd 12
11Apr87—Bumped steadied start
Jun 24 Hol 5f ft 1:003 h Jun 19 Hol 4f ft :491 h Jun 3 Hol 5f ft 1:012 h ●May 18 Hol 7f ft 1:241 h

This was a $24,000 allowance race for three-year-olds and upward, run at a mile and one sixteenth on the dirt course.

Mark Chip broke his maiden nicely on May 20th, and then ran last at odds of 2:1 on June 5. His speed ratings and workouts are good, but Mark Chip's tendency to finish third (close-up, as in his last race), as well as inexperience at the distance, are serious negatives.

Athlone has a terrible win, place, show record. This horse can be confidently bet against.

Lord Turk has been away since May 23. The colt's last very hard race at low odds may have taken something out of him. Trainer Jones rested his charge for 17 days before the slowish four furlong work on June 9. Since then, Lord Turk has had two average six furlong works. Chris McCarron, a top rider, retains the mount.

Lord Turk is not likely to run his best race, because of the inactivity and modest training jaunts. The sharp last two races and the services of McCarron are likely to produce a big underlay.

Danski has also been inactive for 35 days, with only mediocre works in the interim. The colt has had heavy support in the past three races, but failed each time. Danski's win, place, show ratio leaves much to be desired. This colt should be overbet because of the close-up but fading finishes and the drop in class. The layoff, poor works, and weak win record are serious negatives.

Patient King has only mediocre speed ratings and mediocre workouts. The move up in class will hurt him as well. No factor.

Bigbadandmean is moving way up in class after a fading fourth place finish in slow time. This horse is not a contender.

Magna Plus blew by his opposition last race to win by nine under heavy support. While the time of that race was not impressive, the manner of victory was. The final time and fractions from Magna Plus's next to last race were more impressive, exceeding those of Athlone's next to last race. The way this colt has run his three races is more important that the final times. This three-year-old is improving and in a bullish mode. He can stand the hike up in class.

There are four contenders: Athlone, Lord Turk, Danski, and Magna Plus. Athlone and Danski will be overbet because of close-up finishes and poor win records. Lord Turk's last race speed rating and finish will generate much support unjustified by the layoff. These three overbet horses will produce an overlay on the remaining logical contender. Magna Plus is in bullish, improving form and will run well. This is not the place to hang your hat on speed ratings. Lord Turk, Danski, and Athlone will not run back to their ratings; Magna Plus will likely improve. Forget the ratings, judge the other factors here.

Magna Plus ended up at 6:1 because Lord Turk and Danski were heavily overbet. He was an excellent bet.

SEVENTH RACE
Hollywood
JUNE 27

1 $\frac{1}{16}$ MILES. (1.41%) ALLOWANCE. Purse $24,000. 3-year-olds and upward which have not won $3,000 other than maiden, claiming or starter. Weights, 3-year-olds, 114 lbs.; older, 122 lbs. Non-winners of a race other than claiming at a mile or over since May 1 allowed 3 lbs.; such a race since April 1, 5 lbs.

Value of race $24,000; value to winner $13,200; second $4,800; third $3,600; fourth $1,800; fifth $600. Mutuel pool $302,710. Exacta pool $345,017.

Last Raced	Horse	Eqt.	A.	Wt	PP	St	¼	½	¾	Str	Fin	Jockey	Odds $1
7Jun87 4Hol1	Magna Plus	b	3	114	7	3	4³	4³	4²	12½	1²	Meza R Q	6.70
5Jun87 7Hol5	Mark Chip	b	4	117	1	5	3⁴	3¹	3½	3¹½	2¹½	Pincay L Jr	11.30
10Jun87 9Hol4	Bigbadandmean		4	112	6	1	2²	2⁵	1ʰᵈ	2ʰᵈ	3ʰᵈ	Gryder A T⁵	37.00
17Jun87 7Hol4	Athlone	b	5	117	2	7	7	6²	5ʰᵈ	4²½	4³	Delahoussaye E	5.90
23May87 9Hol2	Lord Turk	b	3	115	3	6	5½	5¹½	6³½	6²	5⁶	McCarron C J	.90
6Jun87 5Hol1	Patient King		3	109	5	4	6²	7	7	7	6²¾	Shoemaker W	11.60
22May87 6Spt3	Danski	b	4	119	4	2	1ʰᵈ	1ʰᵈ	2⁴	5¹½	7	Stevens G L	3.60

OFF AT 4:44. Start good for all but ATHLONE. Won handily. Time, :22⅖, :45⅗, 1:10½, 1:36⅗, 1:43 Track fast.

$2 Mutuel Prices:	7-MAGNA PLUS	15.40	7.40	5.80
	1-MARK CHIP		10.00	7.20
	6-BIGBADANDMEAN			7.40

$2 EXACTA 7-1 PAID $153.60.

Money Management

Money Management

Common sense dictates that the best wagering scheme is the one that is the simplest and safest, i.e., bets of equal amounts. Most progression or parlay methods can turn losses into disasters very quickly for anyone except the most experienced, controlled operator. Even for this person, the financial pressures connected with progressive betting schemes can occasionally lead to gross errors of judgment and eventual ruin.

A policy of varying the dollar amounts according to the strength of conviction for the bet is not a sound idea either, because it introduces the elements of fear and greed into money management—fear acting to keep a bet too low, greed contributing to a bet excessively large. Emotional whims have no place in a serious horseplayer's betting method. It is hard enough to simply decide between betting and not betting, leave alone the confusion introduced by varying the amounts.

It is true that bets have associated with them degrees of profit potential, i.e., some are larger overlays than others; and it is also a fact that bettors have varying amounts of confidence in each bet, sometimes having great expectations, other times having little more than hope. But in the short time before a bet is placed, when a decision under pressure is required as to betting or not betting, it is very difficult to make another decision based on a quick judgement that is highly subject to bias. I cannot imagine any good player operating in such a way. A professional approach, one that can function well under pressure year after year, is geared toward the elimination of as many subjective elements as possible. A serious bettor hates to be confused five minutes to post time.

Win, Place, or Show

Where should the bet go? Much thought and study has gone into the answer to this question, by horseplayers, system developers, and other authors. The clear answer is that the win spot provides the highest overall return and should therefore be favored; however, place bets should at least be profitable in any approach that provides at least a 30 percent return on money bet to win. My experience is that the place profit, corresponding to a well-established 30 percent win bet return on the dollar, is of the order of 20 percent of every dollar bet. Corresponding show profits average 5 percent or less.

Some horseplayers are not temperamentally suited to cope with the long losing streaks (10 to 20 losses in a row), which are possible when using straight win betting. For these players I recommend splitting the bet evenly between win and place. An approach showing a 50 percent place percentage has only about one chance in one hundred of encountering a streak of at least seven consecutive losses. Overall profit will be lower by perhaps one quarter, an amount that can be considered as the premium for a psychological insurance policy. Win and show betting should not be considered unless profit margins are very high, perhaps 20 percent or more. Heavy show bets can reduce the return in a self-defeating way, because of the relative smallness of the show pool.

Exclusive place or show betting is not recommended even if long-term results demonstrate that, while not as profitable as win betting, they produce positive returns. The reason for this advice is that handicapping to place or show tends to uncover more potential bets, because the concern is not whether the horse is best but rather will the horse be close. As a result, handicapping to place and show will uncover more contenders, sometimes two or three or more in a race. This means simply that there is more room for error, and this means, in the long run, lower profits or larger losses.

If place or show betting must be done, it should normally be done in combination with win handicapping and win betting, and not simply because a horse should finish near the front of the pack. However, there have been methods proposed that attempt to take advantage of overlays that appear in the place and show betting pools. The overlay is detected by comparing the amount of monies bet on a horse in the win, place, and show pools. If the ratio of win-to-show amounts for a horse is significantly greater than the ratio of win-to-show amounts for the entire pool, then the assumptions are that (a) there is serious win money being bet on the horse in question, enhancing its chances, and (b) there is an overlay in the show betting on that horse. The conclusion is that the horse should then be bet to show—similarly for the place position, if overlaid.

There is merit in this approach. Overlays can arise in the win, place, or show betting positions. I do spot them and play them occasionally; however, a player can become so obsessed with seeking out and betting these situations that the real meat arising from win position overlays and underlays gets missed. The real money is to be made by betting win position overlays. The fact that show and place betting overlays may exist should be used primarily as another of several ways to confirm that a horse's connections expect their horse to run well enough to win the race.

Size of Bankroll

The size of the bankroll required depends on (a) the usual cashing percentage, (b) the average unit return per winning bet, and (c) the size of the bets. I go along with the traditional recommendation of a bankroll at least 25 to 30 times the size of the bets for an approach with a cashing percentage of 25 percent or higher and a modest 20 percent profit return. Below a 25 percent cashing percentage, a bankroll of 50 times the bet size is more prudent. The chance of ruin in these instances would then be less than 5 percent.

A word of warning in this regard should be mentioned, however. A method of play that shows a steady year-to-year winning percentage may experience lengthy periods during which the average declines drastically, perhaps to as low as one half to two thirds the usual figure. These runs usually correspond with a significant change in racing conditions for the local colony of horses, such as a change in venue, unusual long-term weather conditions, an influx of outside horses, and so on. Sometimes these periods of unformful racing are inexplicable.

When my results fall off dramatically from one week to the next, without apparent reason, I will exercise extreme caution or take a vacation until things start making sense again. Taking time off at these junctures can be useful in two ways. First, the layoff can prevent potential losses, and second, periodic rests are highly beneficial for recharging the emotional and mental batteries. Contrary to the popular view of racing as a lazy man's get-rich-quick scheme, serious horseplaying can be quite exhausting, with fatigue of the mind and body accumulating over extended periods. This is particularly true during difficult periods such as losing streaks or when good bets are scarce. It requires considerable willpower to break away from the game when things are not going well. The tendency is to want to keep fighting until either things improve or a real financial crisis erupts, necessitating an enforced retrenchment. I have learned over the years to walk away from the game for at least a few days when I find myself fighting the odds. During these short vacations I avoid all contact with racing information. For those who may view these measures as too drastic, my suggestion is to cut back on the number of bets and/or the amounts until results improve.

Exactas, Trifectas, Pick Six, et cetera

These exotic bets were developed by racing associations to encourage patrons to bet more money more often, since velocity of turnover of the money walking around in pockets and purses correlates with track revenues. Bet hedging, through multiple combinations, is common among exactor and triactor players, and greatly increases the betting handle and therefore the track profit.

As a general rule, I do not utilize multiple-choice bets in my approach. Assessing the win bet odds line usually requires my full attention, leaving little or no time for other considerations. There are two situations arising now and again, however, that can entice an exacta bet from me, providing I notice the opportunities. The most common occurs in small fields in which a heavily bet favorite is clearly overbet, for one or more of the reasons described earlier. Exactor wagering by the public in these situations tends to be strongly weighted toward combinations that include the favorite on top. This kind of betting usually provides large overlays on combinations involving the other horses and on combinations with the favorite as second choice.

My bets, in these situations, are based on the relative merits of the remaining contenders and often include the favorite as the choice to run second. There are no set rules for bets of this kind, although generally speaking, the second choice should receive heavy weighting as the most likely winner. The normal win bet amount should be divided into equal parts in proportion to the number of combinations. A good practice is to avoid making a combined bet of size exceeding the amount of the normal win bet.

The second occasion for a worthwhile exactor bet is on a race that shapes up as a likely speed duel. A speed duel involves two horses that break away from the pack and fight head to head into the stretch, with both finishing well ahead of the rest of the field. One of the two speed candidates is nearly always the favorite, but the other is often much higher priced. When I spot a very likely candidate to provide a fight for a speedy favorite, I will bet the pair in a reverse combination, or in a quinella, provided the favorite is not heavily overbet. If the favorite is overbet, I bet the nonfavorite on top.

Take out percentages are usually increased on the big payoff wagers, such as triactors and pick-sixes, and combined with difficulties inherent in juggling dozens of betting possibilities, making the potential for long-term, consistent profit remote indeed. I cannot imagine anything more frustrating than wheeling six horses and watching my seventh choice be part of a $10,000 payoff. I would rather play the odious lottery game.

This is not intended as a condemnation of high stakes bets, for there must certainly be horseplayers around who do well at them, but rather is intended to make the point that playing the game with single horse wagers or small and well-thought-out combinations, is fundamentally much easier as well as less susceptible to wide profit/loss swings.

The Inner Struggle

The Inner Struggle

Many people try to beat the races; all but a handful fail. Of those failing, there are a significant number who do so in spite of possessing excellent handicapping skills as well as a good understanding of the game.

The simple fact is that success in this endeavor requires a special mix of personal attributes. Unfortunately, in the past, handicappers have been given little help in the development of these characteristics. Many racing books are written by recreational horseplayers who perhaps attempted at times to beat the game but decided that it was too demanding, or that their personality was unsuited to the enforced life-style. Even the better books, those written by outstanding horseplayers, do not adequately delve into the inner struggle that the horseplayer must overcome before consistent profits are possible. There are several personality characteristics that all race track winners share, whether naturally inborn or otherwise acquired. These are discussed below with the intent that their presentation can help serious horseplayers realize what personal skills and attributes must be developed in order to achieve their goal.

Logical Thinking

It does not take a genius to beat the races, but it does require a mind able to work through a puzzle or problem in a reasonably unbiased and logical way. While logical thinking is largely an inborn characteristic, it can be developed through intelligent practice and a desire to understand why a handicapping analysis may have failed. When a race is run in a manner that is at odds with the handicapper's projection, then it is beneficial to go back to the Form and find out where the analysis failed. The mind will absorb the lesson with little effort. Logical thinking is the most important characteristic, because each race is first and foremost a complex puzzle.

Judgment

Judgement at the track refers to the ability to mentally weigh and compare several interrelated tangible and intangible factors and make decisions that, on the average, are correct. Good judgement is paramount in sizing up overlay and underlay situations. Knowledge and experience are prerequisites.

Racetrack judgement can most rapidly be acquired by cultivating a habit of making mental projections about the horses and races even when bets are not made. For example, in my own case, I like to make predictions and observations for every race about (a) the way a race will be run, (b) the chances of specific contenders, and (c) the overlay-underlay makeup of the betting line. If the race is run in a manner that proved my predictions wrong, I usually restudy the form details on the top contenders and pace setters and reevaluate them with respect to the post time betting line. In this way I constantly upgrade my knowledge and experience to the maximum degree. This exercise, while perhaps not having immediate impact, has a positive effect on the long-term thought processes and data bank in the brain. This is the way good judgement is gradually developed.

Ability to Work Hard

An average day's racing card requires about three hours of study before going to the track, and fifteen minutes of additional work between races. All told, that represents four to five hours of intensive concentration each racing day, a tiring workload. I have said this before on other pages, but it bears repeating: The results that a horseplayer achieves are only as good as the amount of time spent studying the Form. Achieving worthwhile profits at the track can be likened to getting good marks at school or running a successful business: hard work is usually rewarded.

In regards to the amount of time spent over the Form, I occasionally find good betting opportunities only in retrospect, because there was not enough time available for a thorough prerace analysis. These situations make me wish that, at least for some races, there were one or two hours available for their assessment. By spending that much time on difficult races, I would miss fewer opportunities.

Decisiveness

The fact that there are less than ten minutes between the time the horses are paraded and the close of betting puts pressures on the decision-making capabilities of the horseplayer. Adding to the pressure is the tendency for odds on the top contenders to move up or down substantially as race time nears, because the heavy betting (which usually determines overlays and underlays) is generally done just before the race is run.

For several years I experienced a great deal of trouble in making last-minute decisions, and it always seemed that I made the wrong one under pressure. Today, last minute decisions are for me easier to make and my record is better, for two reasons.

First, I do not care as much as before about making the perfect decision. Experience has taught me that, in spite of what appear in the immediate postrace period to be errors in judgement, the proportion of good decisions, over many races, compensates adequately for the bad ones. As a result, I do not get as tense about having to make tough decisions, which in turn leads to more objectivity and better judgment.

Secondly, when I examined my record of previous years' results, I found that nail-biting decisions considered in the last five minutes, to bet or not bet a particular horse, were basically a waste of effort, because it would have been more profitable to make the bet. In other words, last minute decisions to not bet were unprofitable. My policy now is to lean toward making a bet when I start sweating out a decision.

Effective decision making at the track has its roots in thorough preparation before going to the track. When fully prepared and familiar with the competitive relationships among the horses, the horseplayer should not find it overly difficult to spot an odds line that is significantly out of proportion.

Persistence

The dictionary defines *persistence* as the ability "to continue firmly in an action in spite of obstacles." The road to profitable horse race betting is piled high with obstacles, some of which include the track take, long boring periods of poor opportunities, periods of emotional and financial hardship during losing streaks, loneliness, hard work, fear-greed cycles, self-doubts, the physical demands of track life (travel, noise, smoke, poor weather), and self-recrimination for mistakes. There are balancing plusses, of course, the main ones being the sense of freedom, the challenge, the potential for large income. These attractions notwithstanding, persistence in large amounts is absolutely essential in order for a prospective professional to overcome the negatives and make the grade. As a wise man said, nothing will substitute for it; talent won't, desire won't, nor will any of the other qualities mentioned here.

Patience

Successful horseplaying entails a lot of waiting for favorable situations. While there may be as many as four or five good bets on some days, on other days there may be none. If the sporadic pattern of bet occurrence is not recognized and accepted, impatience can destroy in a few hours the profits accumulated over weeks.

Impatience is typically a problem of youth, afflicting the older, more mature player less often. In my case, impatience is no longer a factor of importance, although at one time it periodically led to serious collapses. During long dry spells I would often make large bets to relieve the boredom. Boredom? Yes. Playing the horses in a serious way can be rather tedious at times. On some days there are simply no profitable betting opportunities, on other days perhaps only one. Moreover, occurring occasionally are weeks when the racing is so confusing or when profitable prices are so scarce that only a few bets can be made during the entire period. If a high proportion of those bets lose, the racetrack routine can be sheer drudgery. It takes a very patient person indeed to continue along the proper path and to keep a high level of concentration under these conditions.

There are no easy cures for an impatient nature. Maturity, in terms of expectations and experience, is most important in curbing this tendency. The player must be exposed to, and survive, a few long slow periods to gain the experience and perspective to accept them as part of the business. It is beneficial to keep in mind that there will always be a certain number of days when no bets will be made. In other words, expectations about the number of bets available on any given day should be kept modest.

Failure Recognition

Learning begins only after failure is recognized and understood. It is an easy and even natural tendency to blame failure on factors outside the horse-player's realm of control—for example, blaming an unprofitable year on the presumed skulduggery of trainers and jockeys, or on racetrack stewards who supposedly did not do their jobs in enforcing racing rules. Rationalization of results in this way hinders the advancement of knowledge and ability and has no place in a serious horseplayer's set of principles.

Failure patterns and habits are very difficult to change. This is not to suggest in any way that there is no hope for a horseplayer who continues to fall back into comfortable but incorrect methods, but to suggest instead that the road to rational and correct behaviour is long and distinguished by many blind alleys. Progress is measured over years rather than months or weeks. Improvement in results is sporadic with the periodic advances often retarded by pullbacks as a result of renewed failure. But if the failure is recognized early and accepted as part of the process of learning correct methods, the next leg up can occur shortly thereafter. Slowly, but emphatically, the bad habits are broken in this way and replaced by a thinking, rational approach that can withstand any and all pressures.

Reasonable Expectations

Dreams about exciting racetrack events such as betting every race, huge payoffs, winning streaks, and easy money, are common among ordinary horseplayers but do not belong among a winning horseplayer's expectations. The consistent winner has learned over time that, when doing a proper job, the hours are long, the work is intensive, the bets are few, the percentage returns are usually modest, losing days not uncommon, and winning streaks rare.

Consider profit expectations, for example. A reasonable profit expectation can range from 20 to 50 percent of monies wagered for a method that yields two or three plays a day, somewhat higher for an approach that gives fewer plays. Very experienced and expert players can do better than this, of course, just as the top professional players in any sport can consistently earn much more money than the average pro. I am sure that some players would consider these profit goals as too low. Experience, however, suggests otherwise.

The primary reason to foster modest expectations relates to achieving psychological perspective. Having proper perspective implies an ability to remain relatively unaffected by short-term hardships and losses on the one hand, and by good luck and excessively high gains on the other. High expectations force a player to be more extreme: to take excessive risks by wagering on exotic bets and seemingly large but nonexistent overlays. The resulting disappointment can be psychologically defeating, to the extent that it leads to further unreasonable behavior, setting up a vicious circle that terminates in collapse.

To make it as a consistent winner, the player must eventually learn to cope with these inevitable cycles and break out of them before falling apart. The key to achieving this difficult goal is to practice self-suggestion—with constant quiet remainders to slow down, keep calm, and be objective—and to patiently strive for moderation and a smoothly functioning, businesslike operation. Thinking in terms of months, race meetings, and years rather than races, days, and weeks is also important in keeping proper perspective. Expectations about one bet or any series of bets of less than 50 or so are unreasonable, because there is simply no way of knowing which bets are going to produce winners and which are going to produce losers. A player may win 35 percent of all bets, but the sequence of winners and losers is unpredictable. During the course of a year, it is entirely possible that, say,

20 out of the first 100 bets will be winners, while 50 or more of the last 100 might win, thereby keeping the winning average over the first and last 100 bets at 35 percent. Such variation can reasonably be expected during the course of a long season. A player with reasonable expectations should be able to cope with this kind of wide but normal variability of results.

Control of Fear and Greed

These two demons are the downfall of many otherwise good horseplayers. Greed is one of the motivating reasons for nearly all monetary pursuits, including racetrack betting. Fear is an emotion that can hold a player back from committing money to an opinion. A horseplayer can only achieve maximally while these two emotions are kept in check.

Greed is not usually a factor of great importance to a seasoned horse-player, simply because greed is always severely punished at the racetrack, and seasoned horseplayers are not normally fond of pain. A good player learns the lessons of greed early; the bad ones never do. But from time to time greed will affect even the best players, to their ultimate but temporary misfortune. It is almost as if the racetrack had a scheme of providing periodic refresher courses in the sins of avarice.

There are several situations occurring in the normal course of race betting that tend to promote greedy behaviour. One occurs during winning streaks (when everything seems to be going right). The inclination then is to bet more frequently because of the heightened feelings of power and control. Another occurs when a horse appears in the Racing Form with past performance characteristics fitting a favorite handicapping pattern, creating a "can't lose" feeling. The temptation can be to bet the house in this circumstance. Also, coming back to the track after a long absence sometimes produces a euphoric feeling of control, when the bankroll bulges with money and the horseplayer's attitude is fresh and buoyant.

Another greed-enticing situation is presented when a well-liked but unbet selection wins and pays well, creating a view that the money lost by not betting should be recouped from a later race. Disqualification of a winner can have the same effect. Finally, the last race can invite a greed bet at the end of a losing day. All horseplayers like to go home as winners, and as a result, they may do some crazy, greedy betting in the last race to get out on top. That this is true is evident in the change in betting relationship between the win and show pools that occurs between the first and last race of the day. The win pool to show pool dollar ratio in the first race is usually about 2:1. By the last race it increases to about 10:1, indicating a move from conservative betting to desperation betting during the card.

Greedy betting behaviour that is not brought under control in the initial stages usually feeds on itself and can eventually destroy the horseplayer, at least temporarily.

One failed greedy bet usually leads to another larger bet, and so on, until the player decides to make one last bet to get even. By this time, emotion controls judgement so that the last bet is among the worst, guaranteeing the final collapse. Breaking a greed cycle is never easy. Awareness of the problem is the first step, but desperate players are usually so blinded by greed that it never gets recognized. For these people there is not much hope. They will forever fill the role of provider, creating opportunities for more controlled, patient, and astute players. For the good player afflicted with temporary greed bouts, my advice is relax the thought processes with suggestions to slow down and to remember that the track will always be there with new races every day.

Fear sneaks up on a player during losing streaks and stifles normal betting behaviour. It can also surface after several wins if the player starts thinking about how rich he is and to what use the money could be put. The result is the same: a loss of natural, instinctive betting flow.

Making bets of too large a size can have the same effect. It is important to consider both the size of bankroll and the experience factor when deciding on bet size. Highly experienced players can start a season out betting up to 10 percent of the bankroll each time without feeling excessive discomfort, but a less seasoned player is likely to panic under the stress of losing a few 10 percent bets right off the bat.

Increasing bet size when in a winning phase should also be prudently done, so that the increase does not strike fear in the heart of the player. A sudden jump in bet size from, say, $20 to $50 can breed fear and dampen the proper flow of judgement and spontaneity. A prudent method of increasing bets should never be based on expected dollar return but rather on what a player feels comfortable with, so that a 15-race losing streak will not increase the fear level to a point that retards the normal betting process.

Monetary considerations are not always at the root of a fear problem. Potential destruction of self-esteem or confidence when losses occur can be a major factor in the build up of debilitating fear. If success at the game means a great deal to a budding player, then bad streaks can be very discouraging and even depressing, occasionally to the point of immobilizing all action. Recovery is best achieved by taking a break from the action for a few days or weeks and by channelling thoughts about the game in a more rational direction. Inexplicable losing streaks happen to everyone, from the long shot players right on down to the chalk eaters. It is simply a case of numbers coming up the wrong way, in many instances.

The likelihood of fear or greed affecting the betting routine diminishes significantly with experience, coincident with gains in understanding of the real principles of the game. After many years at the track, seasoned players rely more on instinct. When they see an opening on the board, they just step up and bet, without fuss or fanfare. Fear and other emotions, if present at all, get suppressed at that moment, and while a dismal performance by a bet may cause some short-lived anxiety and brooding, it usually has little impact on recognition and action involving future wagers.

Sense of Worth

The pursuit of profits from horse race betting certainly is not an occupation or avocation near the top of the list of most noble professions, nor is it considered at all worthwhile in altruistic terms. In fact, horseplayers as a lot are deemed by the general working public as being lazy, selfish, and greedy thrill seekers. The average person knows that "You can't beat the races," and therefore classifies serious horseplayers simply as "racetrack bums." As a consequence, many are forced to carry on closet life-styles.

There are, in addition to the burden of social stigma, a number of sacrifices that every dedicated horseplayer must make during the proving years. One of the most severe drawbacks is that the really serious player is faced with a restricted social and family life. Full weekends must be devoted to racing since many tracks now run on both Saturday and Sunday. Cash flow can also be a major problem for players early in a career in that financial losses are usually suffered for a few years while learning the game, and initial improvement in results tends to be slow and hesitant.

The other important barrier to success is the age factor. Maturity and experience are of utmost significance in mastering the psychological aspect of the game. In fact, it is unlikely the races can be beaten by youth. The player must experience a long series of ups and downs and go broke a few times before important lessons are learned. So, the result is that success in the game favors the older player with several years of experience and having financial resources sufficient to provide the necessities of life during lengthy assaults on the track. This is not to discourage youth from trying. It is merely to suggest that the journey is long and that expectations should be kept very modest until a few years of experience can be gained.

These difficulties notwithstanding, it is important for the horseplayer to maintain a positive attitude and have confidence that his objectives are worthwhile. This is not an easy task, but it can be made easier by acquiring the proper outlook and goals. Money should not be the ultimate goal. Even the top players view money only as a reward for playing the game properly. Taking a clue from that, then an appropriate goal would be to do the right thing rather than strive for big money. Doing a proper job should be the top priority. Other respectable goals to be kept in mind include mastery of the intricacies of handicapping, and greater understanding and recognition of profitable betting patterns.

It is also helpful in keeping perspective to view the business of horse-playing as a sophisticated puzzle, because it sets up the game in the mind as a lifelong challenge, something to be constantly tinkered with and improved. Imprinting this goal can serve another useful purpose. When someone asks, why do a foolish thing like try to beat the races, answer that it's because of the challenge, that it's your Mount Everest, English Channel, Boston marathon, and more. A response of this kind is usually more effective than one that refers to the monetary aspect, since the truth is that even serious players lose money while learning the art, a fact that can make a budding handicapper look bad and feel even worse.

And even if the player never achieves a profit, the striving is worthwhile. The objective player can learn much about himself—his mental and emotional strengths, weaknesses, and idiosyncracies. He learns about the important role chance plays in the game of horse racing and by extension, the game of life. He receives an education in the value of money and what impact it has on his actions. He acquires knowledge of human psychology and crowd behaviour. And, in the end, whatever the outcome, the player will have enjoyed many hours of a challenging activity.

Publisher's Addendum

Liberty Publishing Company, Inc. was founded in 1977 to publish non-fiction, "how-to" books. LPC is now one of the leading sources of quality products to the rapidly growing market of horse race handicapping. Here is a brief description of our most popular products on thoroughbred and greyhound racing:

NOW IN STOCK AND AVAILABLE...

Winning at the Track $9.95 papbk. 160 pages
David L. Christopher

With the revised and updated Sixth Edition, this book can now be classified a best-seller with nearly 60,000 copies sold. The speed handicapping method offered may be used with or without a computer. The software package, which includes a copy of the book, is priced at $59.95. (Note preference: 5 1/4" or 3 1/2" disc).

Handicap! Finding the Key Horse $12.95 papbk. 172 pages
David L. Christopher / Albert C. Beerbower

A new book that addresses a problem that has forever frustrated serious racing fans: Selecting one key horse from the top three or four contenders. Included are several profitable methods of identifying a key horse from those few potential winners.

"...a great new path to the cashier's window!"
The Inside Track

ADVANCED Speed & Pace HANDICAPPING $12.95 papbk. 144 pages
David L. Christopher

This new guide promises to be another authoritative look at this popular approach to handicapping thoroughbreds. With the help of this book, a racing fan can identify the pacesetters, tell how fast the pace is likely to be, and discover which horses are capable of beating the leaders to the wire. This is MUST reading for any serious racing fan, with or without a computer.

Fast and Fit Horses $9.95 papbk. 172 pages
Bob Heyburn

This classic book on pace and form is now available in paperback!

How Will Your Horse Run Today? $9.95   papbk. 216 pages
William L. Scott

Here is a highly-rated book devoted to solving a problem that many handicappers face: Identifying the horse's "form cycle." Now in its sixth printing!

Total Victory at the Track $12.95   papbk. 288 pages
William L. Scott

Expanding on his earlier work, this widely-read author offers a unique handicapping method involving form and class. This book has just been published in paperback for the first time.

The Complete Guide to Racetrack Betting $9.95 papbk. 168 pages
David K. Rosenthal

Knowing *when* and *how* to bet is almost as important as the selection process itself! The author shows how to maximize profits with the proper betting techniques.

Horses Talk: It Pays to Listen $19.95 papbk. 195 pages
Trillis Parker

Many serious bettors would never recognize a "sore" horse or other problems in the post parade. This fully-illustrated book, with more than 40 photographs, is a comprehensive guide on the conformation and health of today's racehorses.

Ten Steps to Winning $9.95 papbk. 160 pages
Danny Holmes

This book presents a simple handicapping method that *anyone* can use. In addition to discussions on pace, form, and condition, the author presents a unique handicapping approach... a different method for specific types of races. *Ten Steps to Winning* is the product of years of experience as a professional bettor and racehorse owner.

The Mathematics of Horse Racing $9.95 papbk. 144 pages
David B. Fogel

After studying thousands of horses over a period of several years at eight major race tracks, the author, a statistician whose hobby is horse racing, offers startling answers to many key questions that "speed" and "class" handicappers ask daily!

Handicapping Trainers $12.95 papbk. 168 pages
John Whitaker

This book is the result of the most significant study of trainers and their "patterns" that we've ever seen. Included are details for selecting long shots that most racing fans experience only once in a lifetime!

Greyhound Racing for Fun and Profit $9.95 papbk. 144 pages
Tom Walsh

Here is the most comprehensive guide to greyhound racing available today. Included is a seven-point handicapping method that helped the author place 3rd in a national handicapping contest.

FOR FASTER SERVICE:

Liberty Publishing Company prefers to ship its products to its customers using UPS ground service. Therefore, please provide a street address when you order. If you would like to have the product shipped to you more quickly, send $6.00, rather than $3.00, and the package will be sent UPS 2nd Day Air. Thanks!

PLEASE SEND ALL ORDERS TO:

Liberty Publishing Company, Inc.
440 South Federal Highway - Suite 202
Deerfield Beach, Florida 33441

ADDITIONAL QUESTIONS? Contact: Jeff Little, Publisher
(305) 360-9000

ORDER FORM

Enclosed is my check or money order for $ _____, including $3 for mailing and handling, for the title(s) listed below.

Quantity	Title
_____	_____
_____	_____
_____	_____
_____	_____
_____	_____

Name _____

Street _____

City _____ State_____ Zip _____